tHe OCTOBER FaCtioN

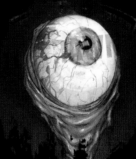

IDW®
www.IDWPUBLISHING.com

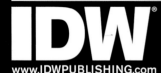

Ted Adams, CEO & Publisher
Greg Goldstein, President & COO
Robbie Robbins, EVP/Sr. Graphic Artist
Chris Ryall, Chief Creative Officer
David Hedgecock, Editor-in-Chief
Laurie Windrow, Senior Vice President of Sales & Marketing
Matthew Ruzicka, CPA, Chief Financial Officer
Lorelei Bunjes, VP of Digital Services
Jerry Bennington, VP of New Product Development

Facebook: **facebook.com/idwpublishing**
Twitter: **@idwpublishing**
YouTube: **youtube.com/idwpublishing**
Tumblr: **tumblr.idwpublishing.com**
Instagram: **instagram.com/idwpublishing**

Originally published as THE OCTOBER FACTION: DEADLY SEASON issues #1–5.

Created by
Steve Niles & **Damien Worm**

Written by **Steve Niles**
Illustrated by **Damien Worm**
Color Assist by **Alyzia Zherno**
Lettered by **Shawn Lee** and **Tom B. Long**

Series Edits by **Chris Ryall** & **David Mariotte**

Cover by **Damien Worm**
Collection Edits by **Justin Eisinger** and **Alonzo Simon**
Collection Design by **Ron Estevez**
Published by **Ted Adams**

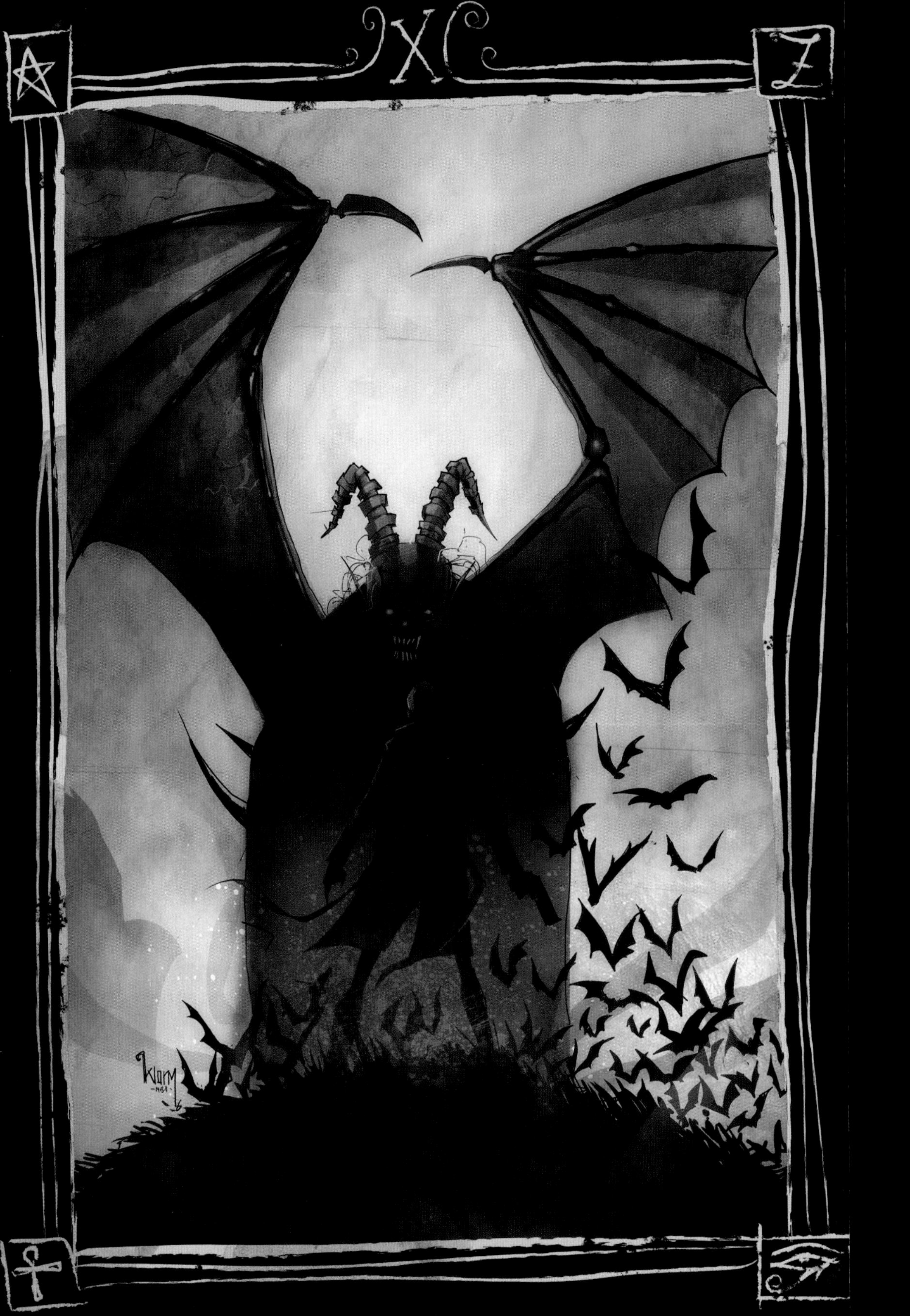
X

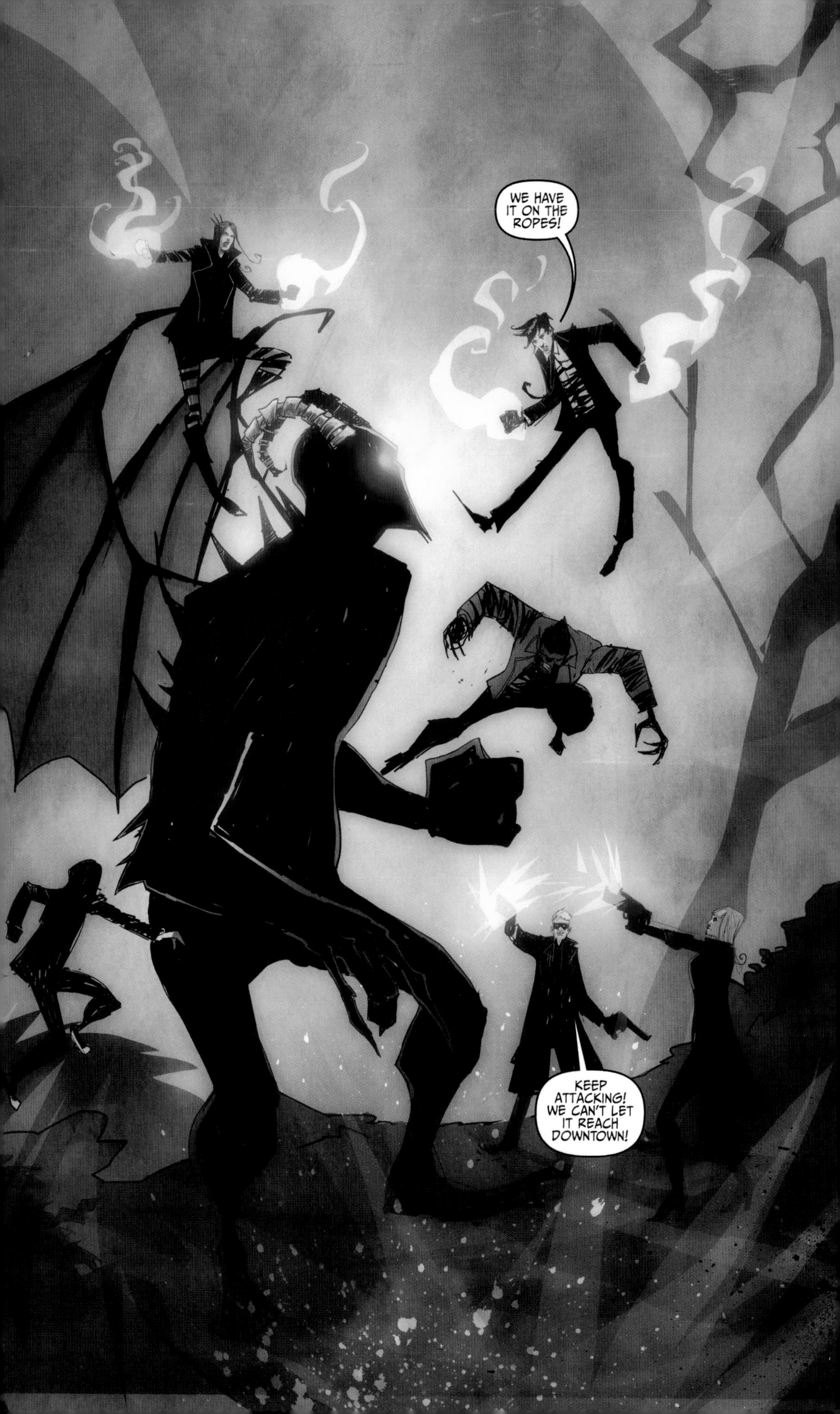
WE HAVE IT ON THE ROPES!
KEEP ATTACKING! WE CAN'T LET IT REACH DOWNTOWN!

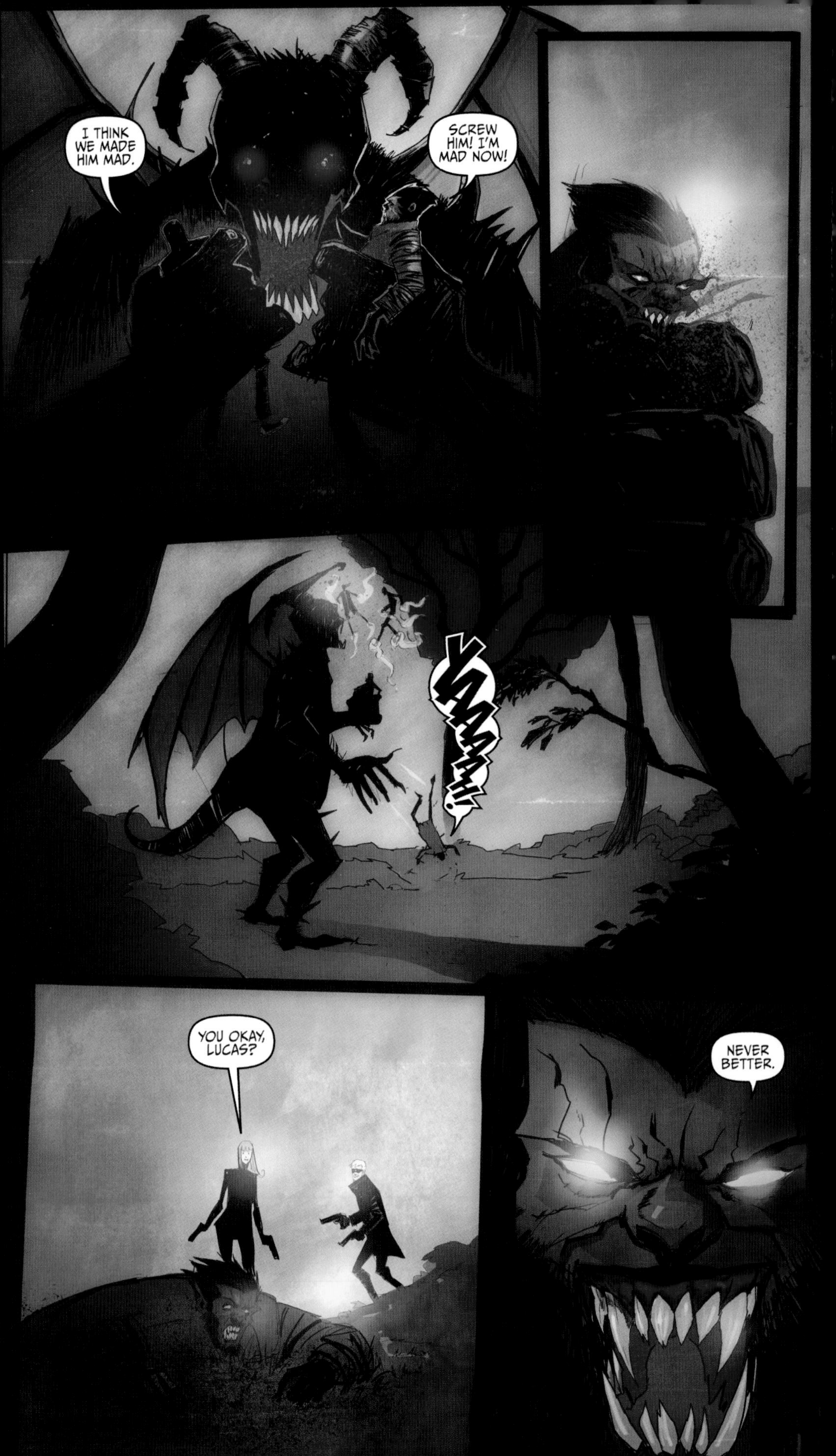
I THINK WE MADE HIM MAD.
SCREW HIM! I'M MAD NOW!
YOU OKAY, LUCAS?
NEVER BETTER.

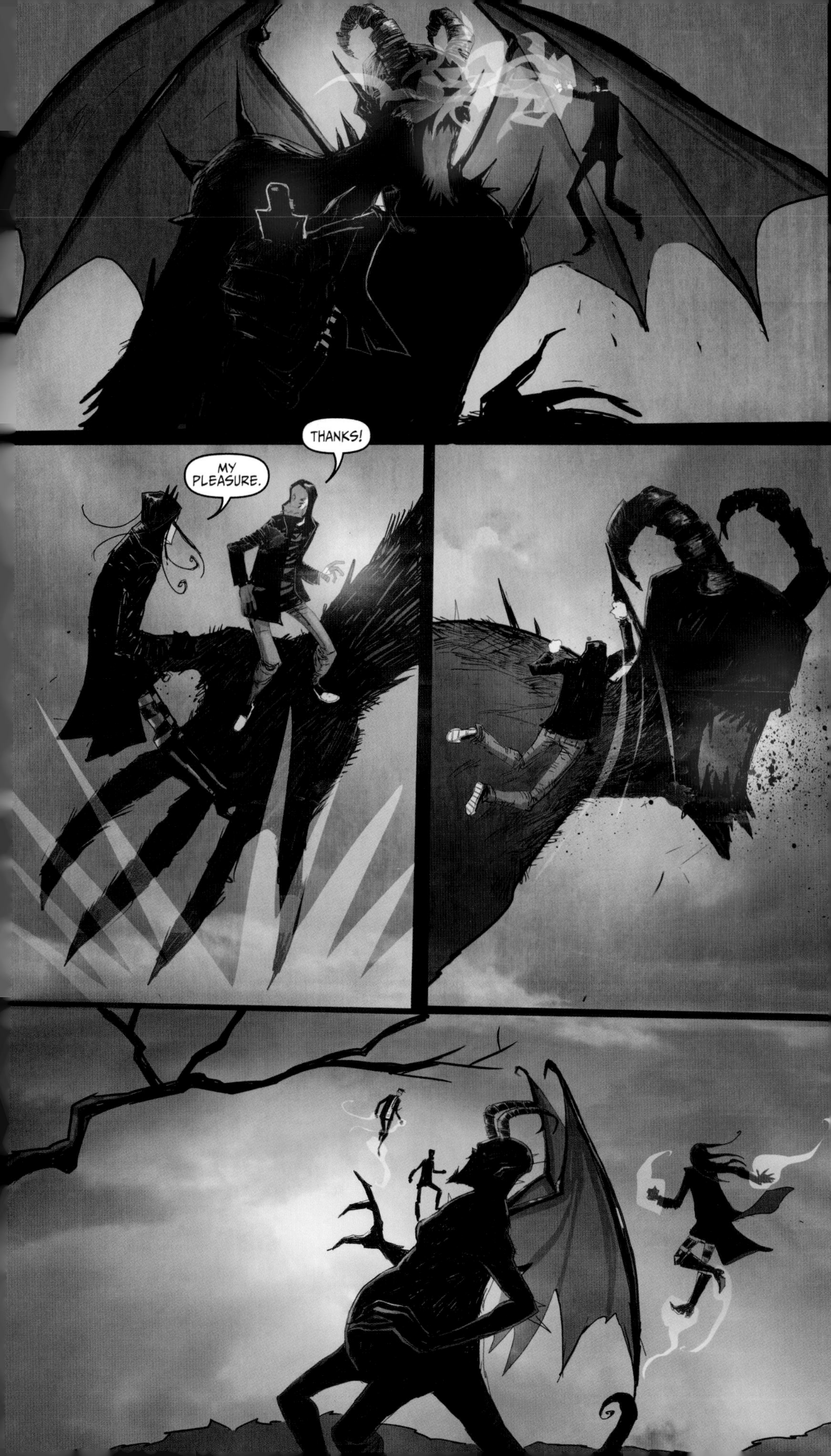
MY PLEASURE.
THANKS!

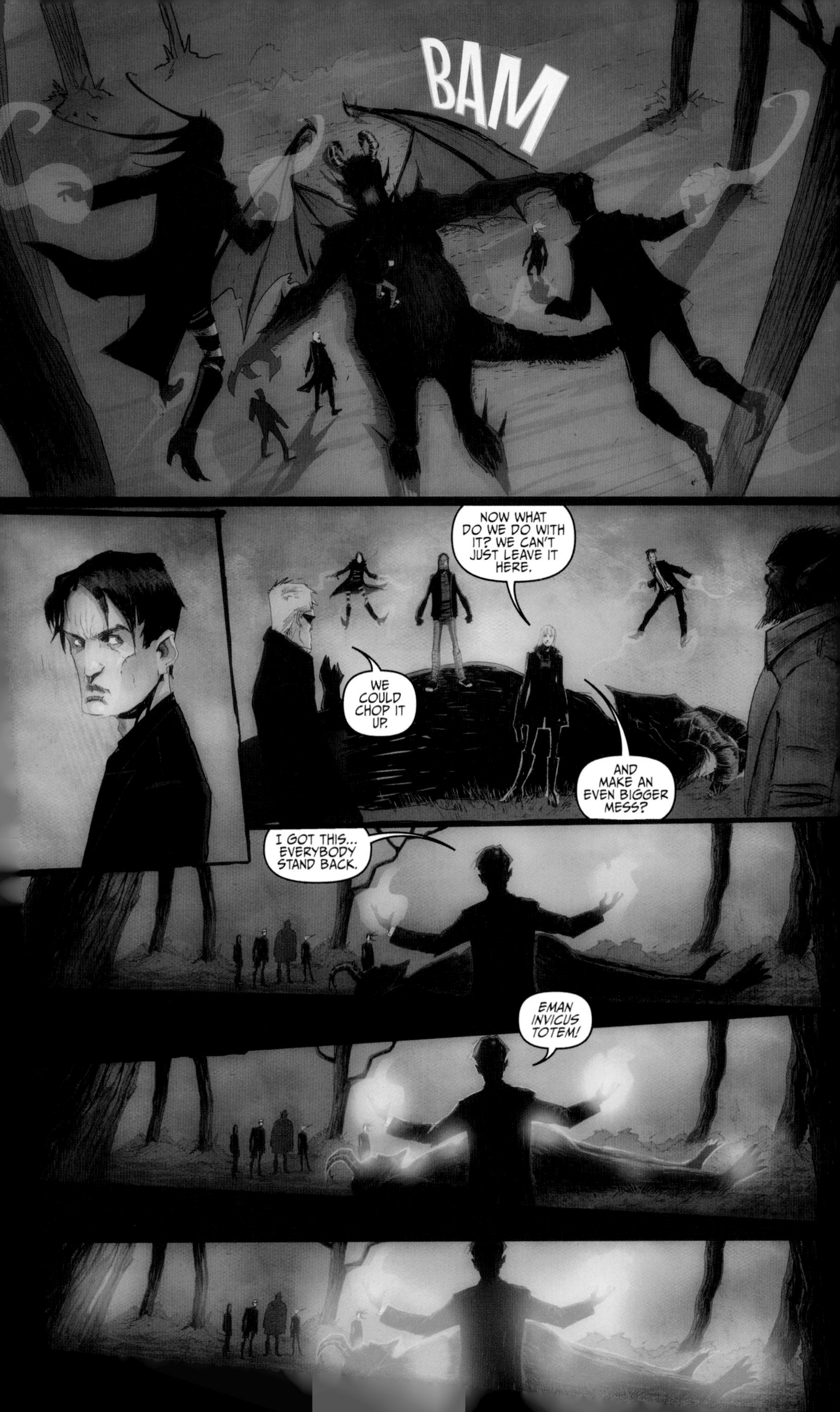
BAM
NOW WHAT DO WE DO WITH IT? WE CAN'T JUST LEAVE IT HERE.
WE COULD CHOP IT UP.
AND MAKE AN EVEN BIGGER MESS?
I GOT THIS... EVERYBODY STAND BACK.
EMAN INVICUS TOTEM!

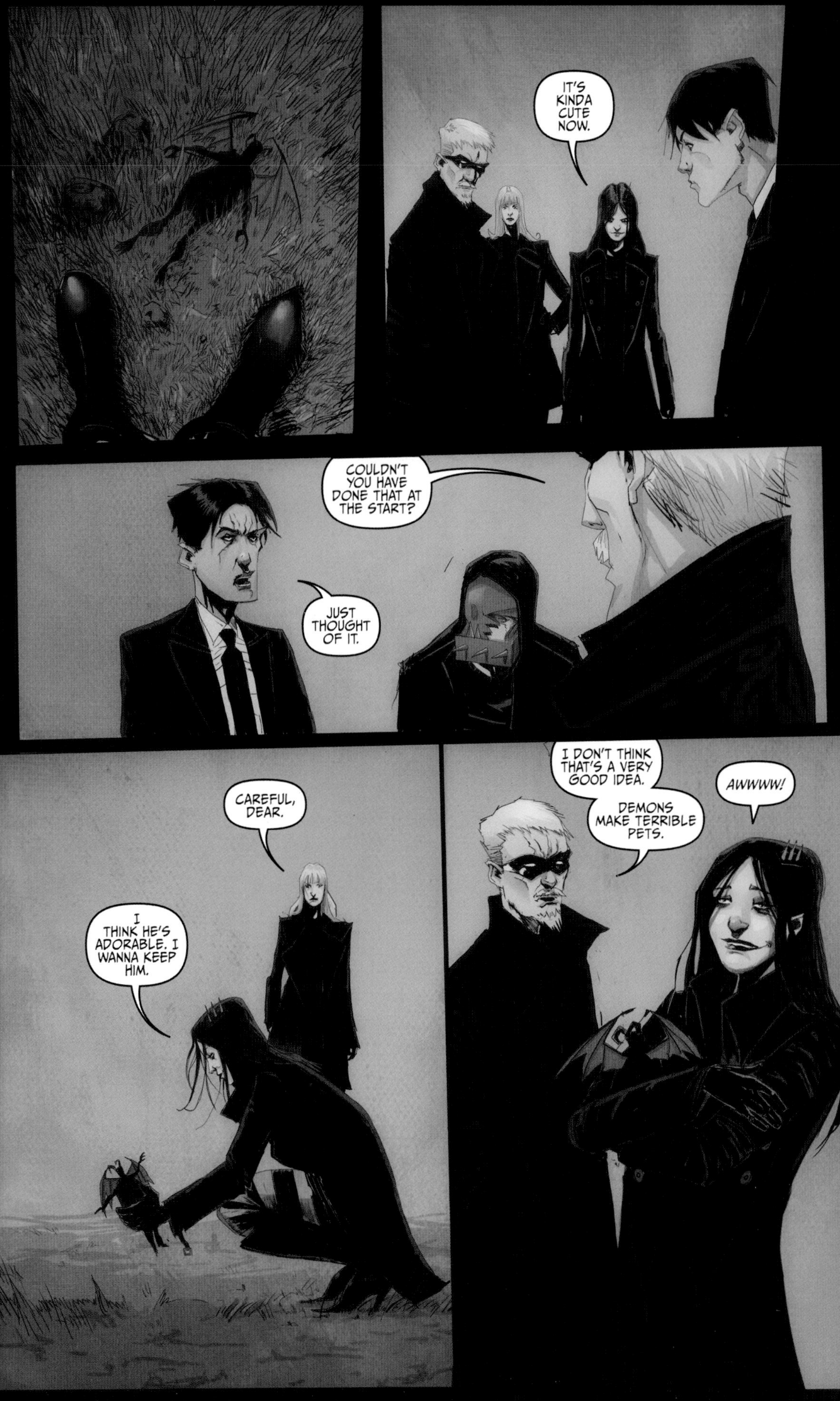
IT'S KINDA CUTE NOW.
COULDN'T YOU HAVE DONE THAT AT THE START?
JUST THOUGHT OF IT.
CAREFUL, DEAR.
I THINK HE'S ADORABLE. I WANNA KEEP HIM.
I DON'T THINK THAT'S A VERY GOOD IDEA.
DEMONS MAKE TERRIBLE PETS.
AWWWW!

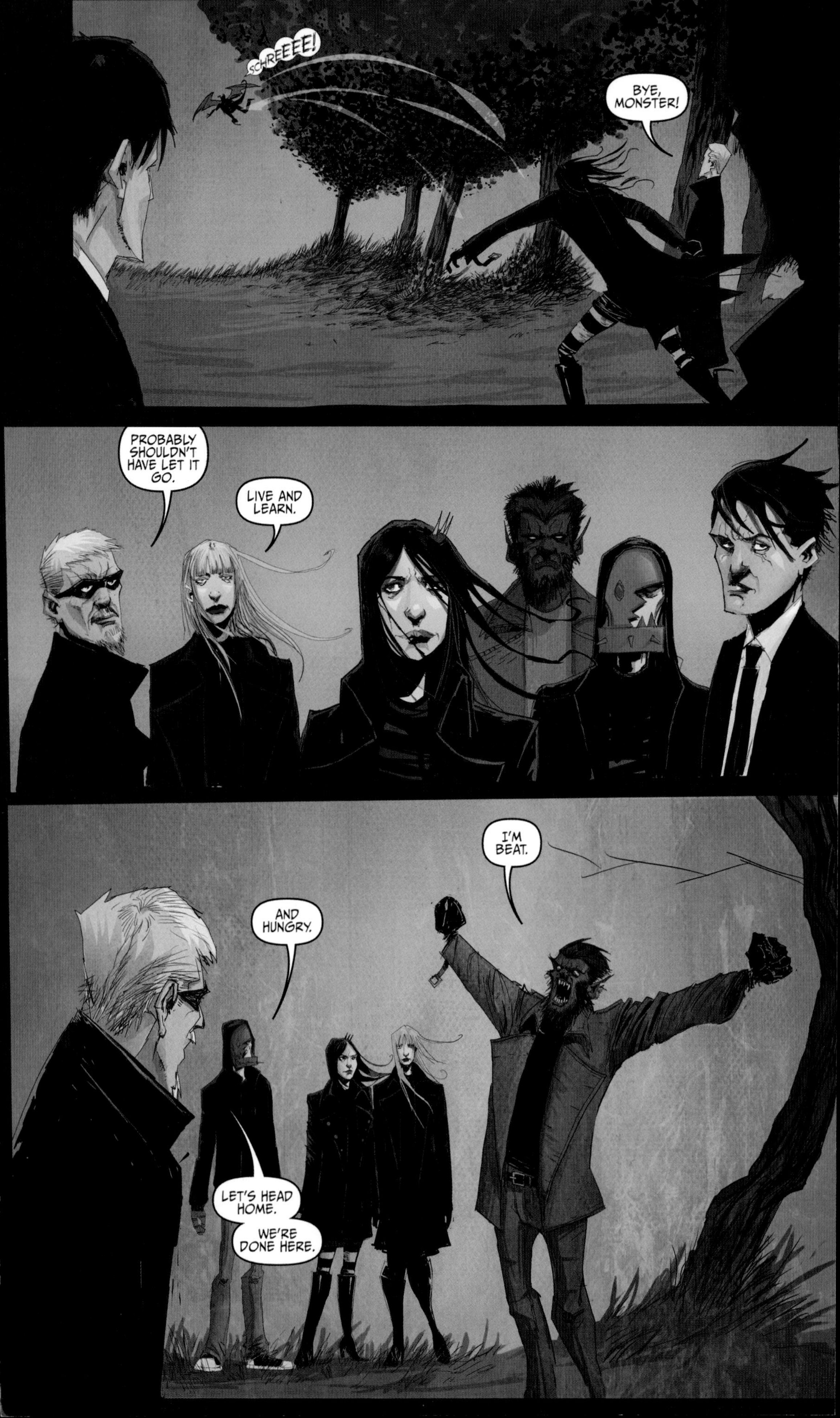
SCHREEEE!
BYE, MONSTER!
PROBABLY SHOULDN'T HAVE LET IT GO.
LIVE AND LEARN.
I'M BEAT.
AND HUNGRY.
LET'S HEAD HOME.
WE'RE DONE HERE.

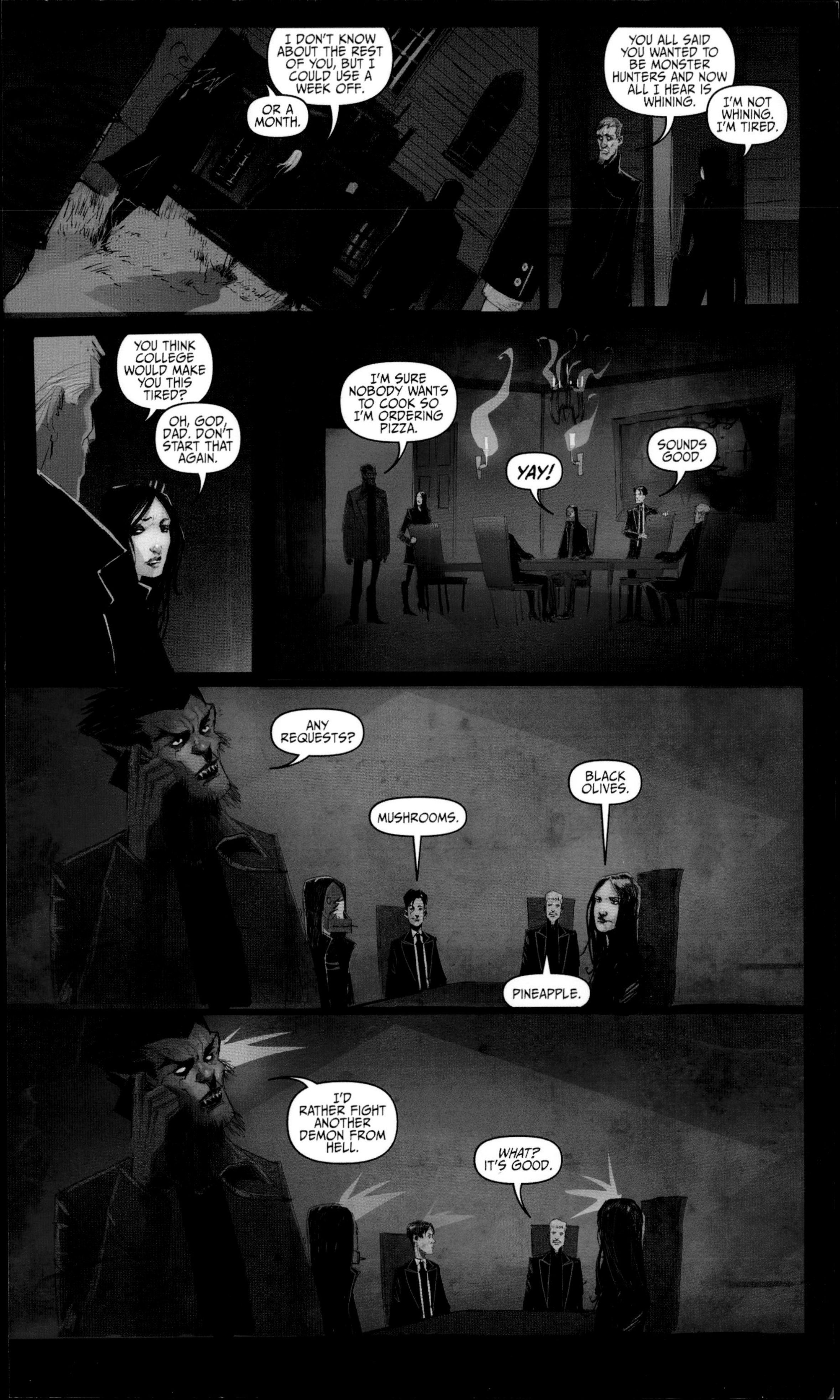
I DON'T KNOW ABOUT THE REST OF YOU, BUT I COULD USE A WEEK OFF.
OR A MONTH.
YOU ALL SAID YOU WANTED TO BE MONSTER HUNTERS AND NOW ALL I HEAR IS WHINING.
I'M NOT WHINING. I'M TIRED.
YOU THINK COLLEGE WOULD MAKE YOU THIS TIRED?
OH, GOD, DAD. DON'T START THAT AGAIN.
I'M SURE NOBODY WANTS TO COOK SO I'M ORDERING PIZZA.
YAY!
SOUNDS GOOD.
ANY REQUESTS?
MUSHROOMS.
BLACK OLIVES.
PINEAPPLE.
I'D RATHER FIGHT ANOTHER DEMON FROM HELL.
WHAT? IT'S GOOD.

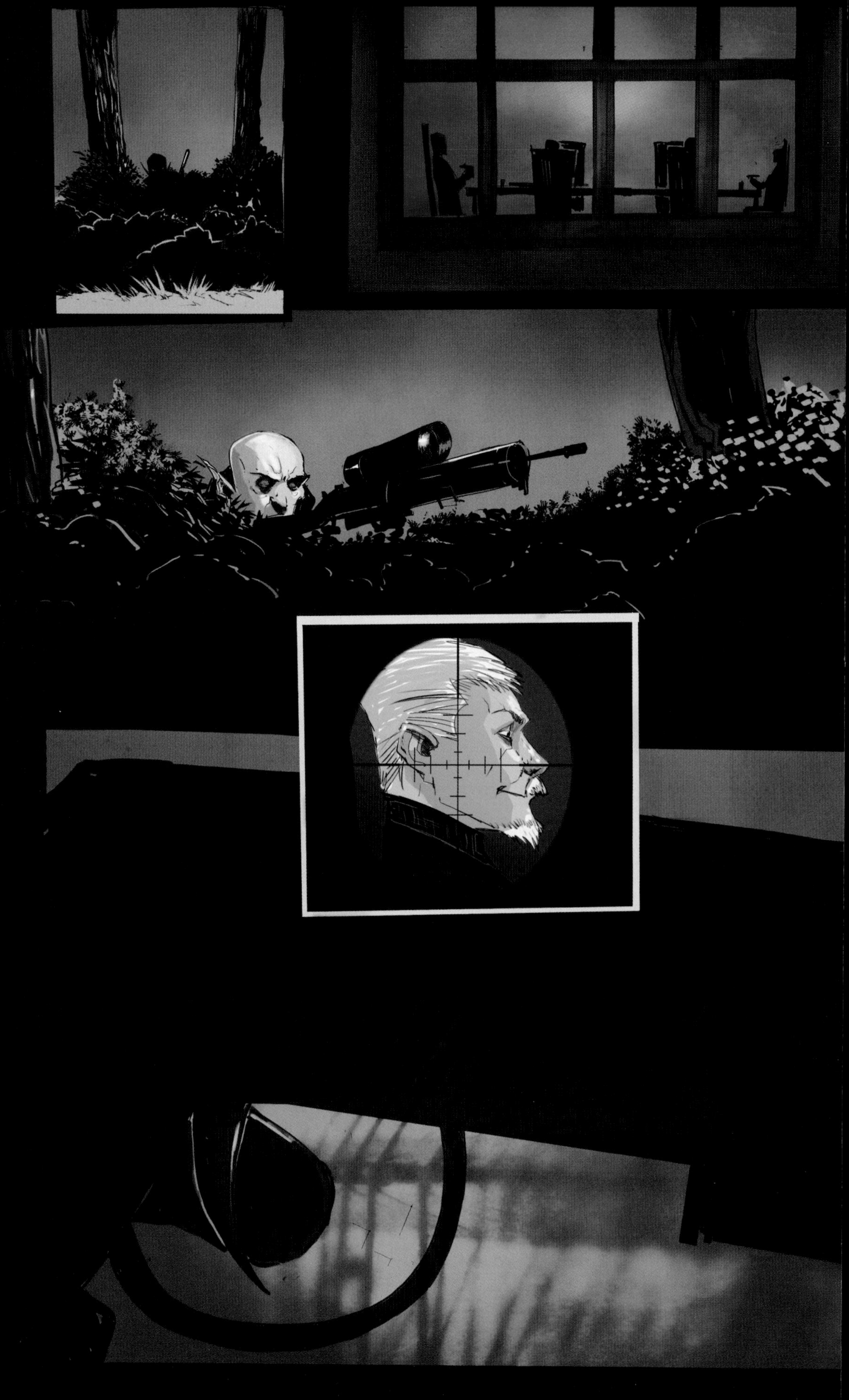

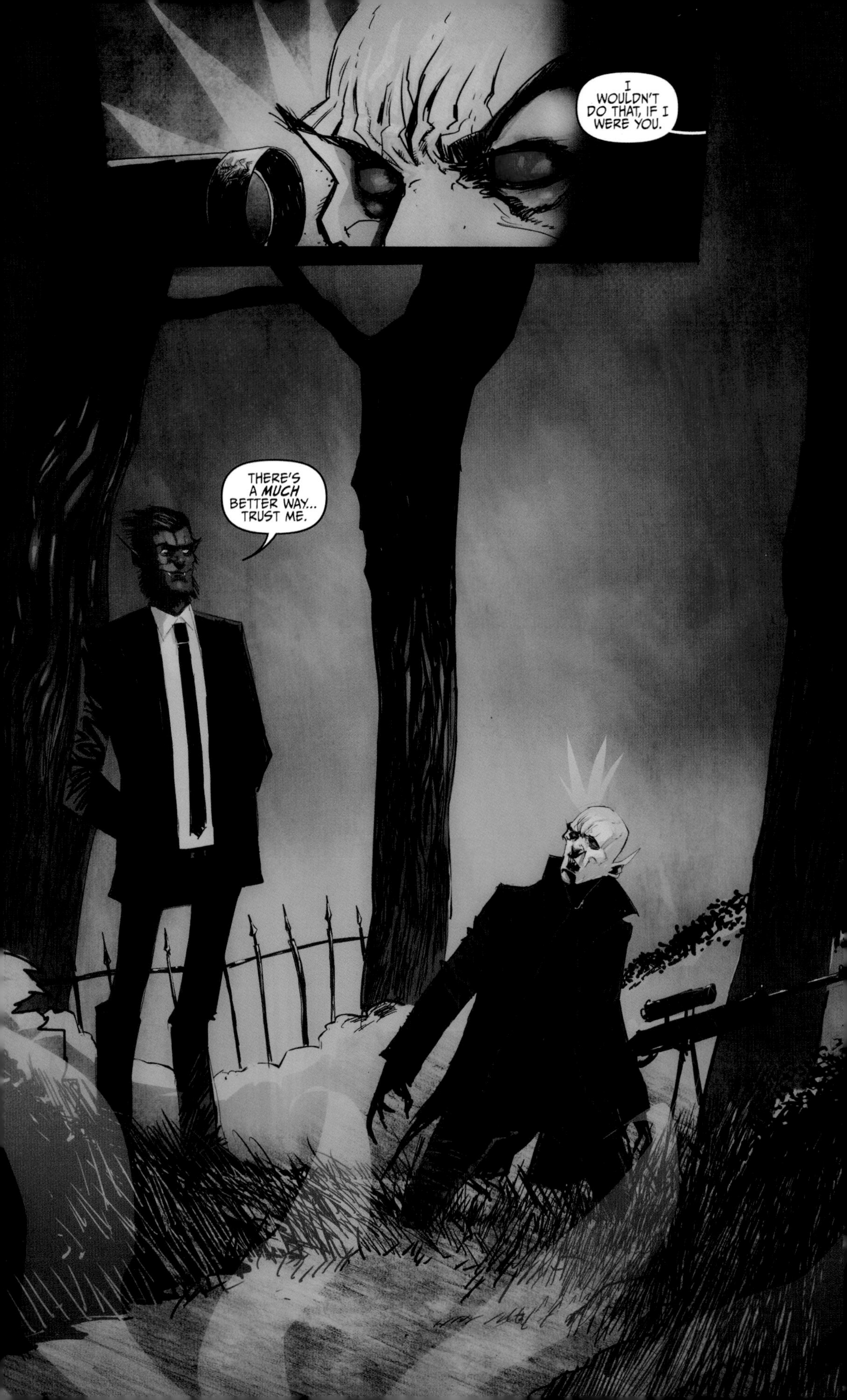
I WOULDN'T DO THAT, IF I WERE YOU.
THERE'S A *MUCH* BETTER WAY... TRUST ME.

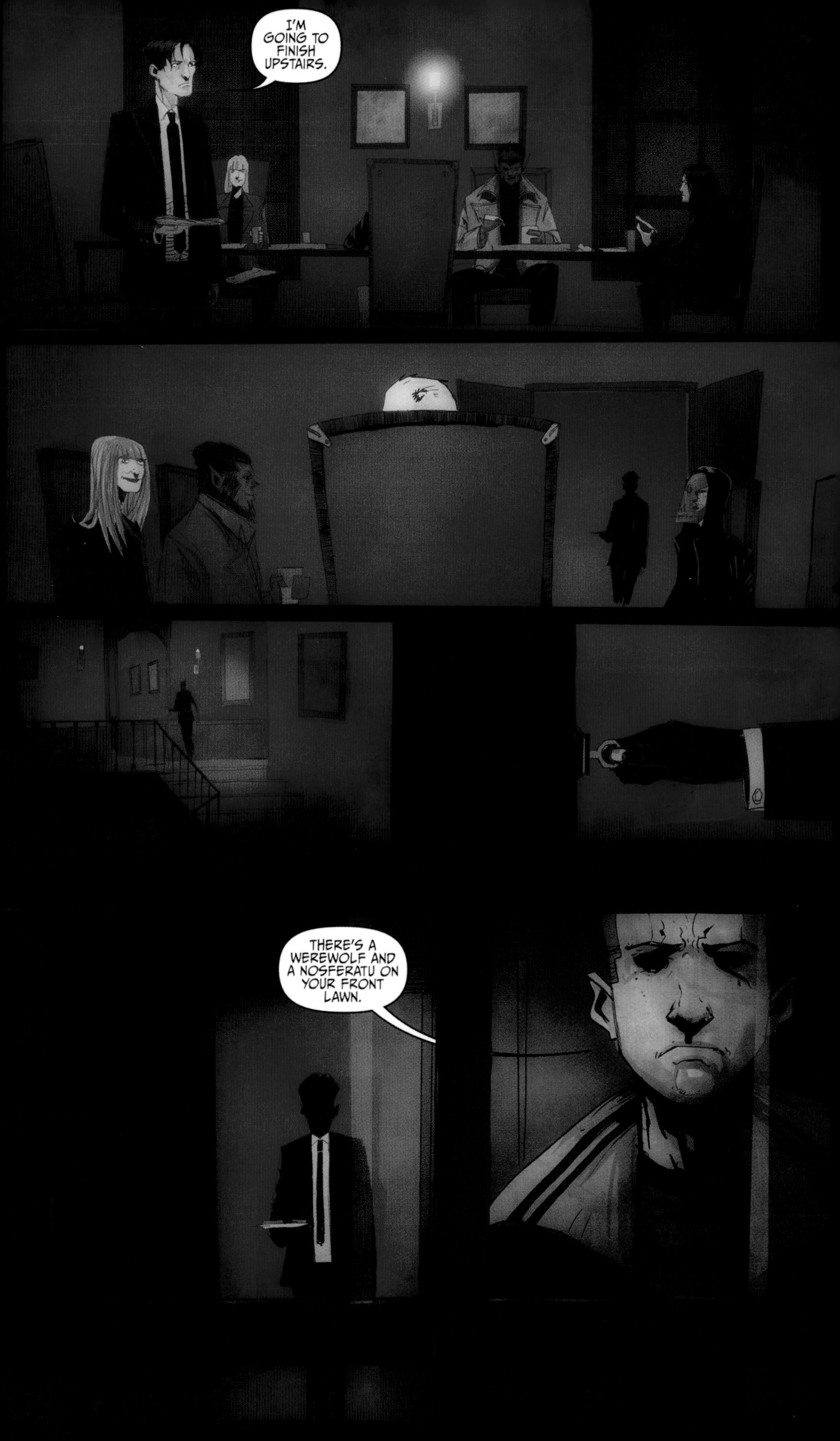
I'M GOING TO FINISH UPSTAIRS.
THERE'S A WEREWOLF AND A NOSFERATU ON YOUR FRONT LAWN.

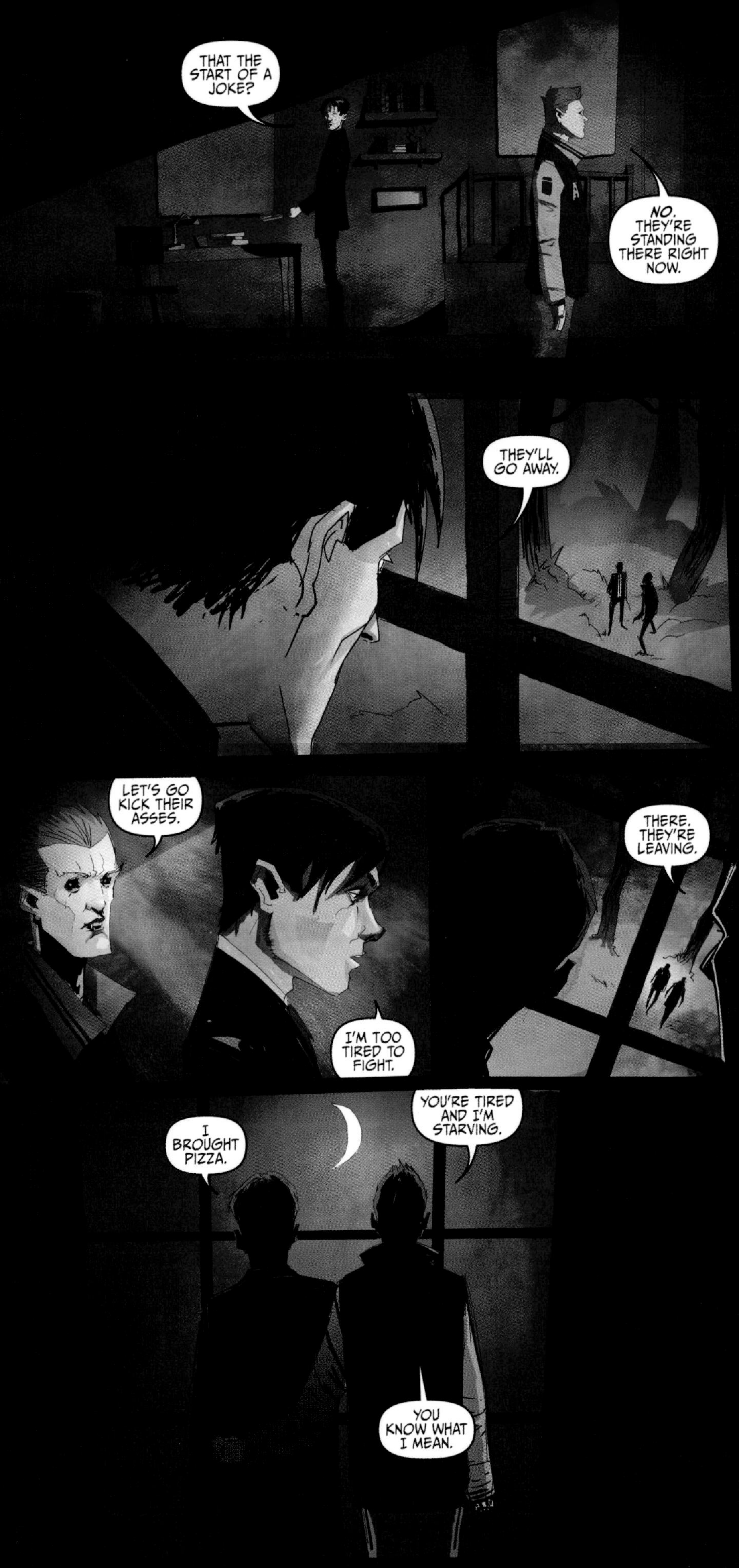
THAT THE START OF A JOKE?
NO. THEY'RE STANDING THERE RIGHT NOW.
THEY'LL GO AWAY.
LET'S GO KICK THEIR ASSES.
I'M TOO TIRED TO FIGHT.
THERE. THEY'RE LEAVING.
I BROUGHT PIZZA.
YOU'RE TIRED AND I'M STARVING.
YOU KNOW WHAT I MEAN.

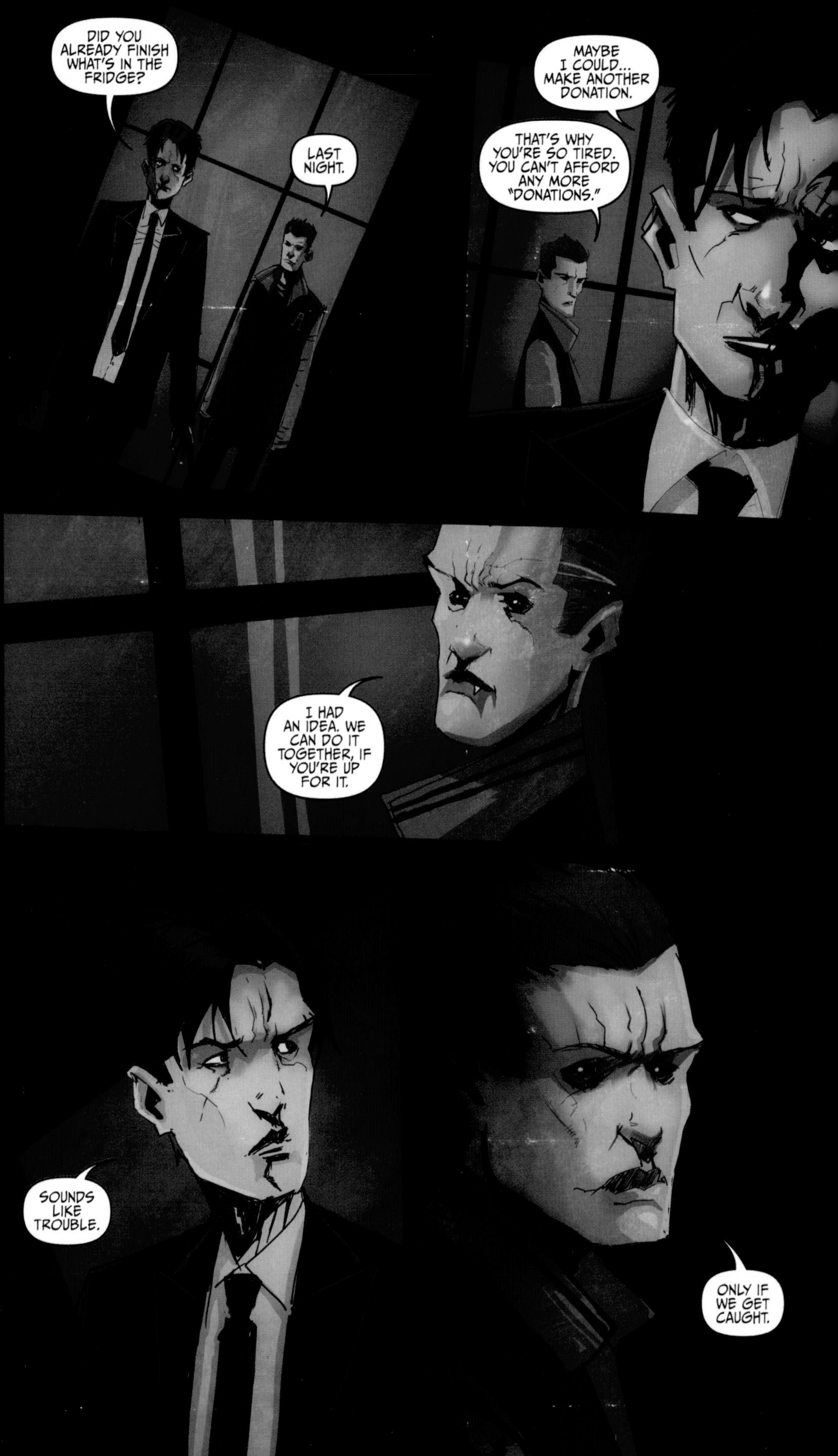
DID YOU ALREADY FINISH WHAT'S IN THE FRIDGE?
LAST NIGHT.
MAYBE I COULD... MAKE ANOTHER DONATION.
THAT'S WHY YOU'RE SO TIRED. YOU CAN'T AFFORD ANY MORE "DONATIONS."
I HAD AN IDEA. WE CAN DO IT TOGETHER, IF YOU'RE UP FOR IT.
SOUNDS LIKE TROUBLE.
ONLY IF WE GET CAUGHT.

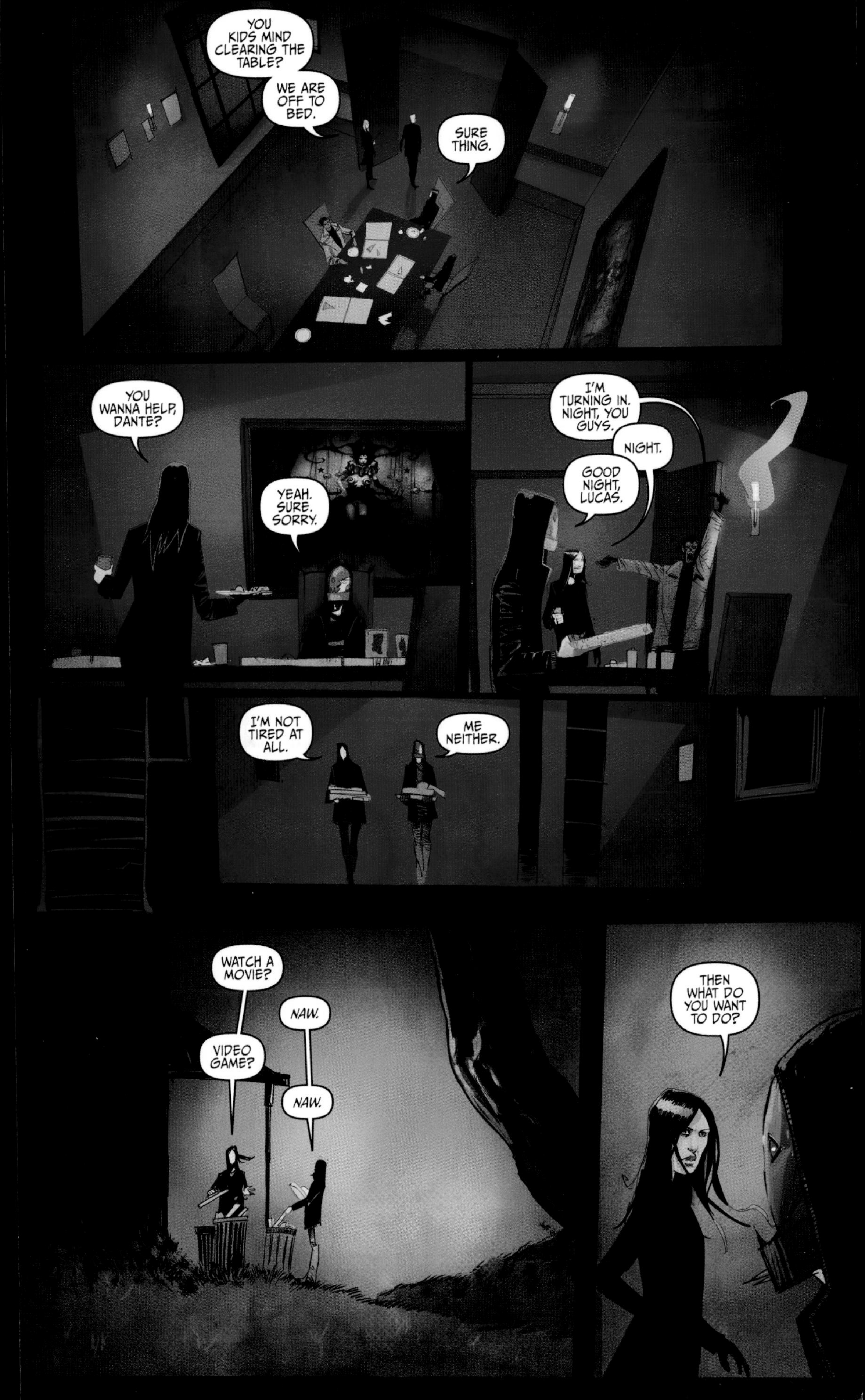
YOU KIDS MIND CLEARING THE TABLE?
WE ARE OFF TO BED.
SURE THING.
YOU WANNA HELP, DANTE?
YEAH. SURE. SORRY.
I'M TURNING IN. NIGHT, YOU GUYS.
NIGHT.
GOOD NIGHT, LUCAS.
I'M NOT TIRED AT ALL.
ME NEITHER.
WATCH A MOVIE?
NAW.
VIDEO GAME?
NAW.
THEN WHAT DO YOU WANT TO DO?

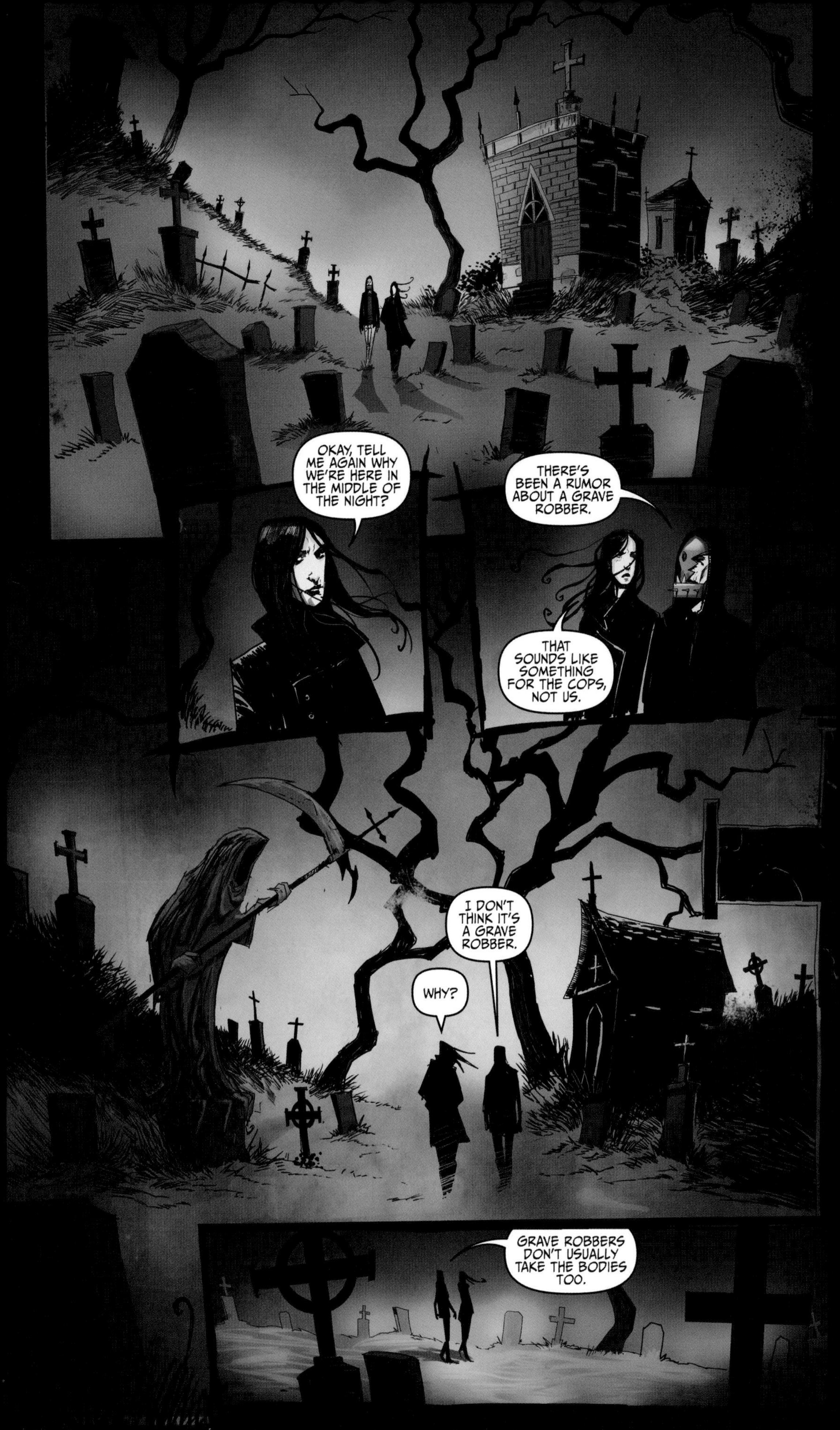
OKAY, TELL ME AGAIN WHY WE'RE HERE IN THE MIDDLE OF THE NIGHT?
THERE'S BEEN A RUMOR ABOUT A GRAVE ROBBER.
THAT SOUNDS LIKE SOMETHING FOR THE COPS, NOT US.
I DON'T THINK IT'S A GRAVE ROBBER.
WHY?
GRAVE ROBBERS DON'T USUALLY TAKE THE BODIES TOO.

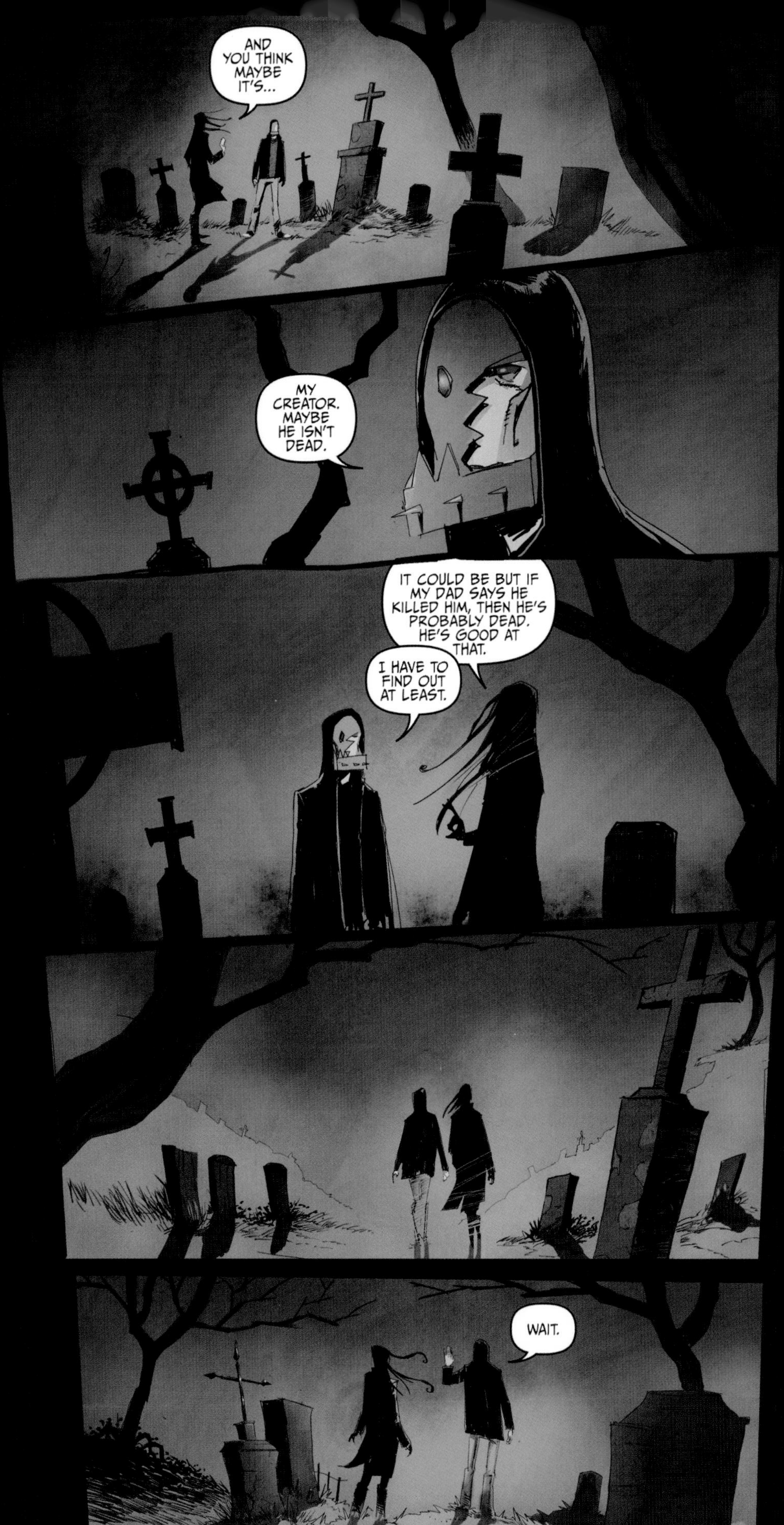
AND YOU THINK MAYBE IT'S...
MY CREATOR. MAYBE HE ISN'T DEAD.
IT COULD BE BUT IF MY DAD SAYS HE KILLED HIM, THEN HE'S PROBABLY DEAD. HE'S GOOD AT THAT.
I HAVE TO FIND OUT AT LEAST.
WAIT.

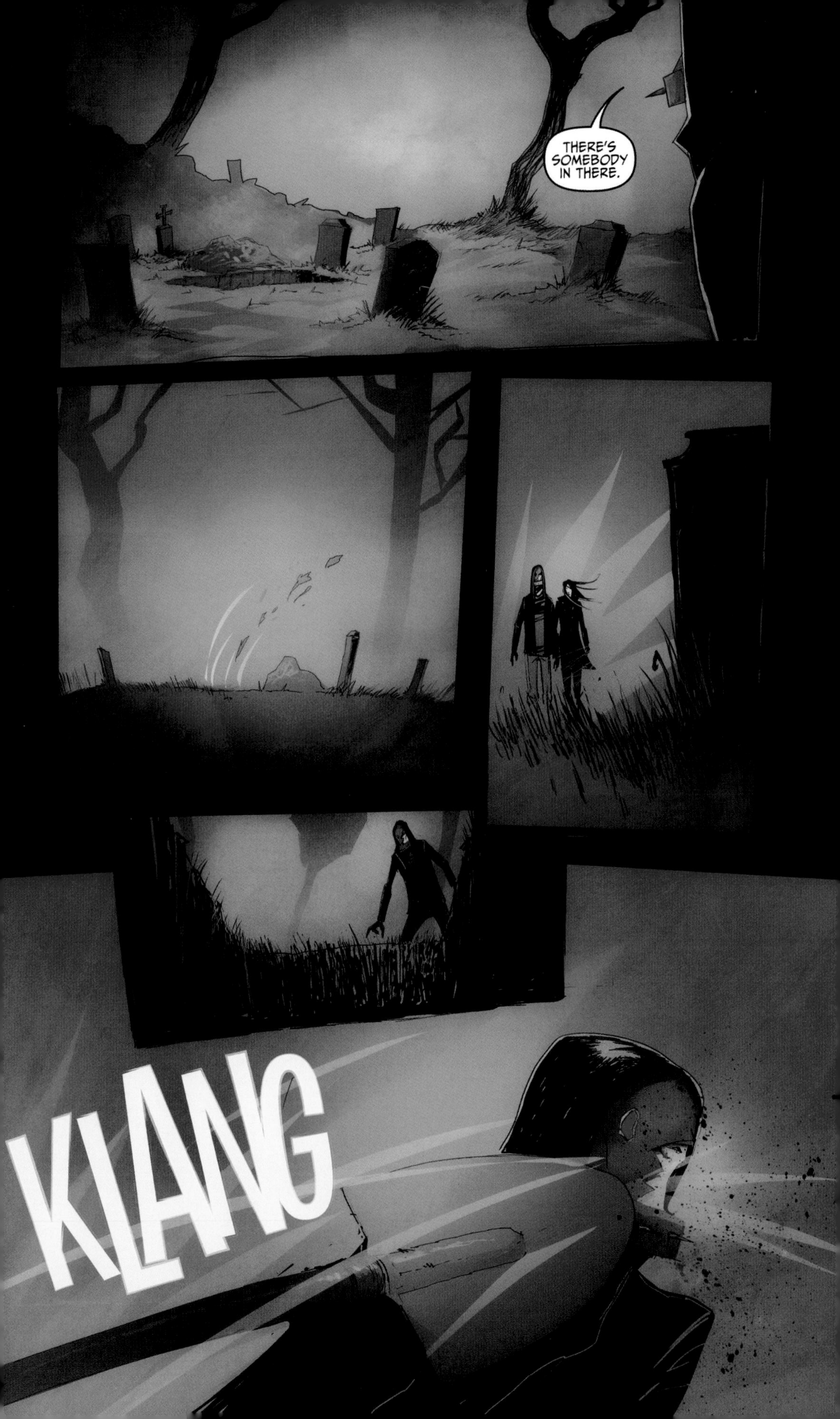
THERE'S SOMEBODY IN THERE.
KLANG

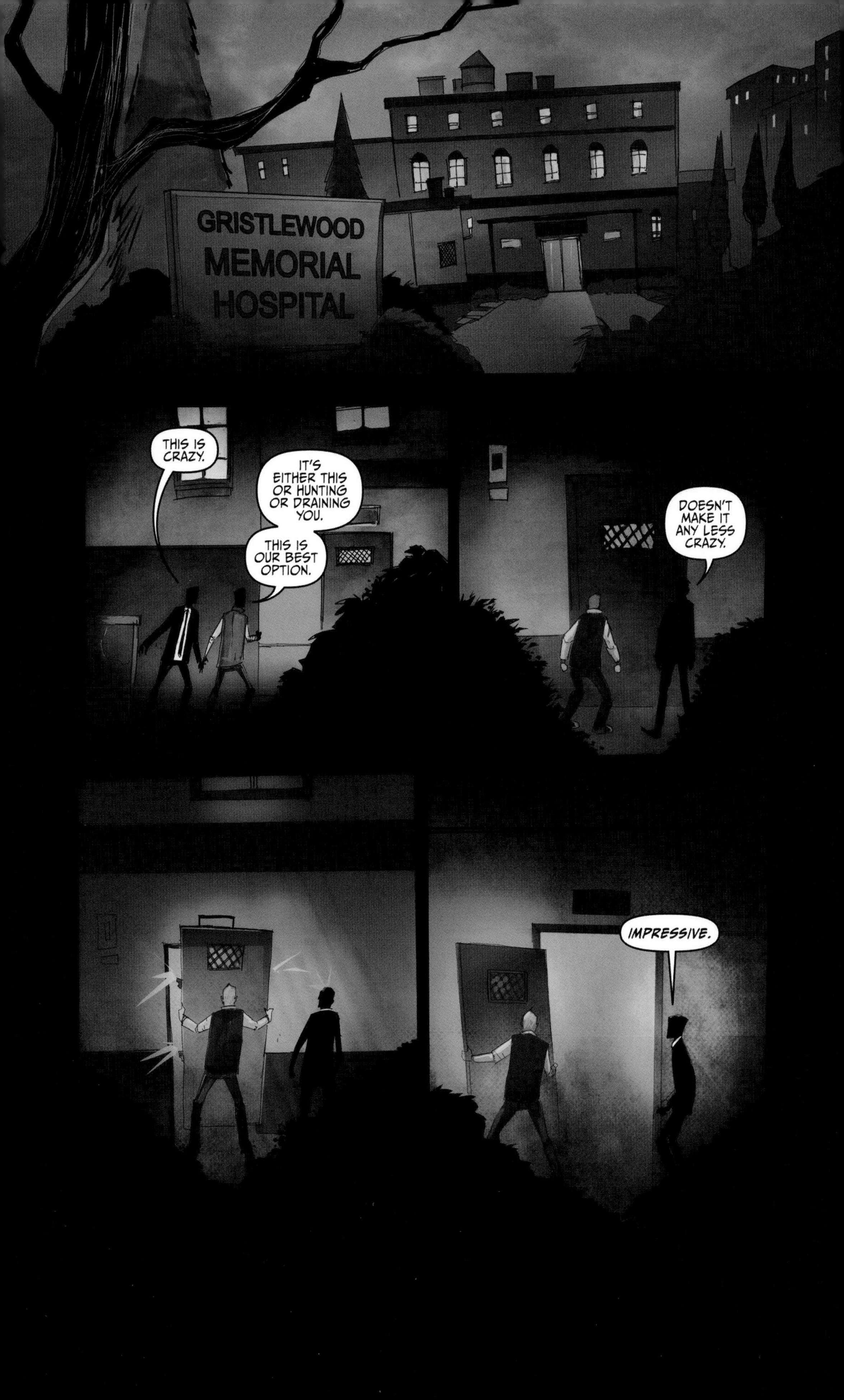
GRISTLEWOOD MEMORIAL HOSPITAL
THIS IS CRAZY.
IT'S EITHER THIS OR HUNTING OR DRAINING YOU.
THIS IS OUR BEST OPTION.
DOESN'T MAKE IT ANY LESS CRAZY.
IMPRESSIVE.

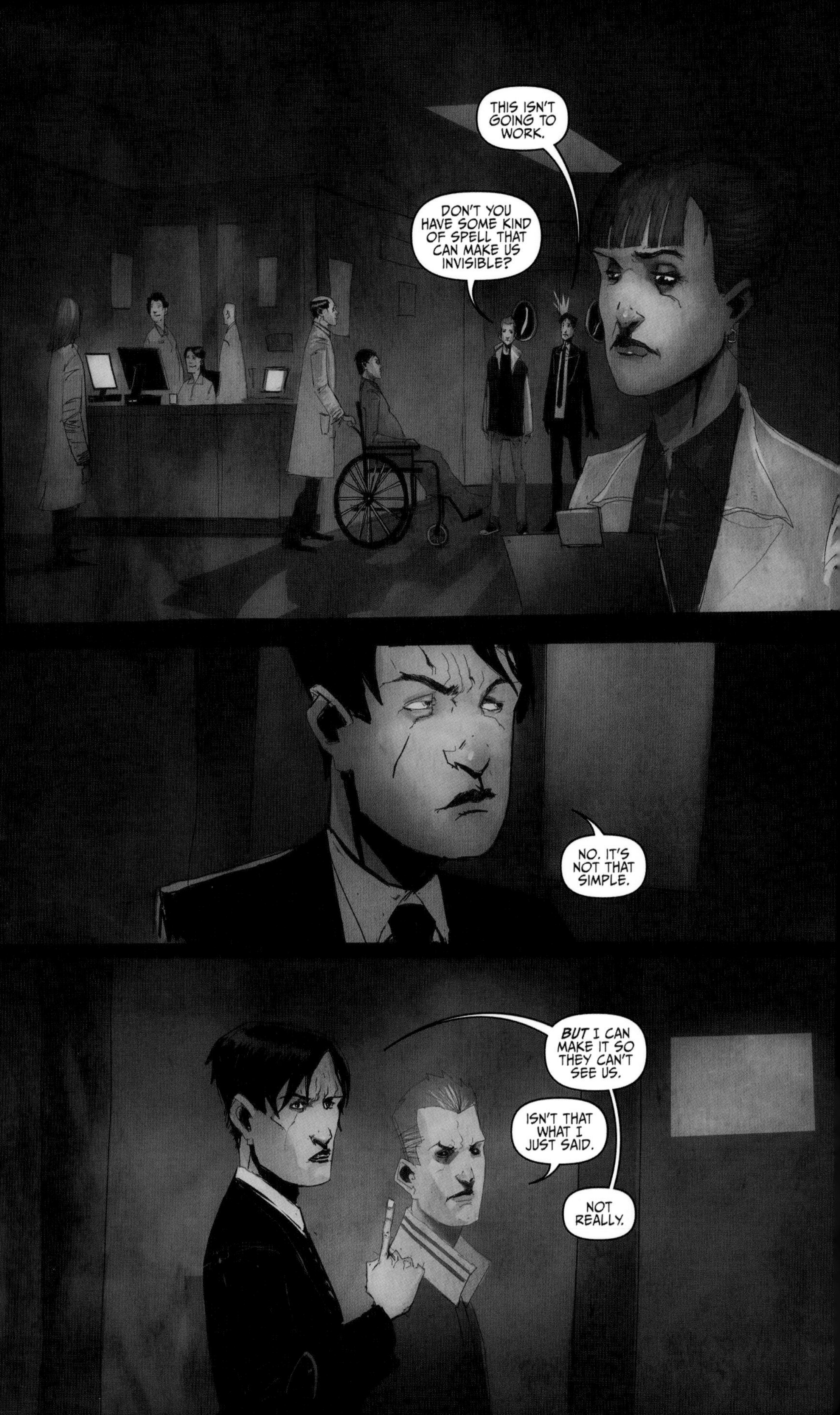
THIS ISN'T GOING TO WORK.
DON'T YOU HAVE SOME KIND OF SPELL THAT CAN MAKE US INVISIBLE?
NO. IT'S NOT THAT SIMPLE.
BUT I CAN MAKE IT SO THEY CAN'T SEE US.
ISN'T THAT WHAT I JUST SAID.
NOT REALLY.

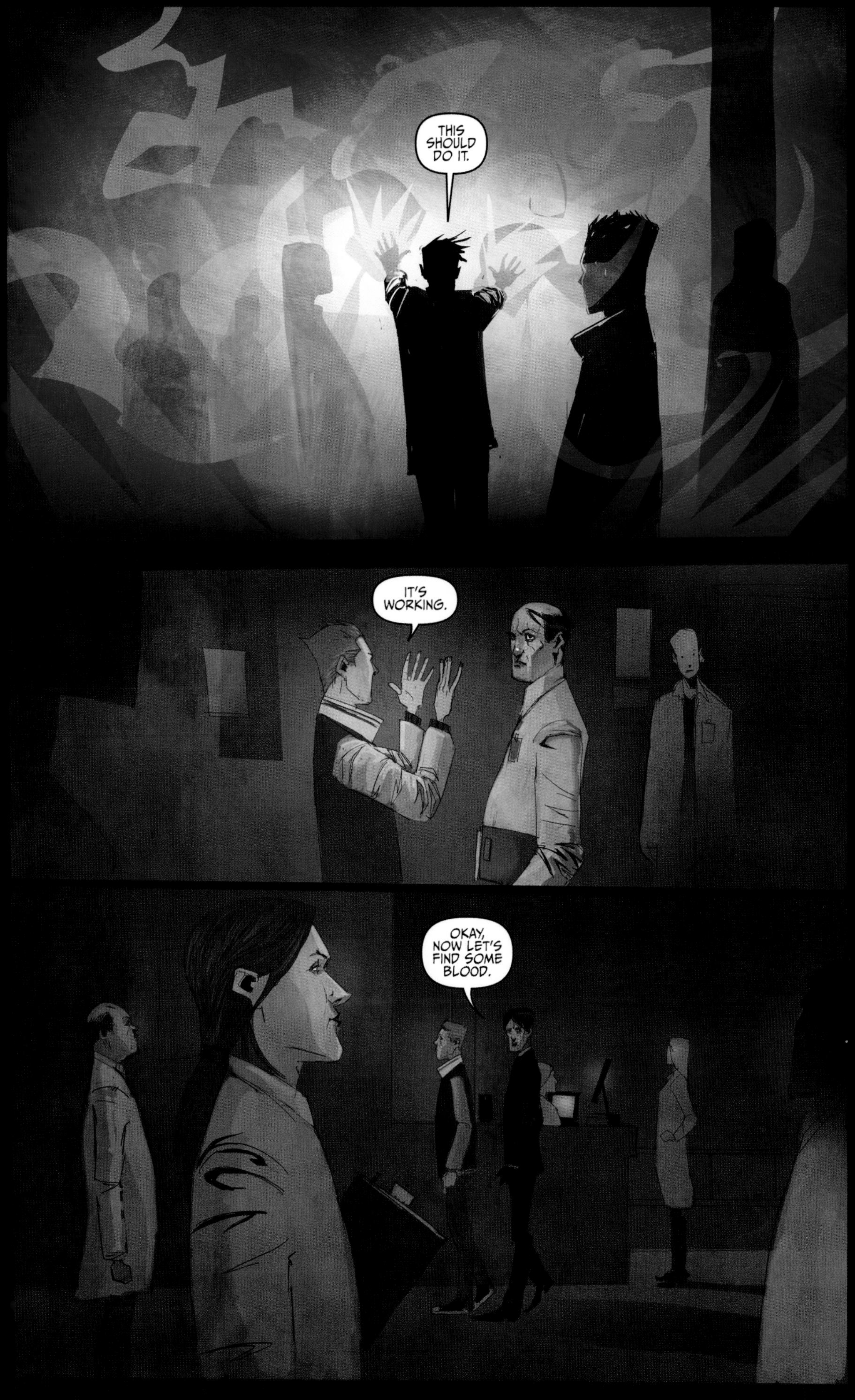
THIS SHOULD DO IT.
IT'S WORKING.
OKAY, NOW LET'S FIND SOME BLOOD.

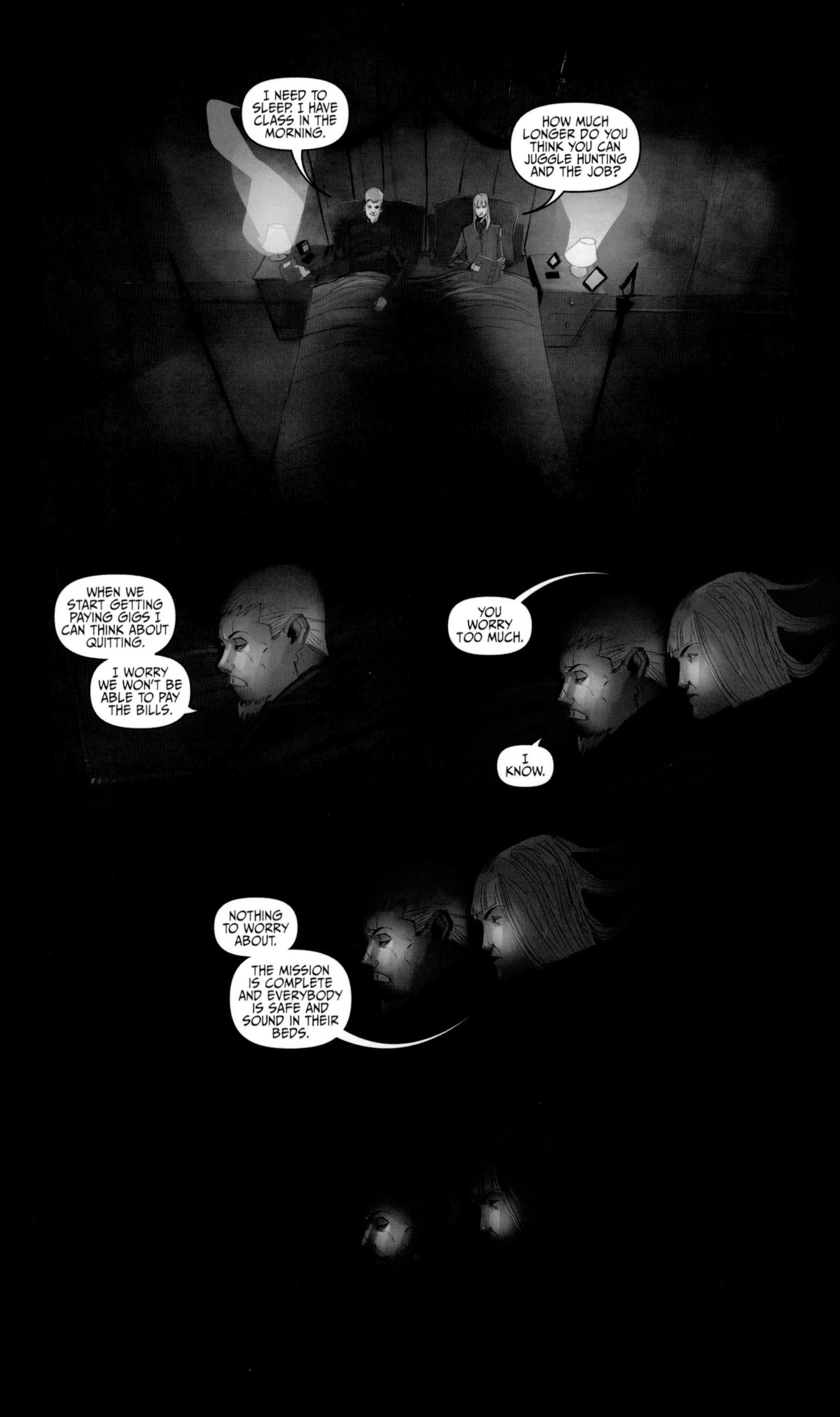
I NEED TO SLEEP. I HAVE CLASS IN THE MORNING.
HOW MUCH LONGER DO YOU THINK YOU CAN JUGGLE HUNTING AND THE JOB?
WHEN WE START GETTING PAYING GIGS I CAN THINK ABOUT QUITTING.
I WORRY WE WON'T BE ABLE TO PAY THE BILLS.
YOU WORRY TOO MUCH.
I KNOW.
NOTHING TO WORRY ABOUT.
THE MISSION IS COMPLETE AND EVERYBODY IS SAFE AND SOUND IN THEIR BEDS.

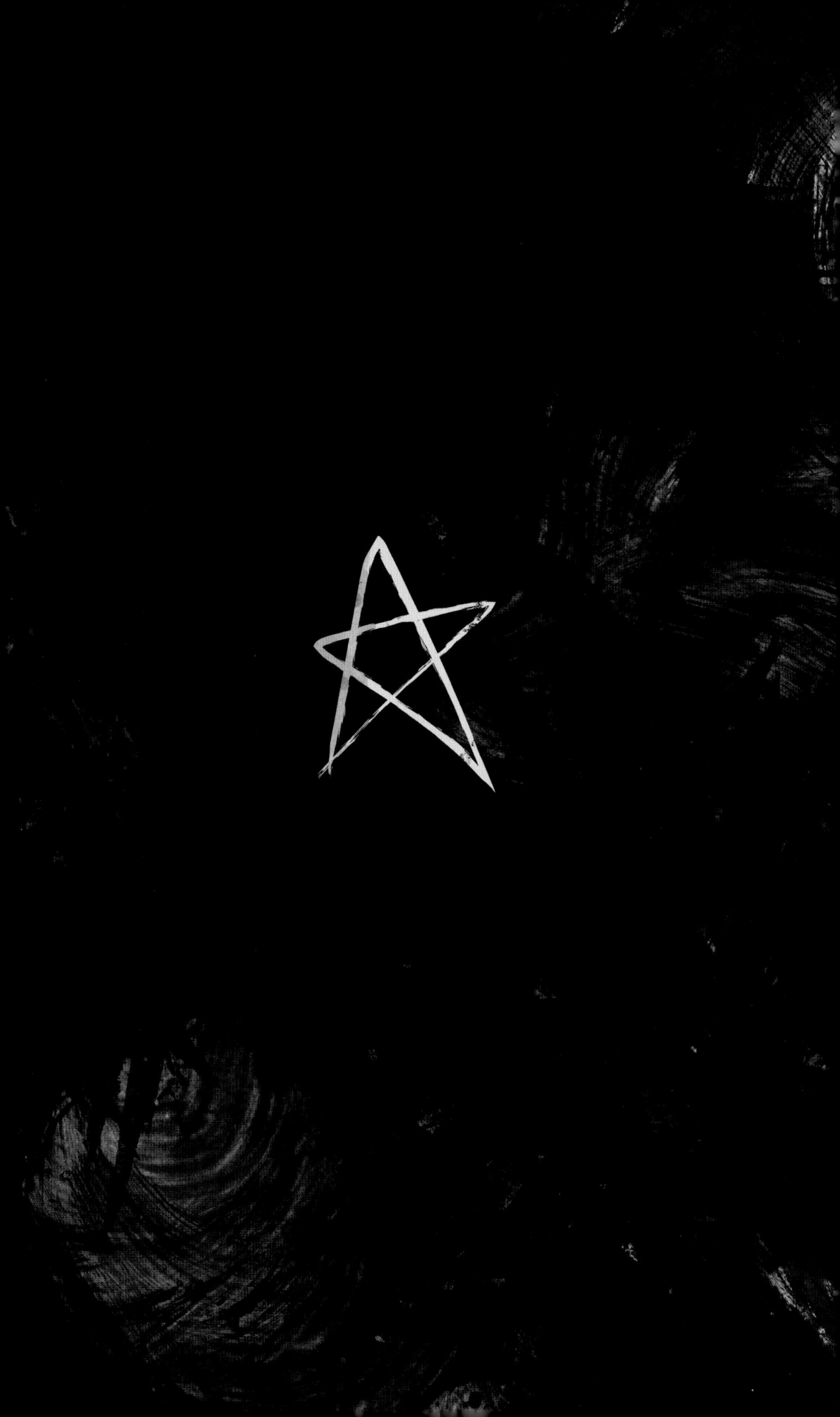

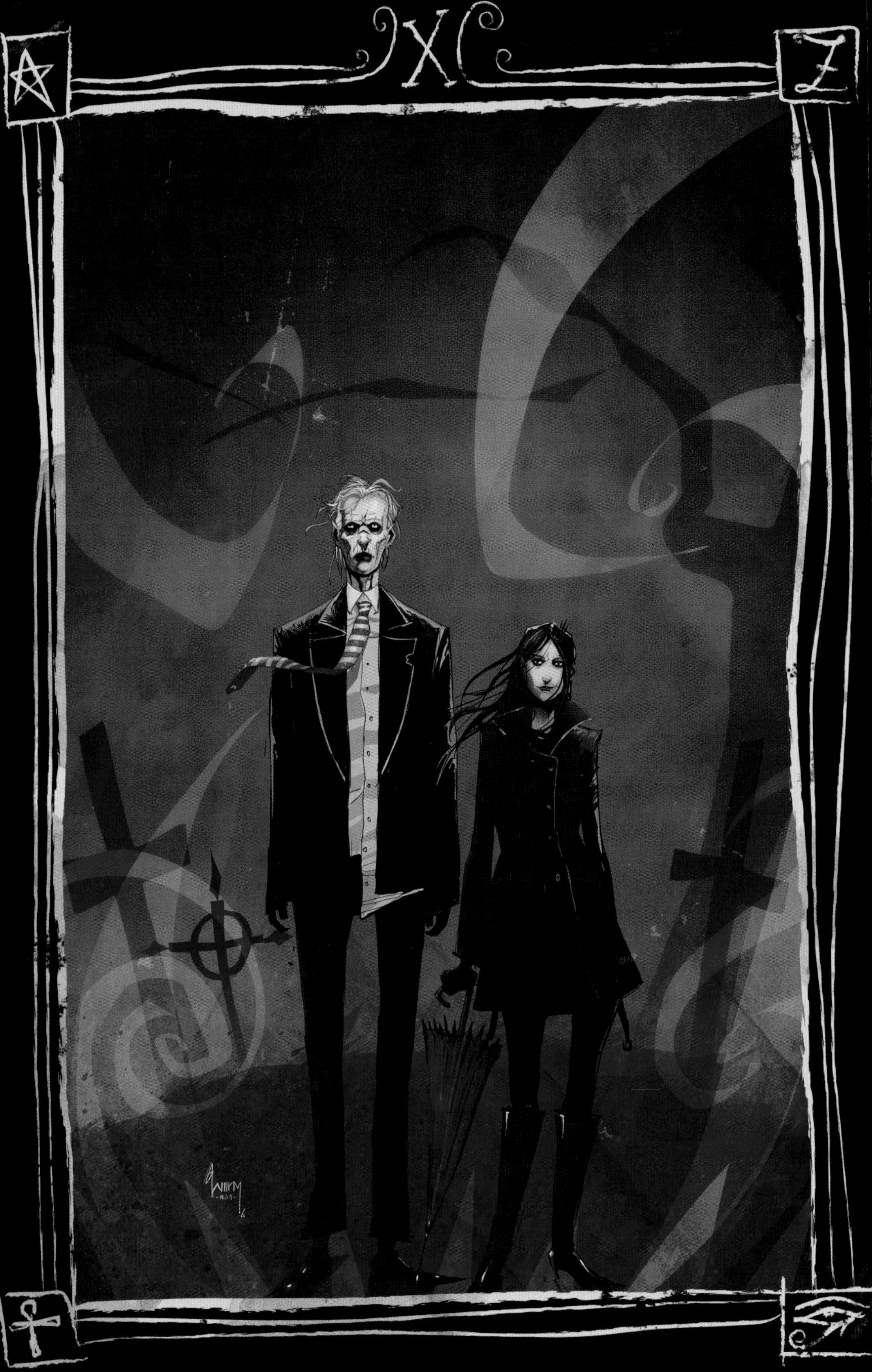
X

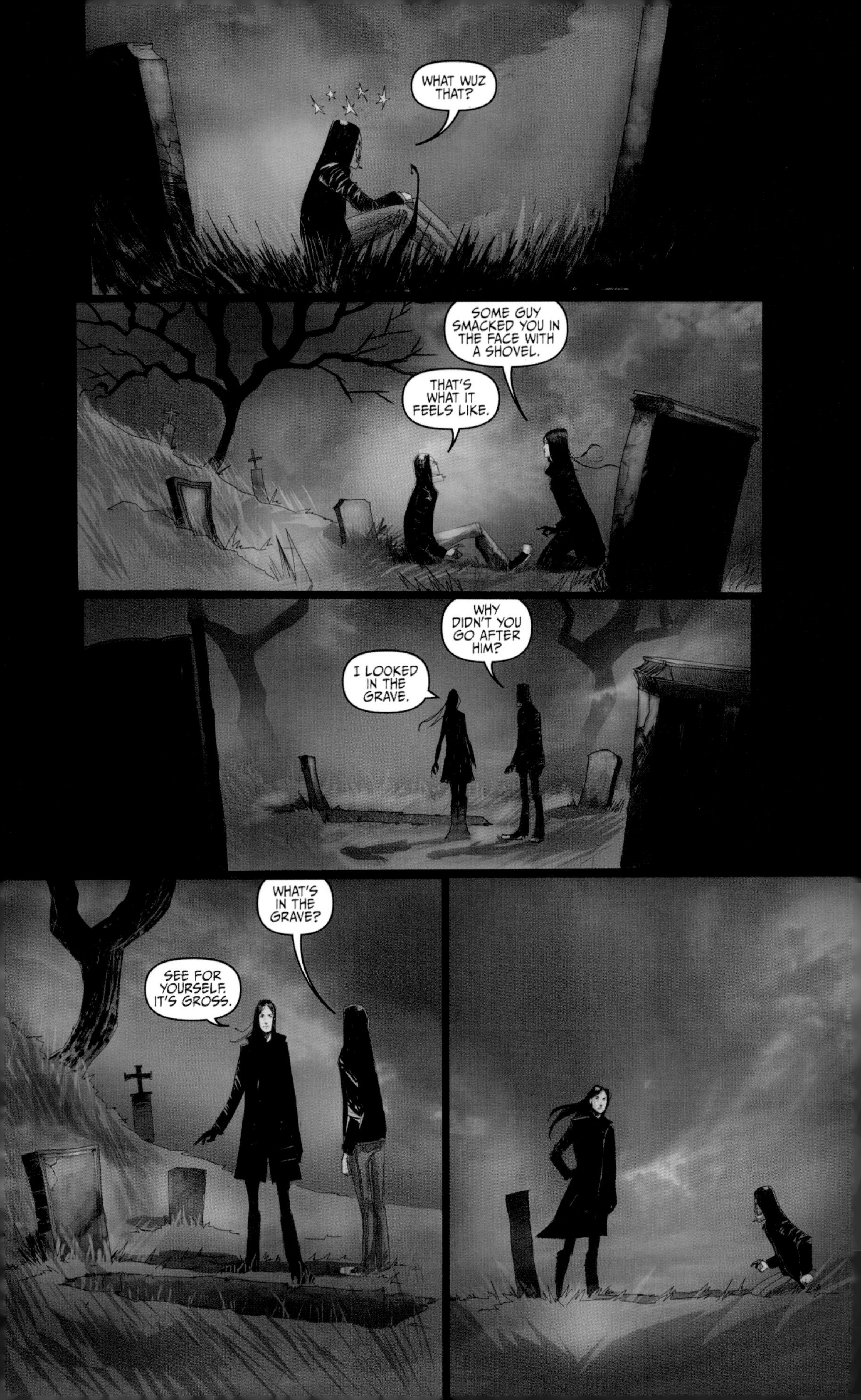
WHAT WUZ THAT?
SOME GUY SMACKED YOU IN THE FACE WITH A SHOVEL.
THAT'S WHAT IT FEELS LIKE.
WHY DIDN'T YOU GO AFTER HIM?
I LOOKED IN THE GRAVE.
WHAT'S IN THE GRAVE?
SEE FOR YOURSELF. IT'S GROSS.

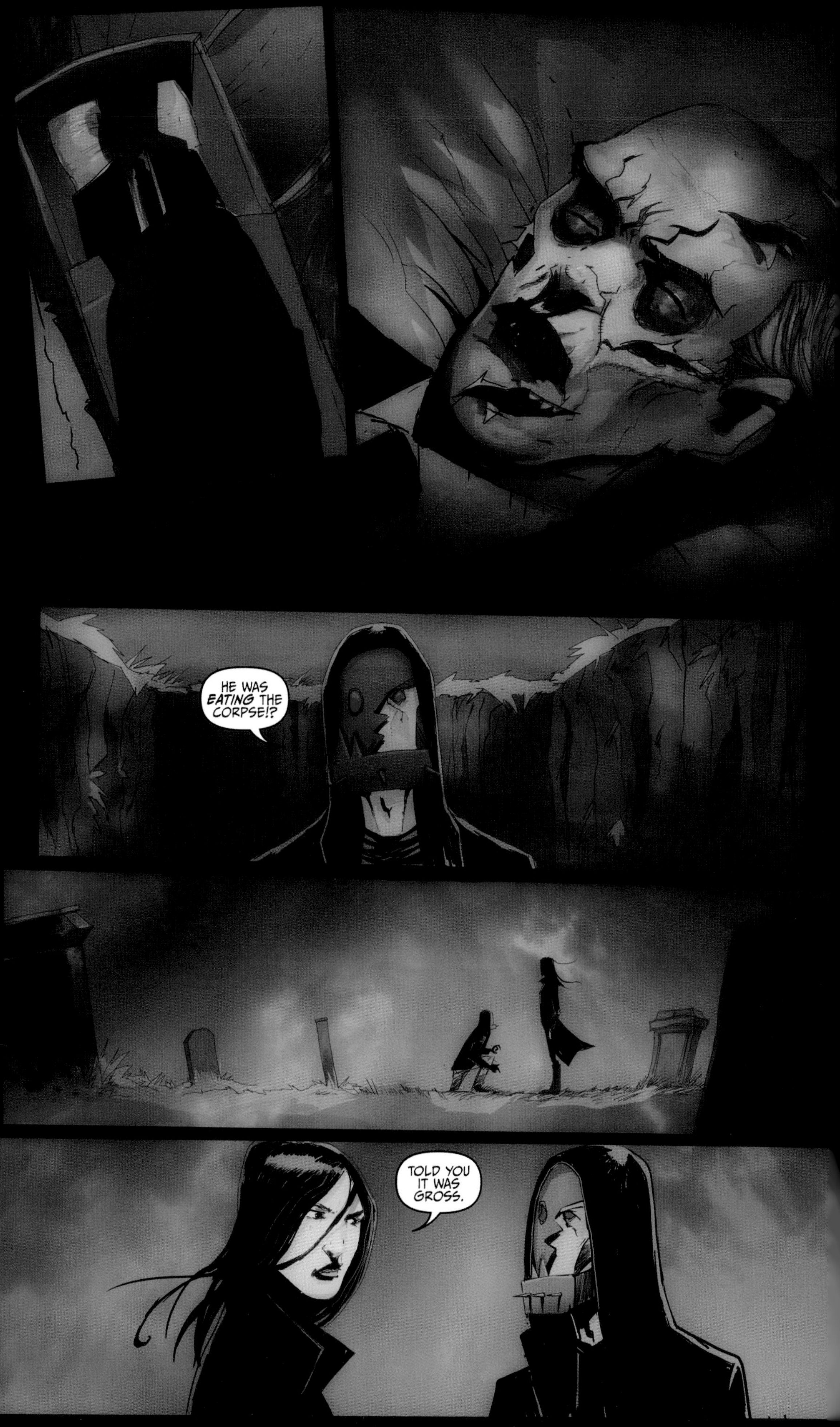
HE WAS EATING THE CORPSE!?
TOLD YOU IT WAS GROSS.

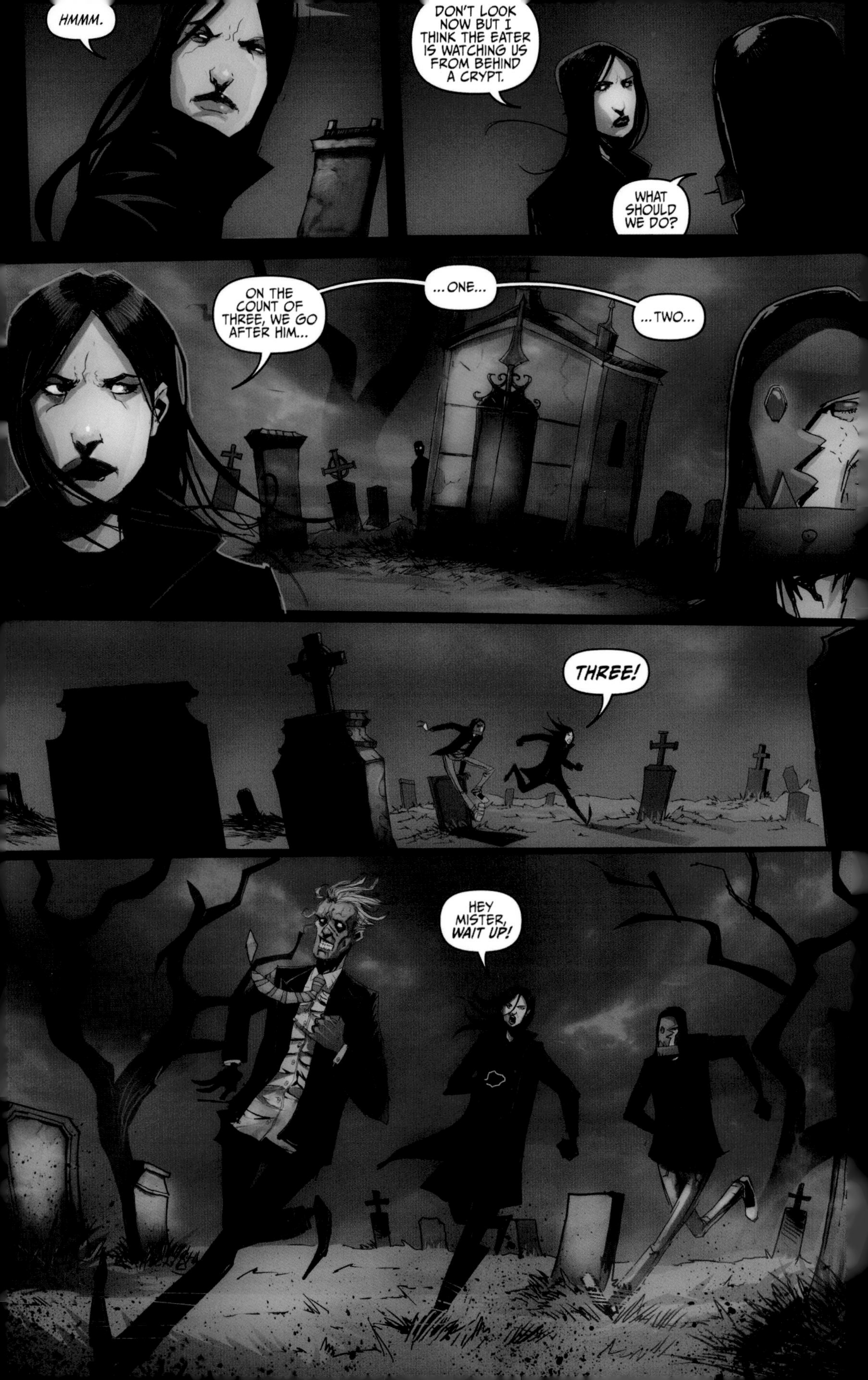
HMMM.
DON'T LOOK NOW BUT I THINK THE EATER IS WATCHING US FROM BEHIND A CRYPT.
WHAT SHOULD WE DO?
ON THE COUNT OF THREE, WE GO AFTER HIM...
...ONE...
...TWO...
THREE!
HEY MISTER, WAIT UP!

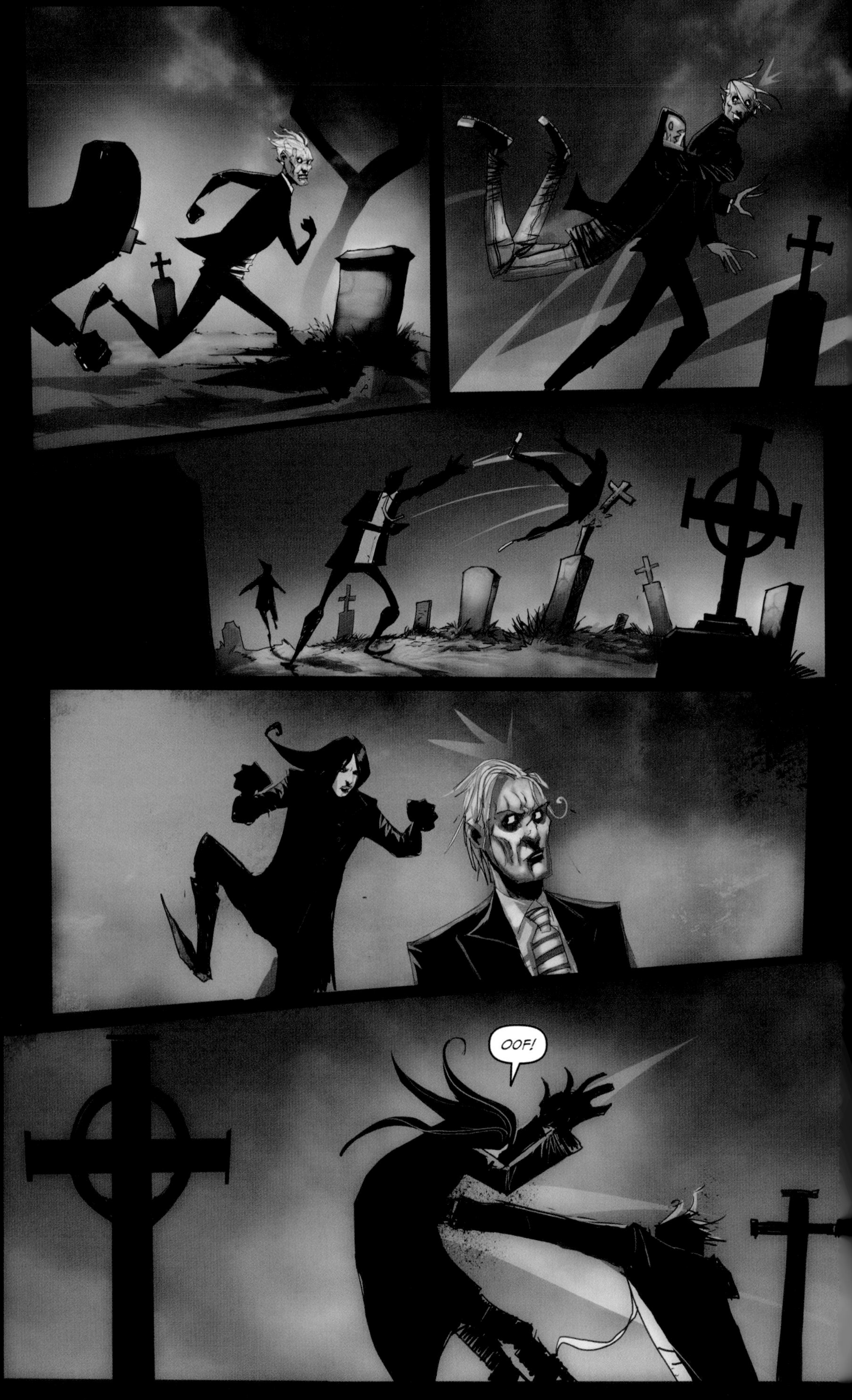
OOF!

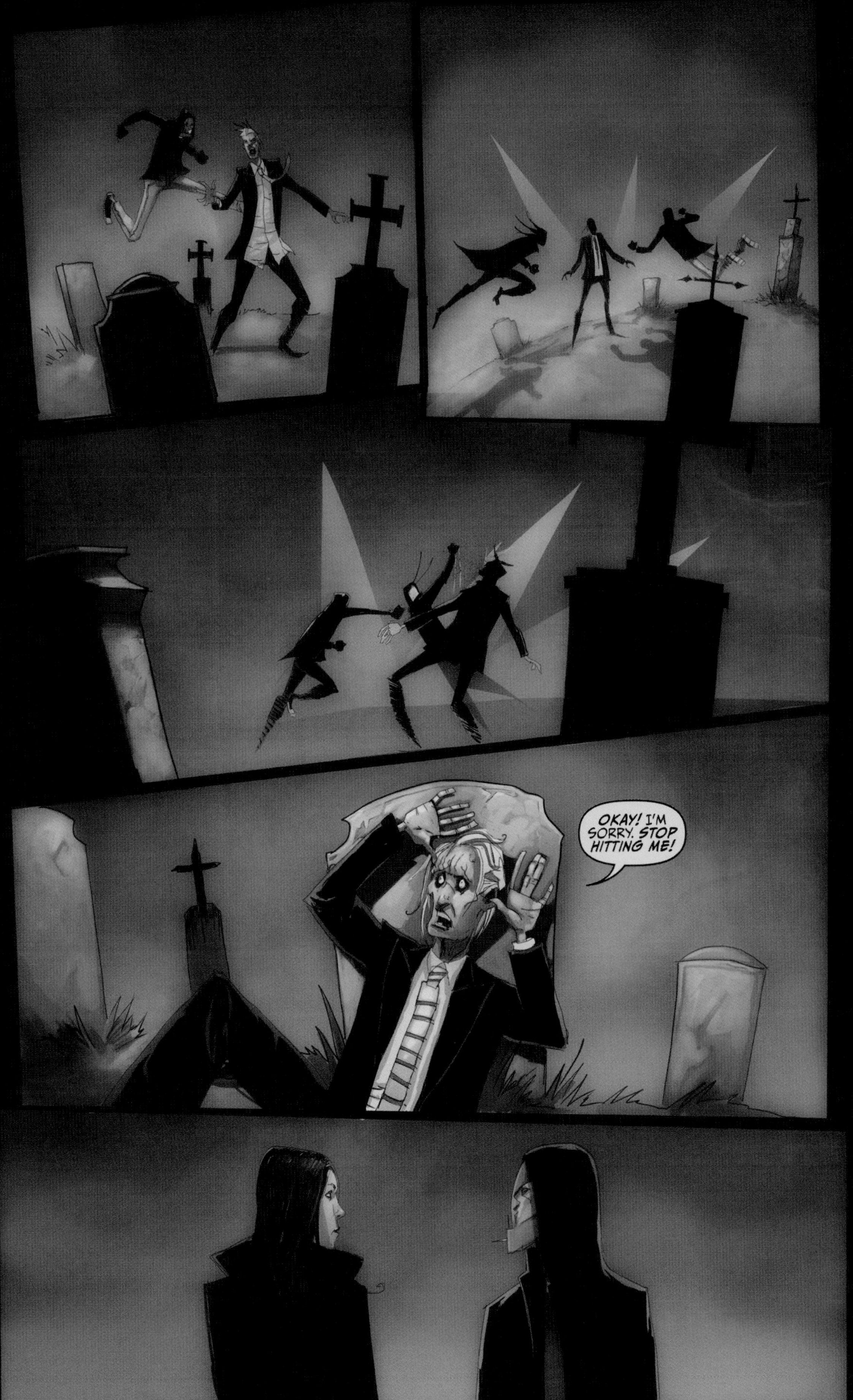
OKAY! I'M SORRY. STOP HITTING ME!

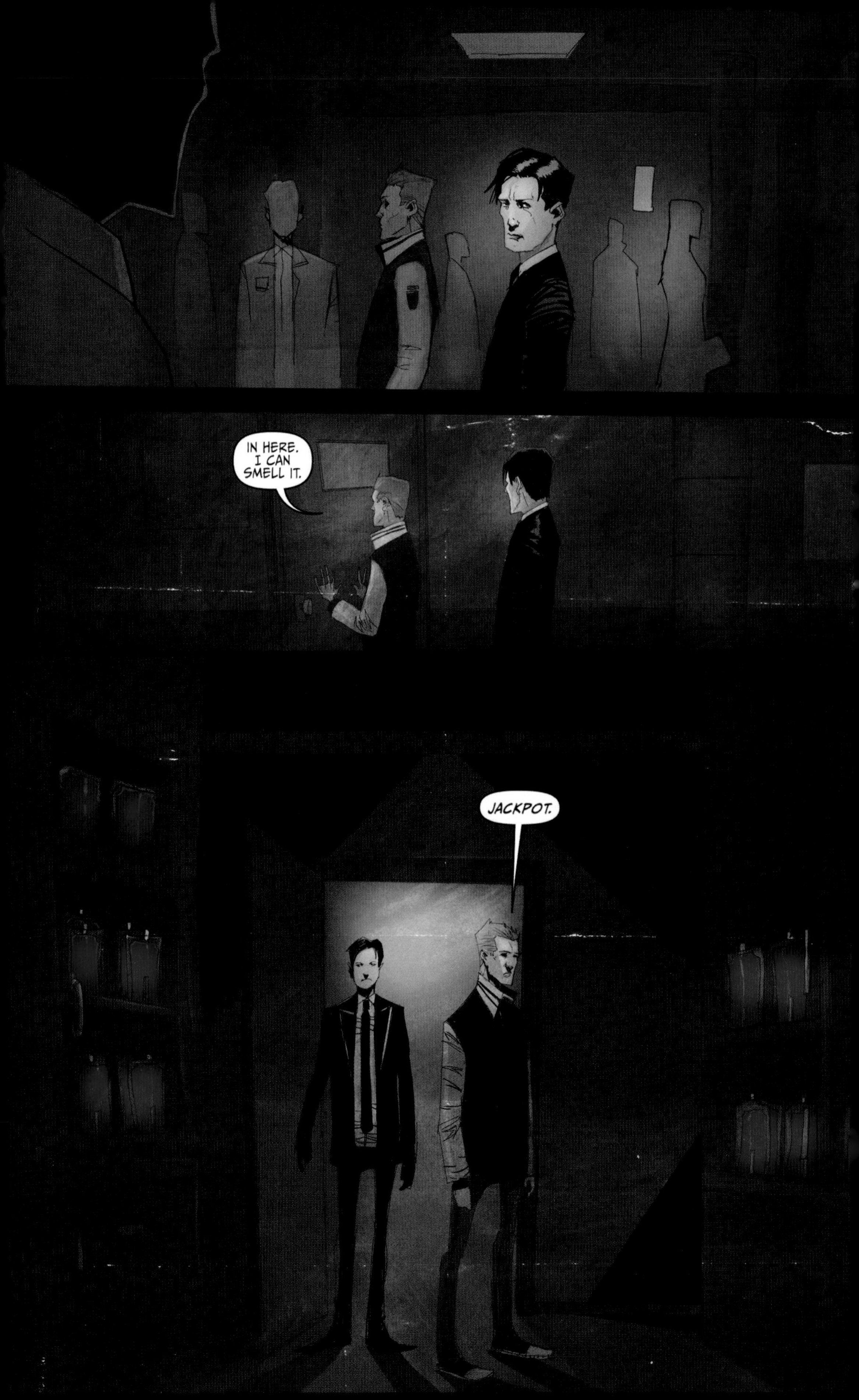
IN HERE. I CAN SMELL IT.
JACKPOT.

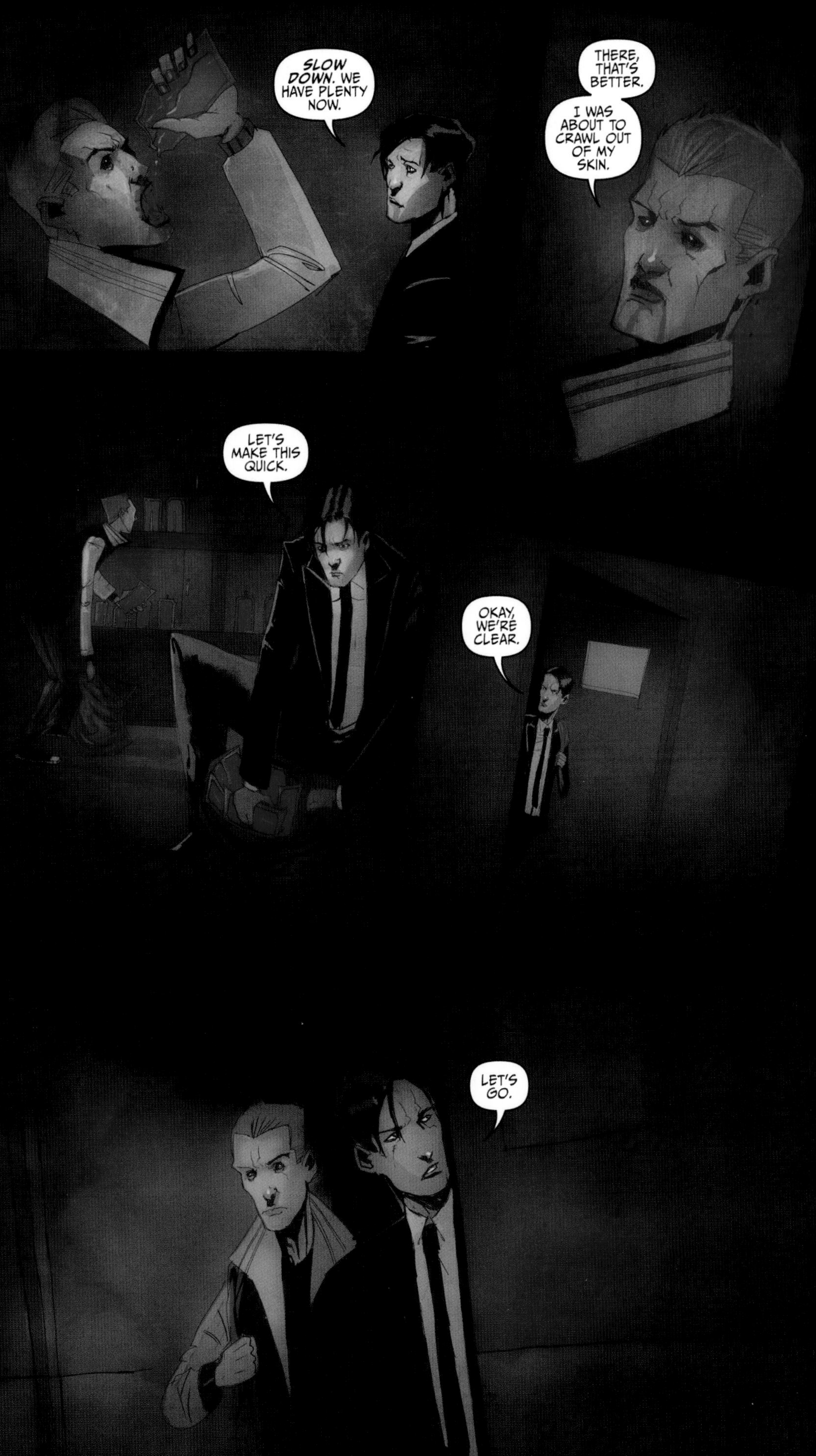
SLOW DOWN. WE HAVE PLENTY NOW.
THERE, THAT'S BETTER.
I WAS ABOUT TO CRAWL OUT OF MY SKIN.
LET'S MAKE THIS QUICK.
OKAY, WE'RE CLEAR.
LET'S GO.

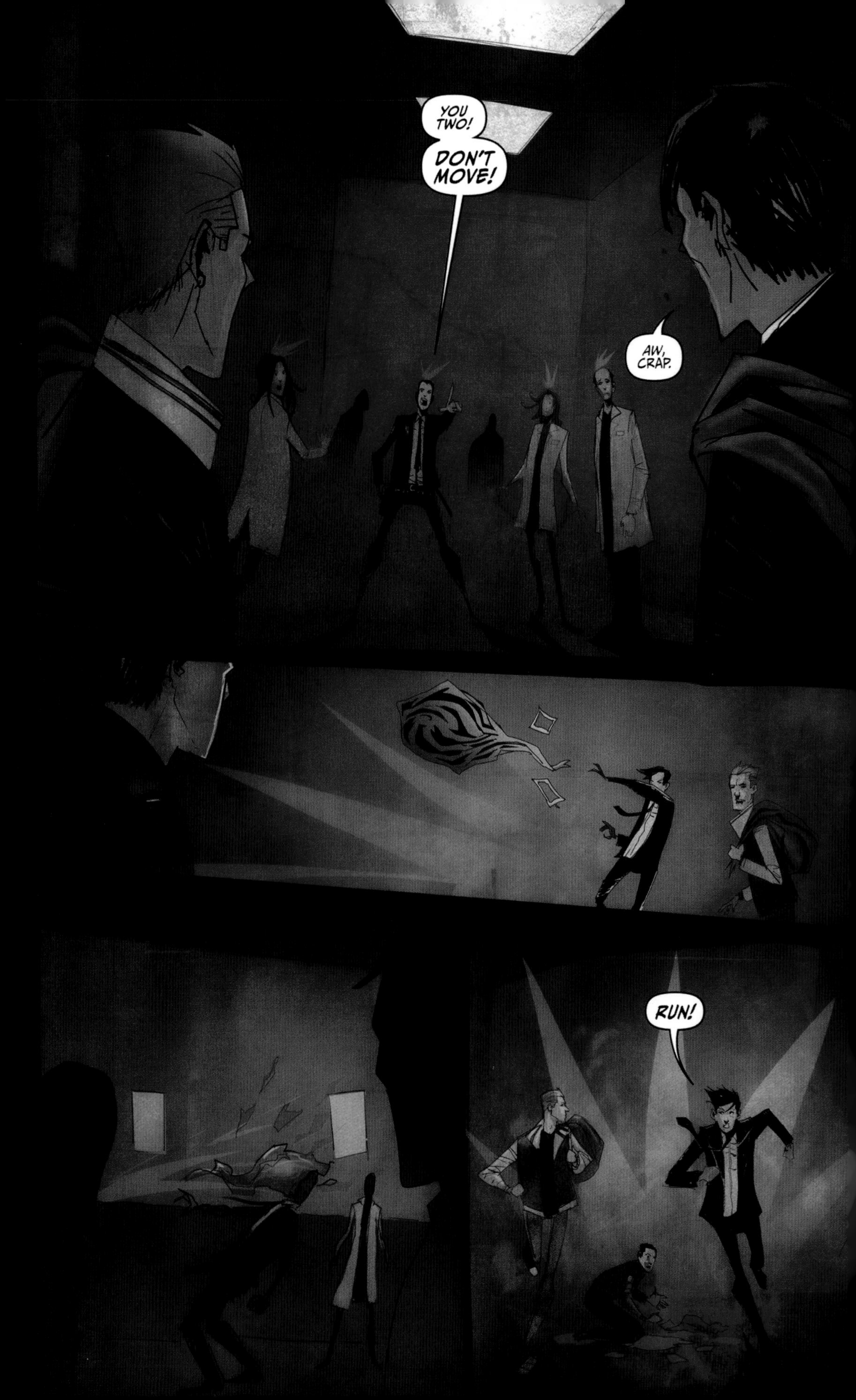
YOU TWO!
DON'T MOVE!
AW, CRAP.
RUN!

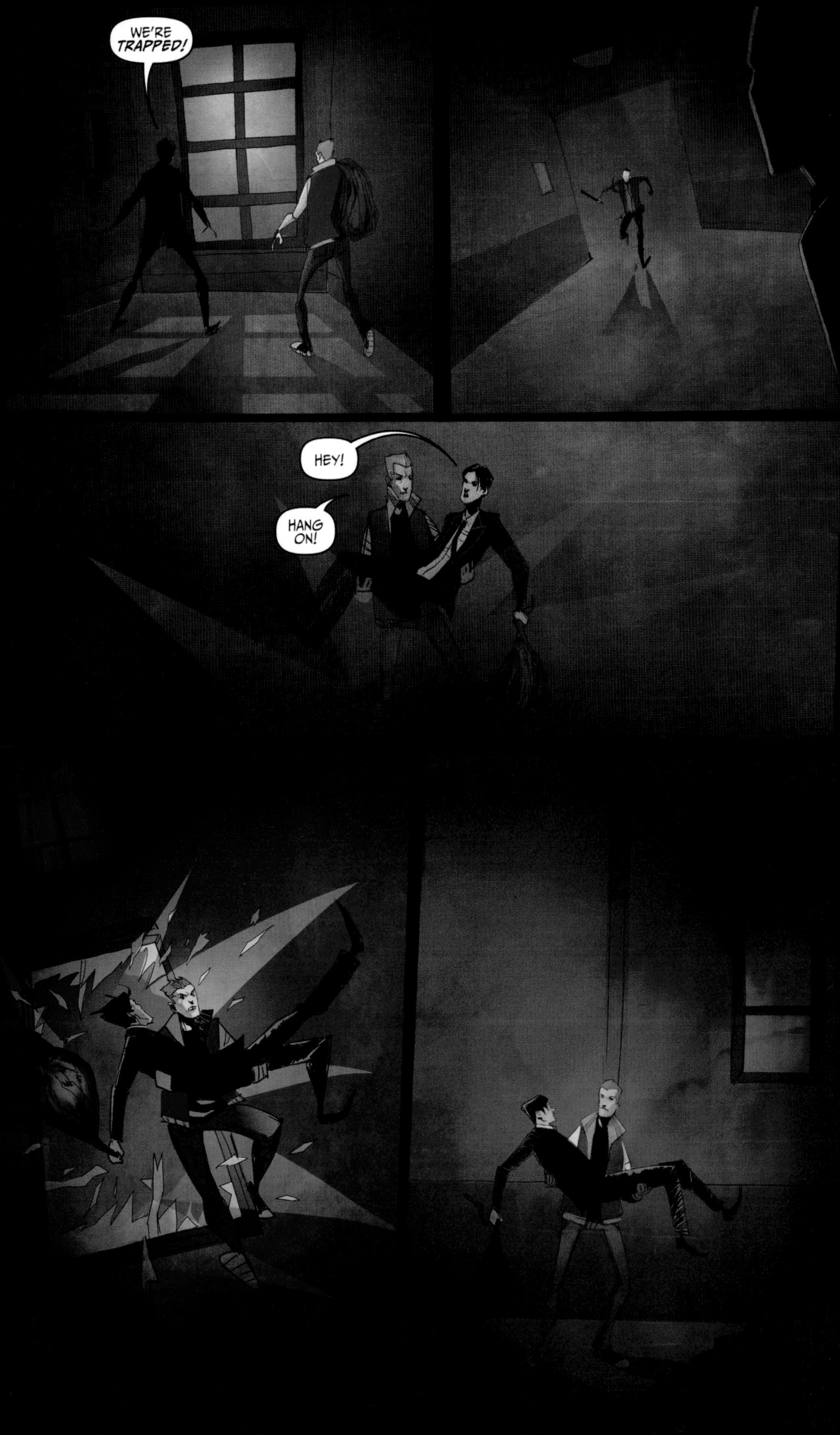
WE'RE TRAPPED!
HEY!
HANG ON!

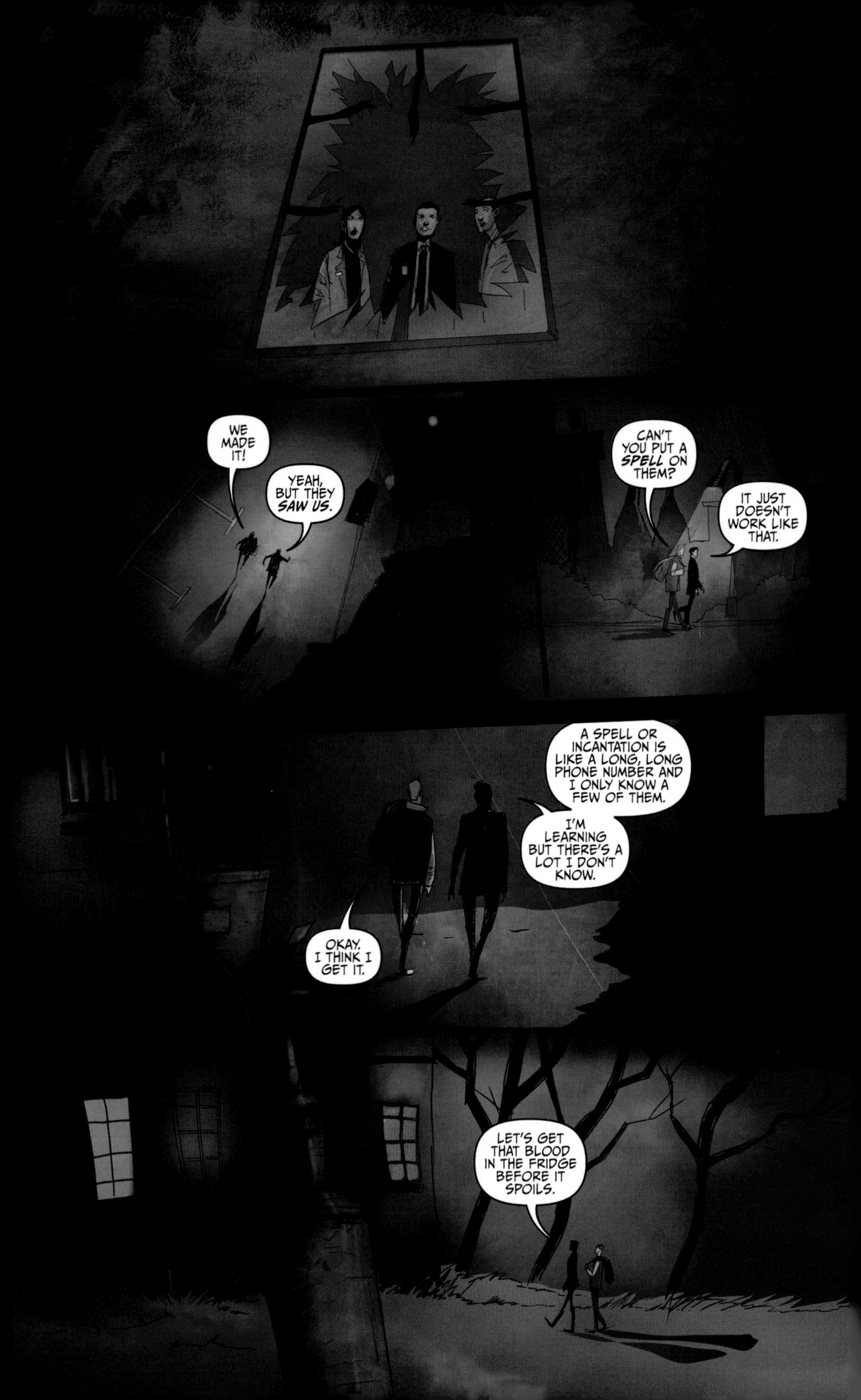
WE MADE IT!
YEAH, BUT THEY SAW US.
CAN'T YOU PUT A SPELL ON THEM?
IT JUST DOESN'T WORK LIKE THAT.
A SPELL OR INCANTATION IS LIKE A LONG, LONG PHONE NUMBER AND I ONLY KNOW A FEW OF THEM.
I'M LEARNING BUT THERE'S A LOT I DON'T KNOW.
OKAY. I THINK I GET IT.
LET'S GET THAT BLOOD IN THE FRIDGE BEFORE IT SPOILS.

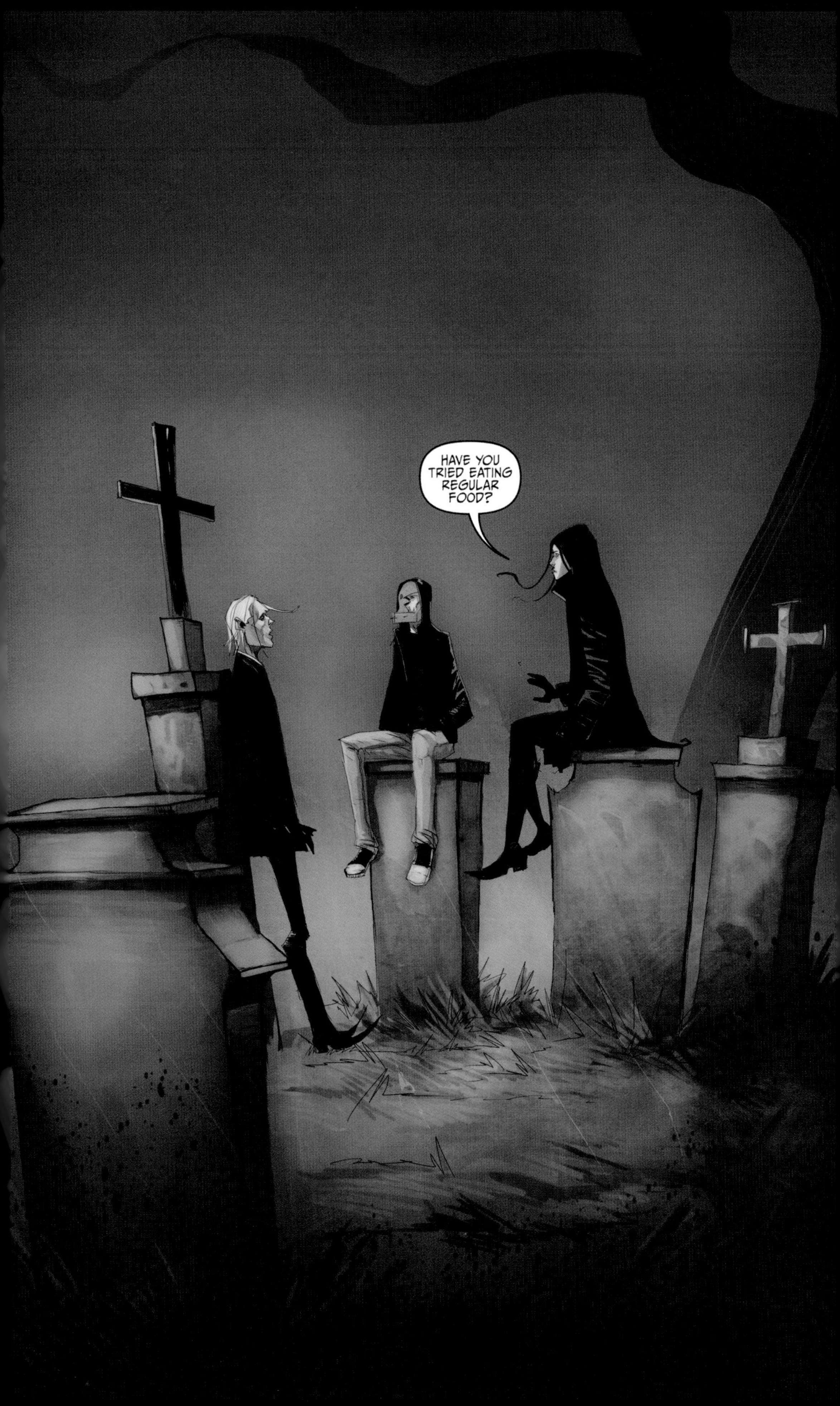
HAVE YOU TRIED EATING REGULAR FOOD?

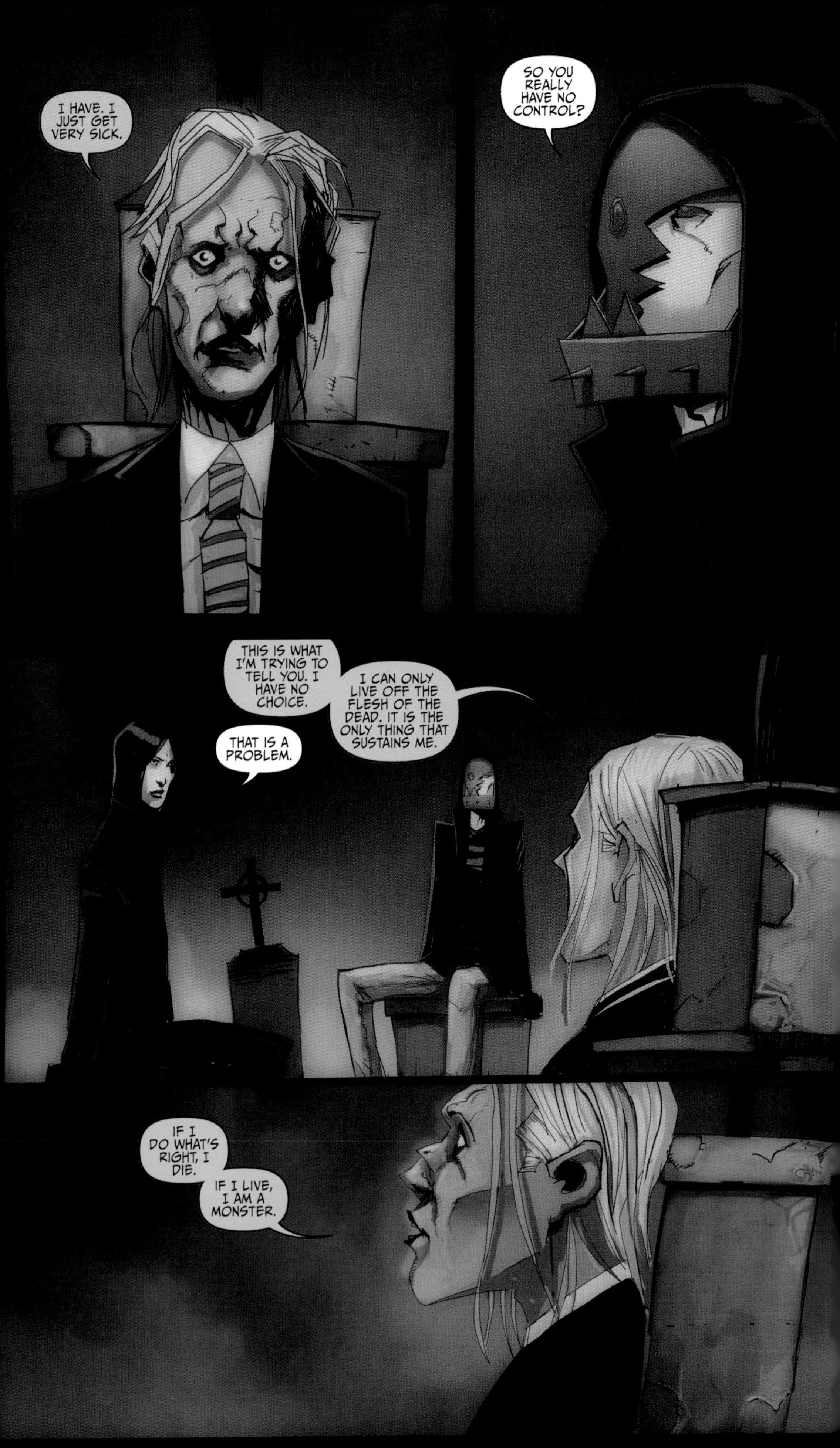
I HAVE. I JUST GET VERY SICK.
SO YOU REALLY HAVE NO CONTROL?
THIS IS WHAT I'M TRYING TO TELL YOU. I HAVE NO CHOICE.
I CAN ONLY LIVE OFF THE FLESH OF THE DEAD. IT IS THE ONLY THING THAT SUSTAINS ME.
THAT IS A PROBLEM.
IF I DO WHAT'S RIGHT, I DIE.
IF I LIVE, I AM A MONSTER.

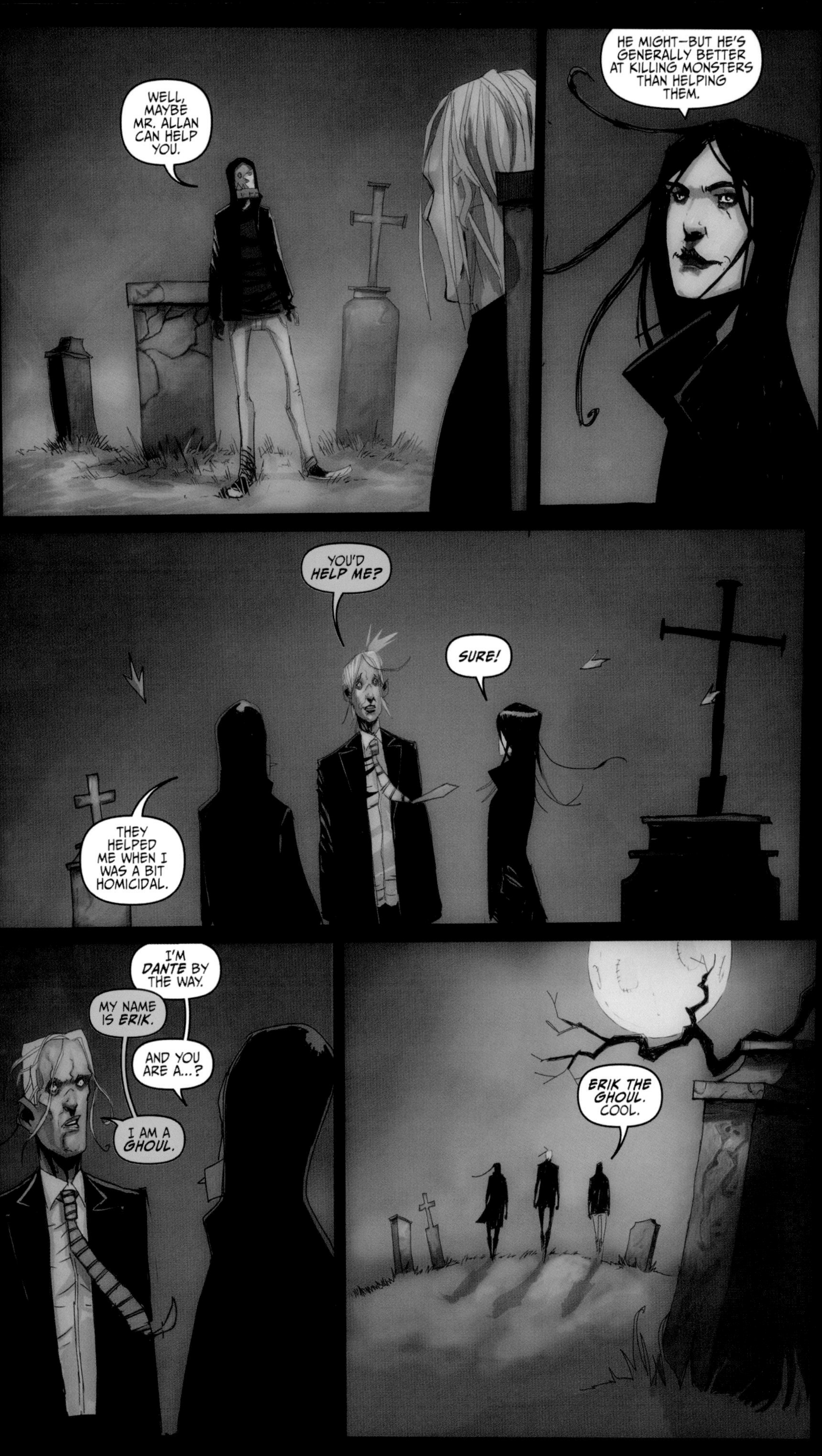
WELL, MAYBE MR. ALLAN CAN HELP YOU.
HE MIGHT—BUT HE'S GENERALLY BETTER AT KILLING MONSTERS THAN HELPING THEM.
YOU'D HELP ME?
SURE!
THEY HELPED ME WHEN I WAS A BIT HOMICIDAL.
I'M DANTE BY THE WAY.
MY NAME IS ERIK.
AND YOU ARE A...?
I AM A GHOUL.
ERIK THE GHOUL. COOL.

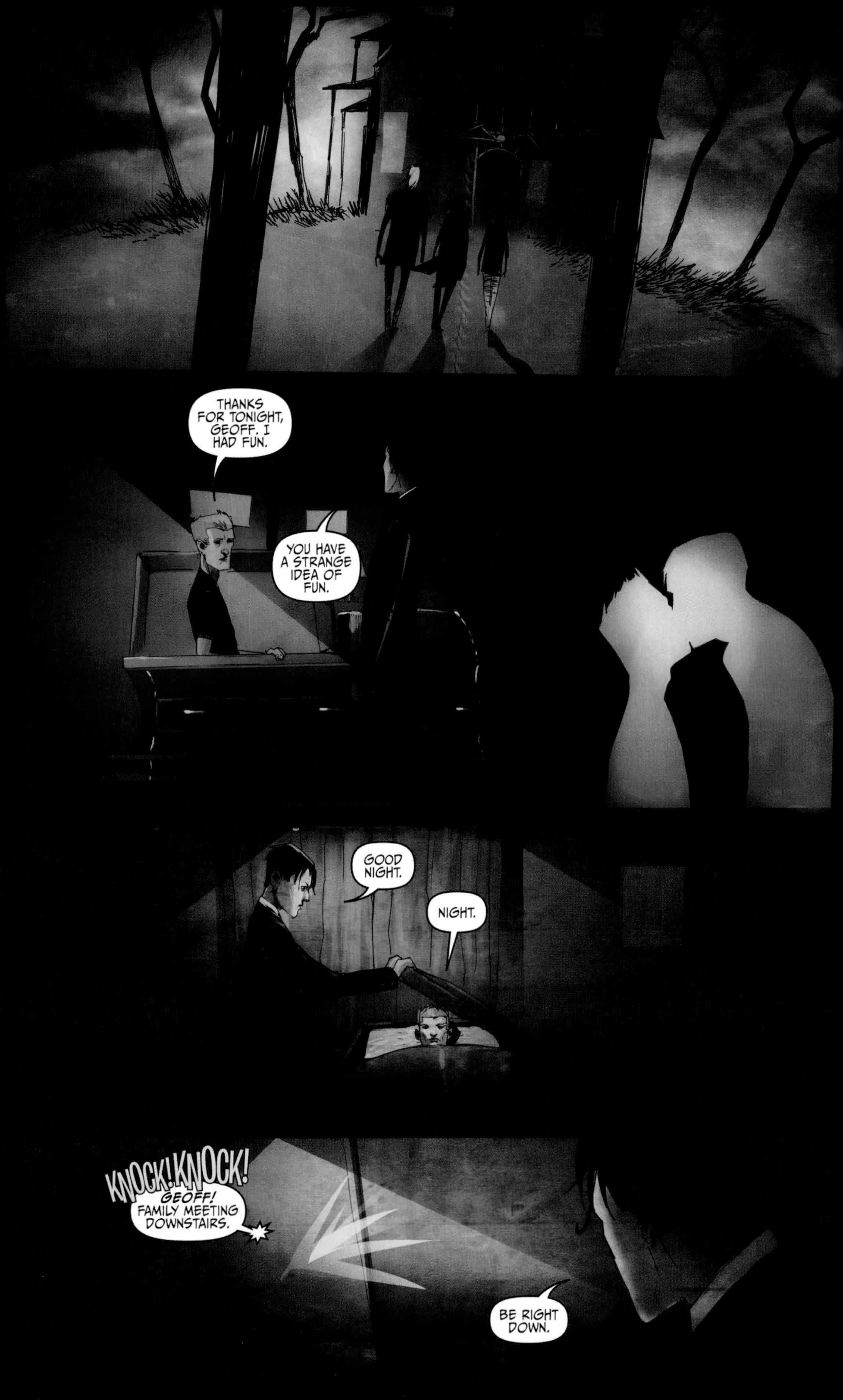
THANKS FOR TONIGHT, GEOFF. I HAD FUN.
YOU HAVE A STRANGE IDEA OF FUN.
GOOD NIGHT.
NIGHT.
KNOCK! KNOCK!
GEOFF! FAMILY MEETING DOWNSTAIRS.
BE RIGHT DOWN.

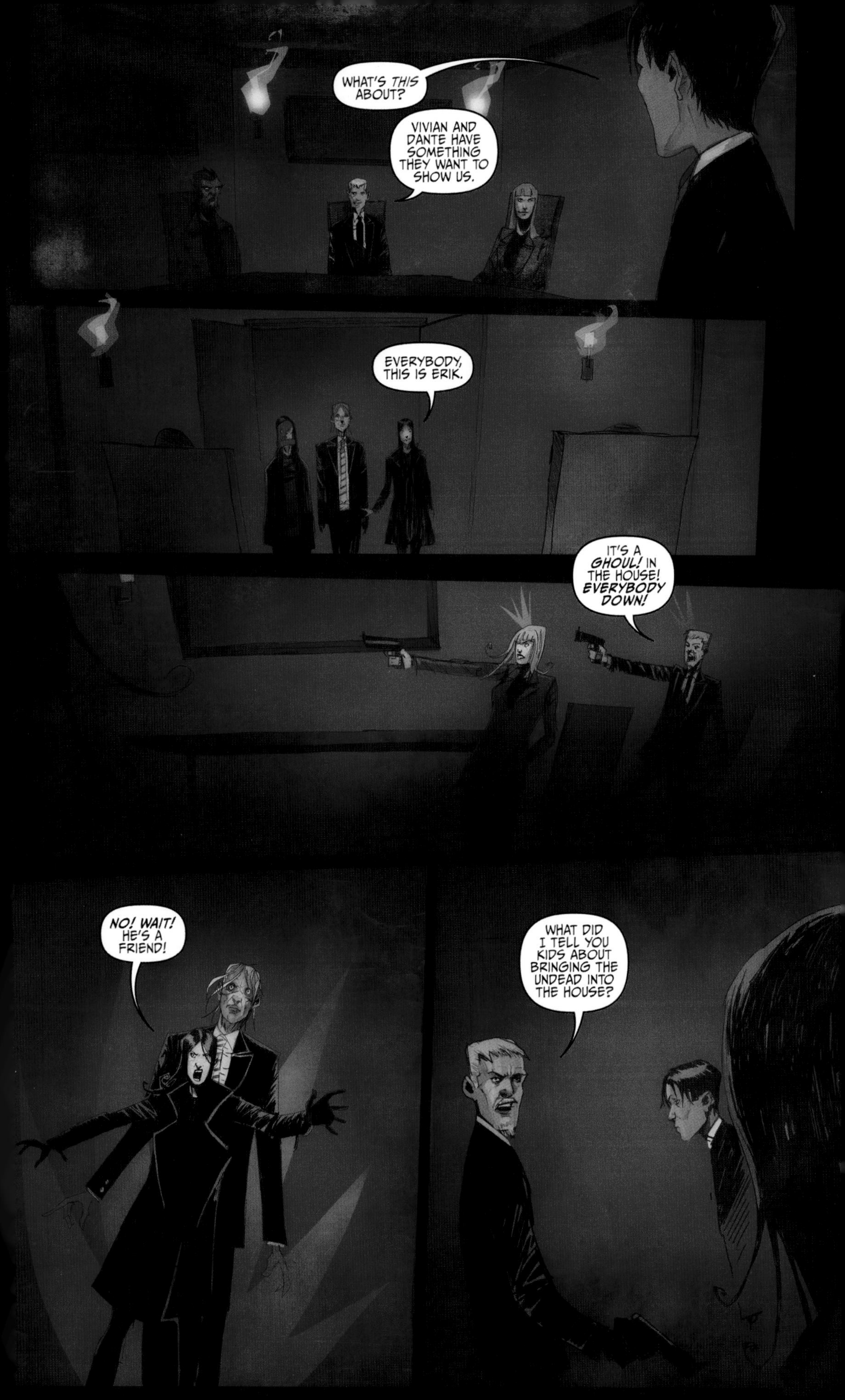
WHAT'S *THIS* ABOUT?
VIVIAN AND DANTE HAVE SOMETHING THEY WANT TO SHOW US.
EVERYBODY, THIS IS ERIK.
IT'S A ***GHOUL!*** IN THE HOUSE! ***EVERYBODY DOWN!***
NO! WAIT! HE'S A FRIEND!
WHAT DID I TELL YOU KIDS ABOUT BRINGING THE UNDEAD INTO THE HOUSE?

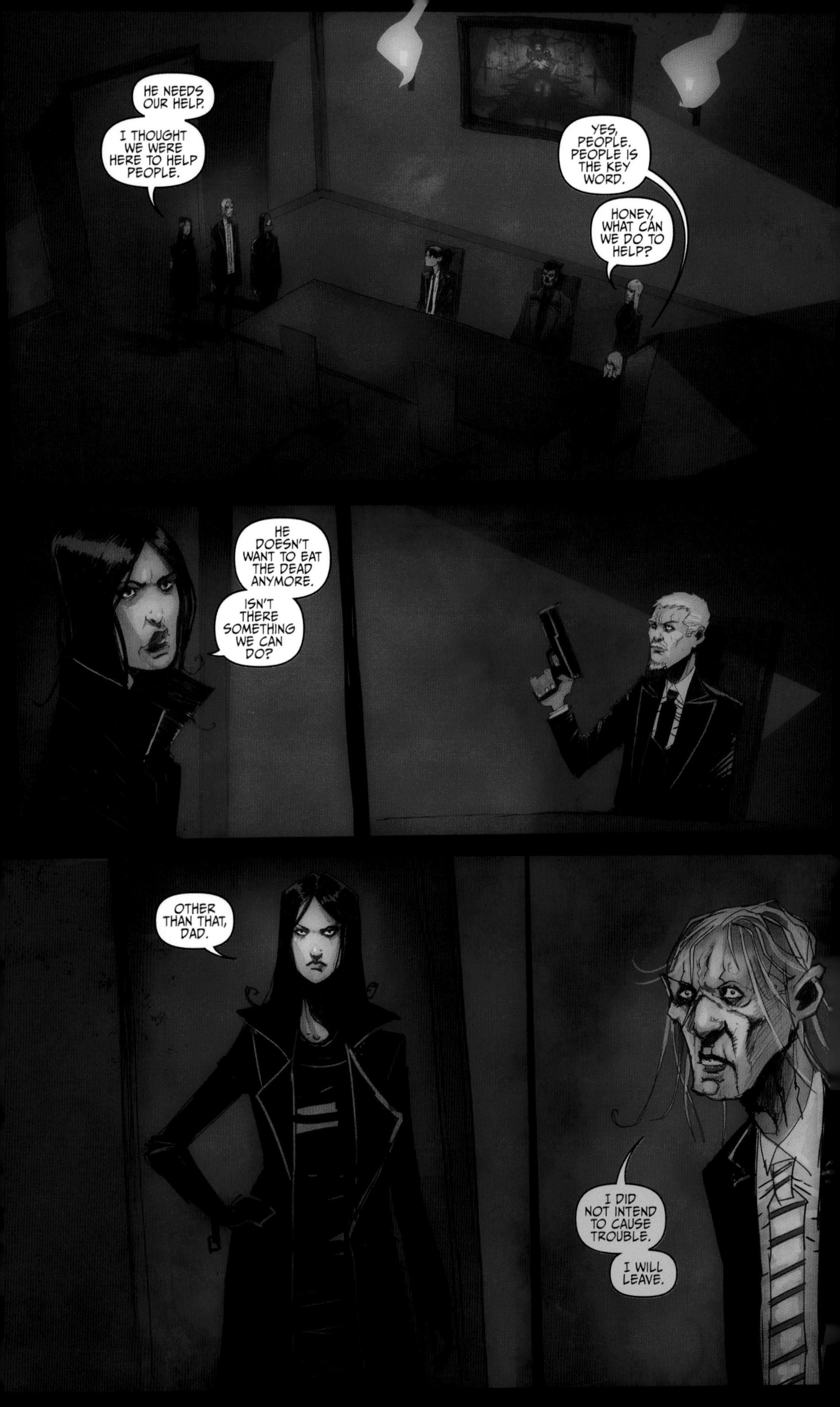

HE NEEDS OUR HELP.
I THOUGHT WE WERE HERE TO HELP PEOPLE.
YES, PEOPLE. PEOPLE IS THE KEY WORD.
HONEY, WHAT CAN WE DO TO HELP?
HE DOESN'T WANT TO EAT THE DEAD ANYMORE.
ISN'T THERE SOMETHING WE CAN DO?
OTHER THAN THAT, DAD.
I DID NOT INTEND TO CAUSE TROUBLE.
I WILL LEAVE.

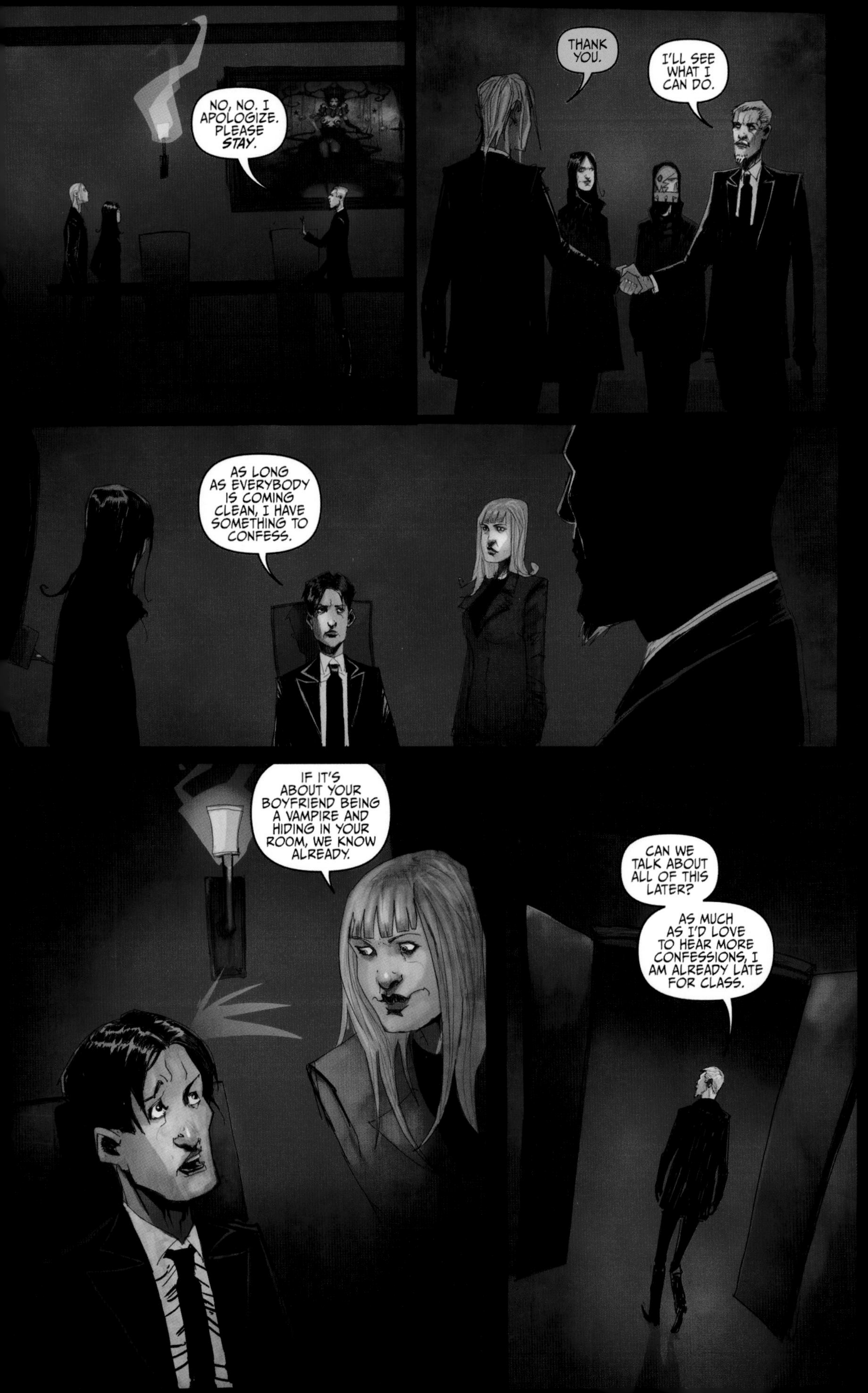
NO, NO. I APOLOGIZE. PLEASE STAY.
THANK YOU.
I'LL SEE WHAT I CAN DO.
AS LONG AS EVERYBODY IS COMING CLEAN, I HAVE SOMETHING TO CONFESS.
IF IT'S ABOUT YOUR BOYFRIEND BEING A VAMPIRE AND HIDING IN YOUR ROOM, WE KNOW ALREADY.
CAN WE TALK ABOUT ALL OF THIS LATER?
AS MUCH AS I'D LOVE TO HEAR MORE CONFESSIONS, I AM ALREADY LATE FOR CLASS.

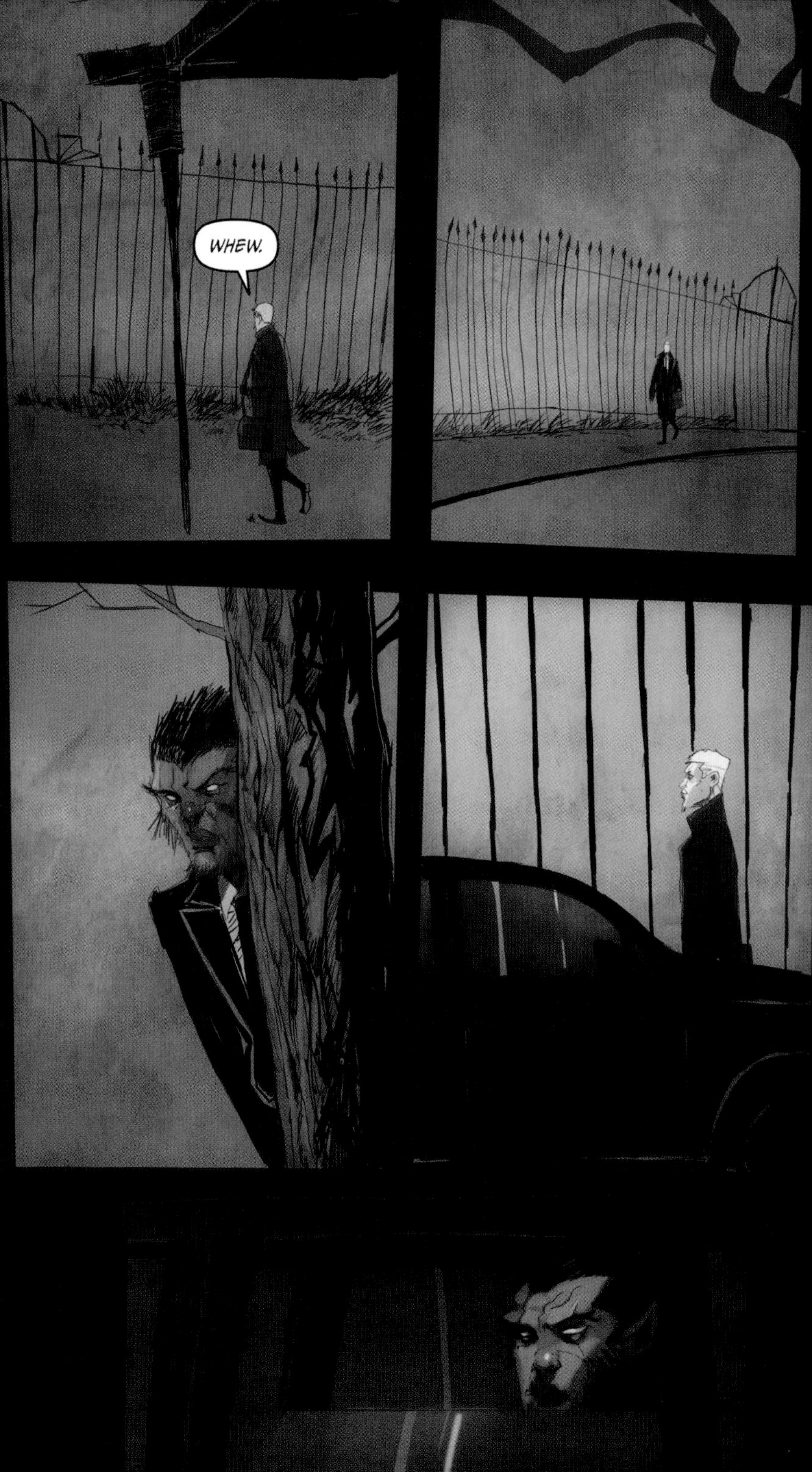
WHEW.

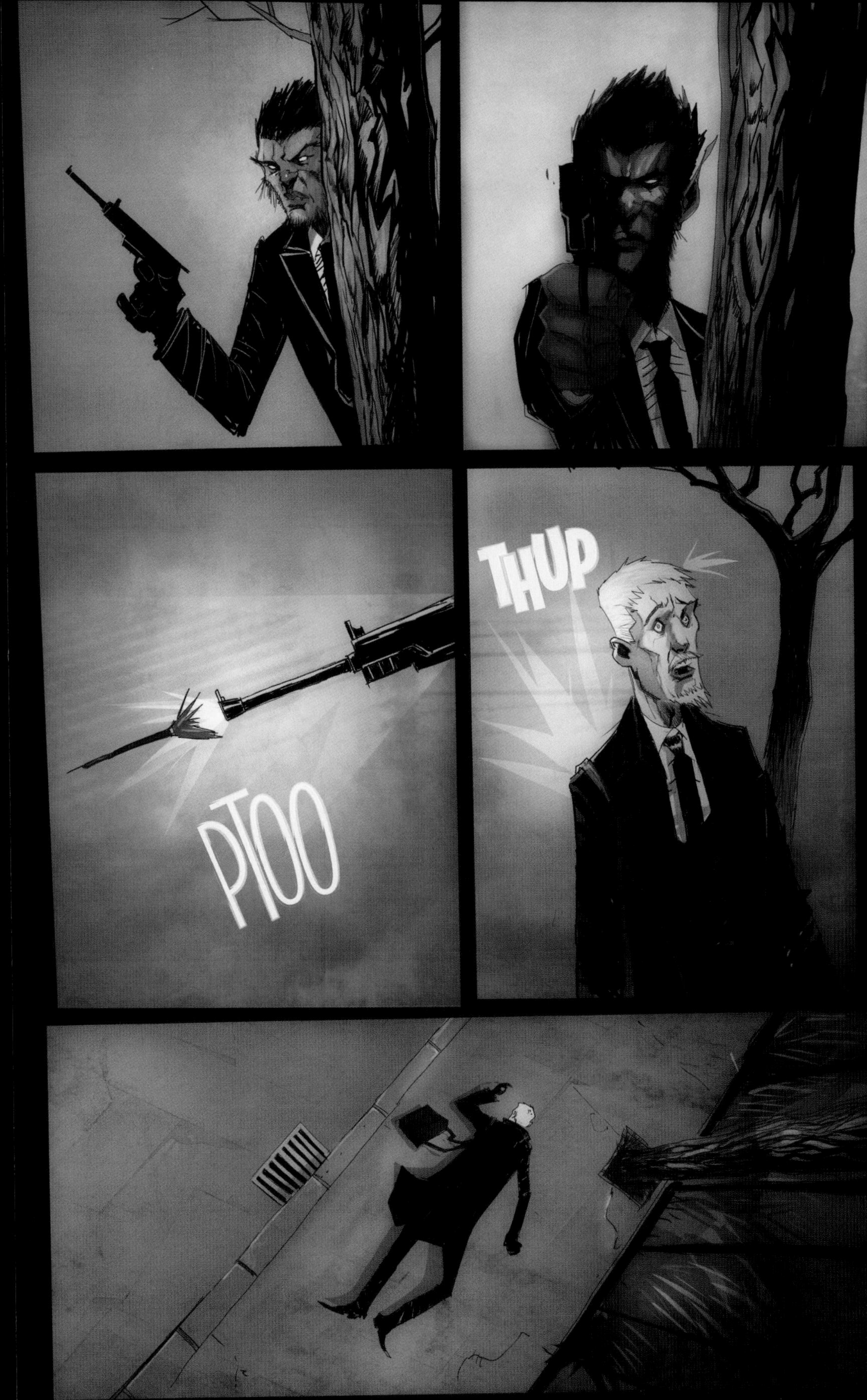
PTOO
THUP

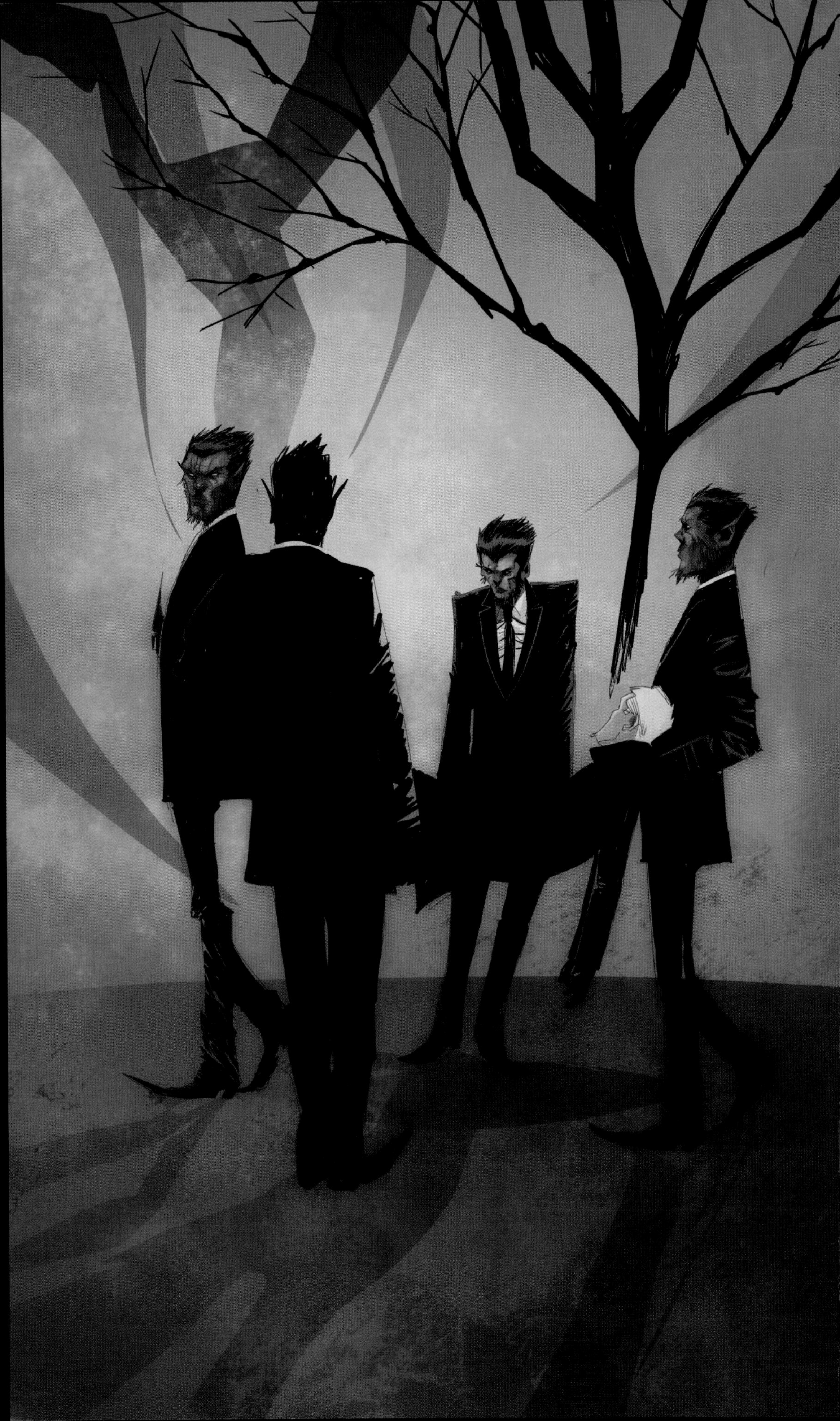

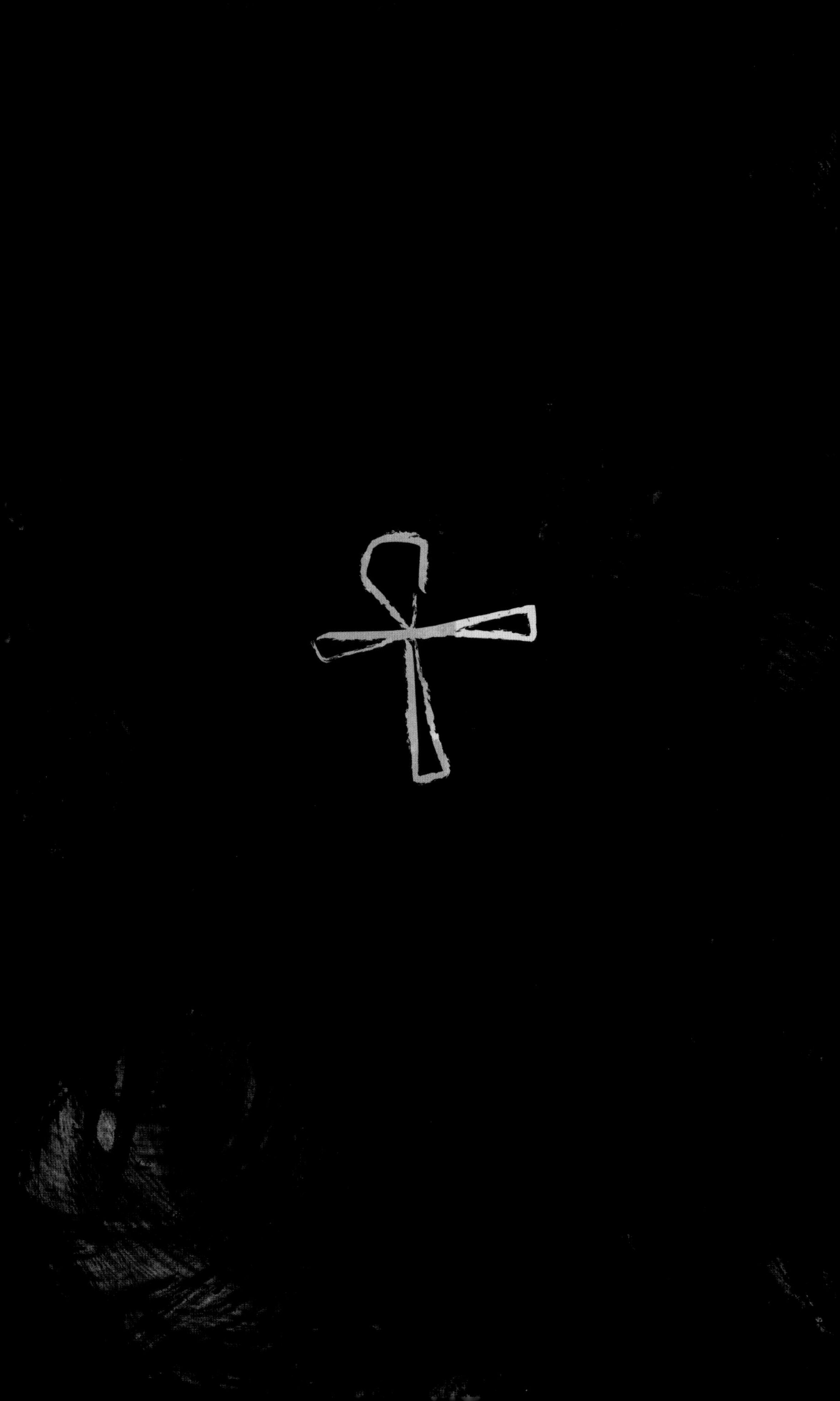

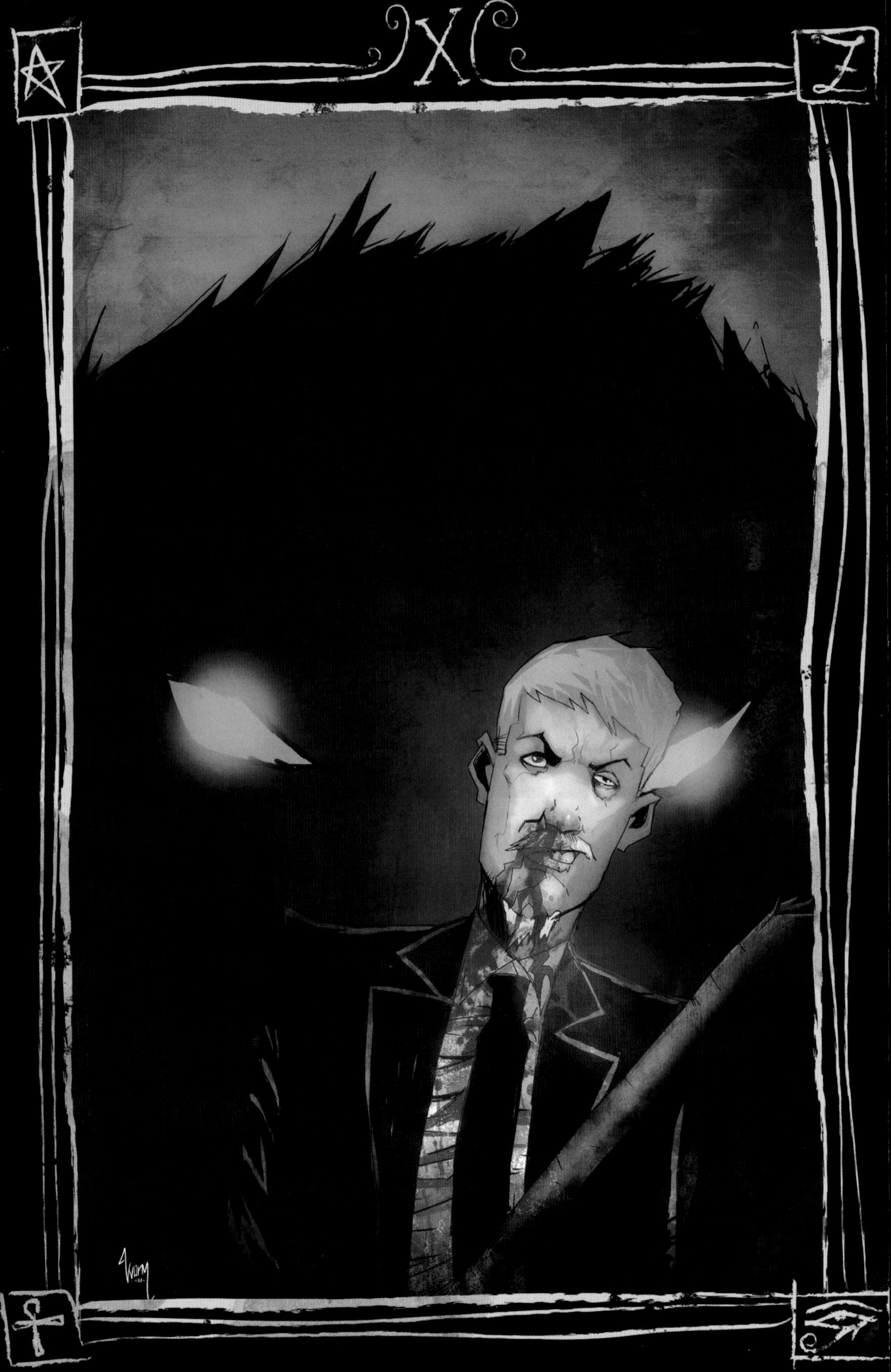
X

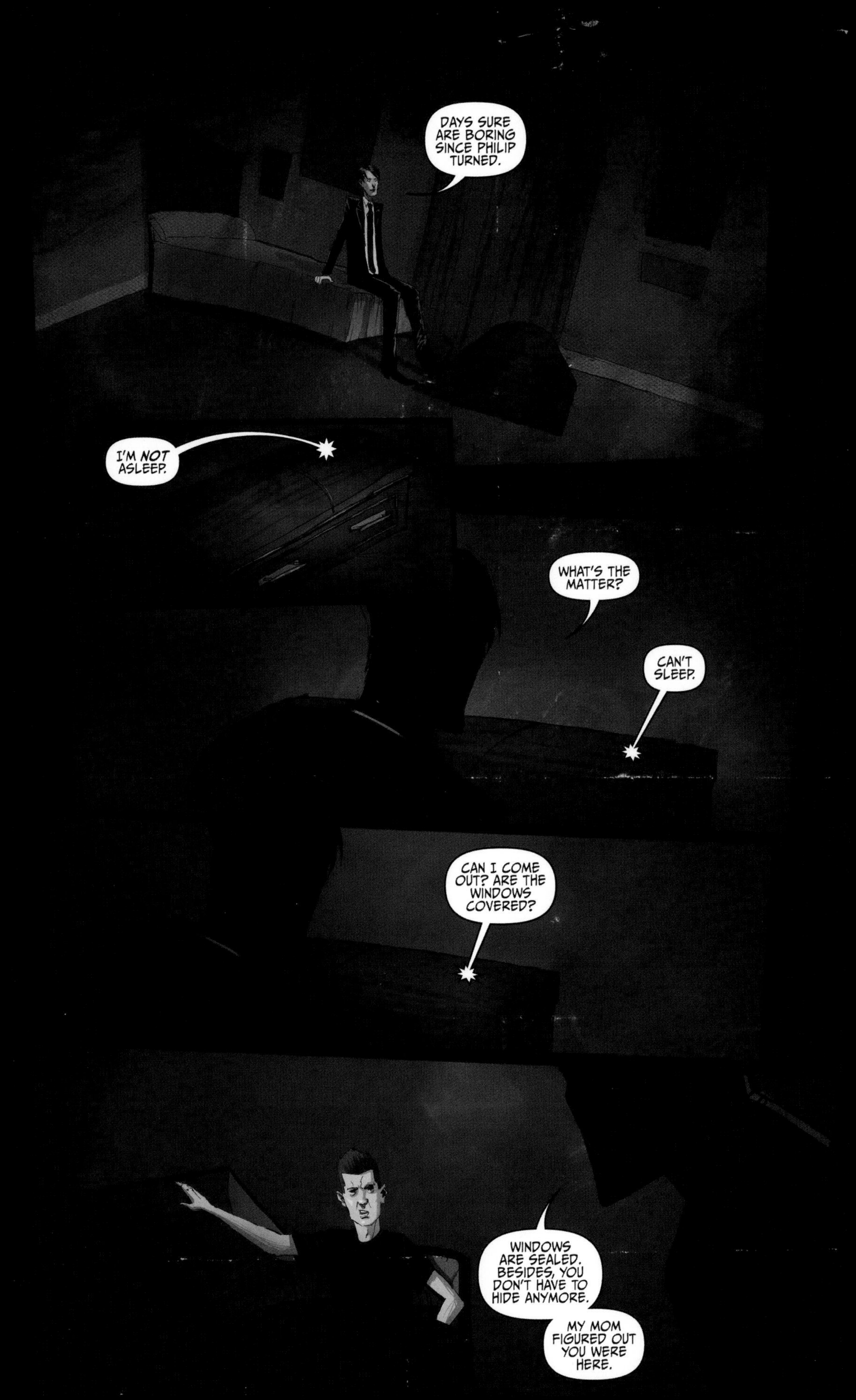
DAYS SURE ARE BORING SINCE PHILIP TURNED.
I'M *NOT* ASLEEP.
WHAT'S THE MATTER?
CAN'T SLEEP.
CAN I COME OUT? ARE THE WINDOWS COVERED?
WINDOWS ARE SEALED. BESIDES, YOU DON'T HAVE TO HIDE ANYMORE.
MY MOM FIGURED OUT YOU WERE HERE.

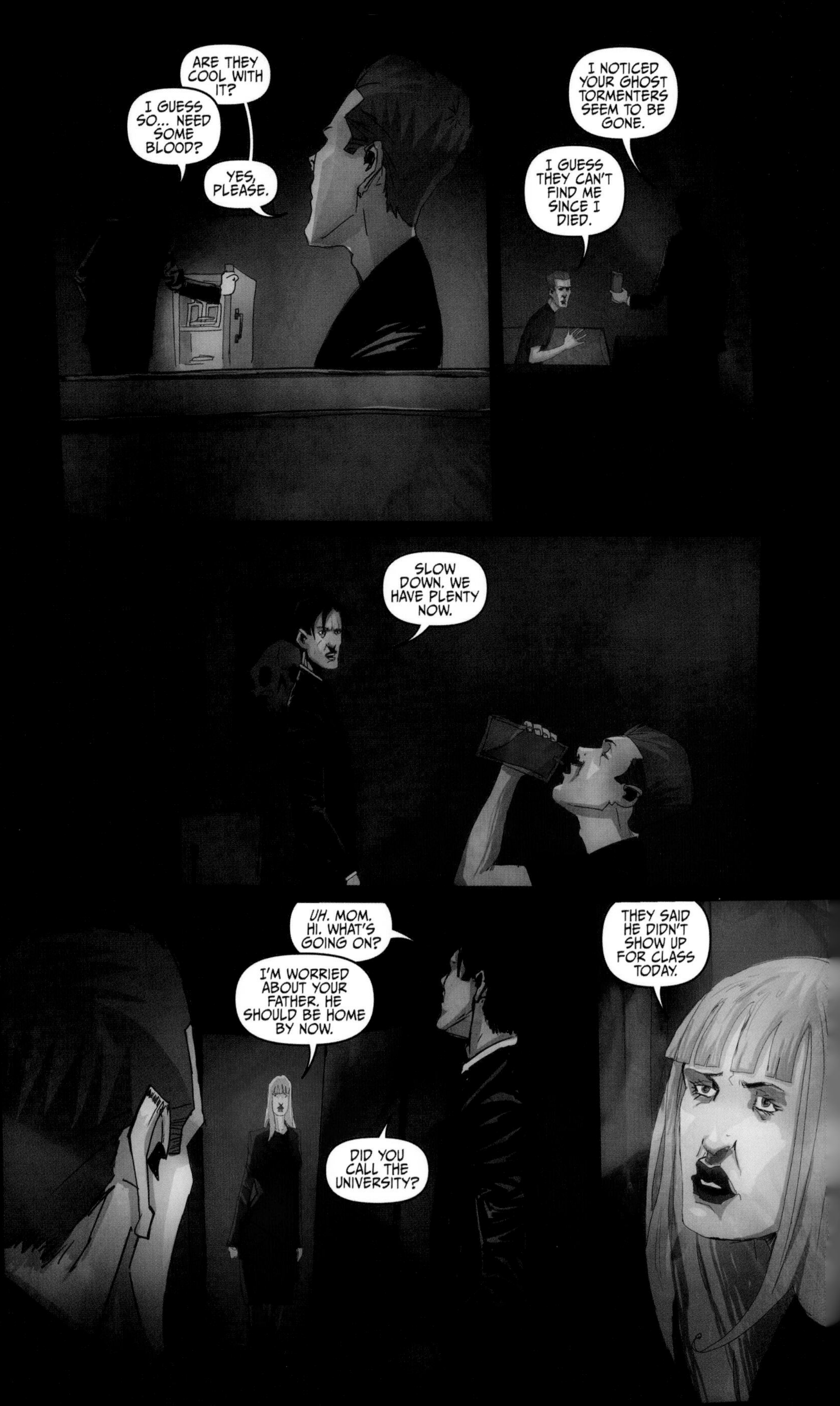
ARE THEY COOL WITH IT?
I GUESS SO... NEED SOME BLOOD?
YES, PLEASE.
I NOTICED YOUR GHOST TORMENTERS SEEM TO BE GONE.
I GUESS THEY CAN'T FIND ME SINCE I DIED.
SLOW DOWN. WE HAVE PLENTY NOW.
UH. MOM. HI. WHAT'S GOING ON?
I'M WORRIED ABOUT YOUR FATHER. HE SHOULD BE HOME BY NOW.
DID YOU CALL THE UNIVERSITY?
THEY SAID HE DIDN'T SHOW UP FOR CLASS TODAY.

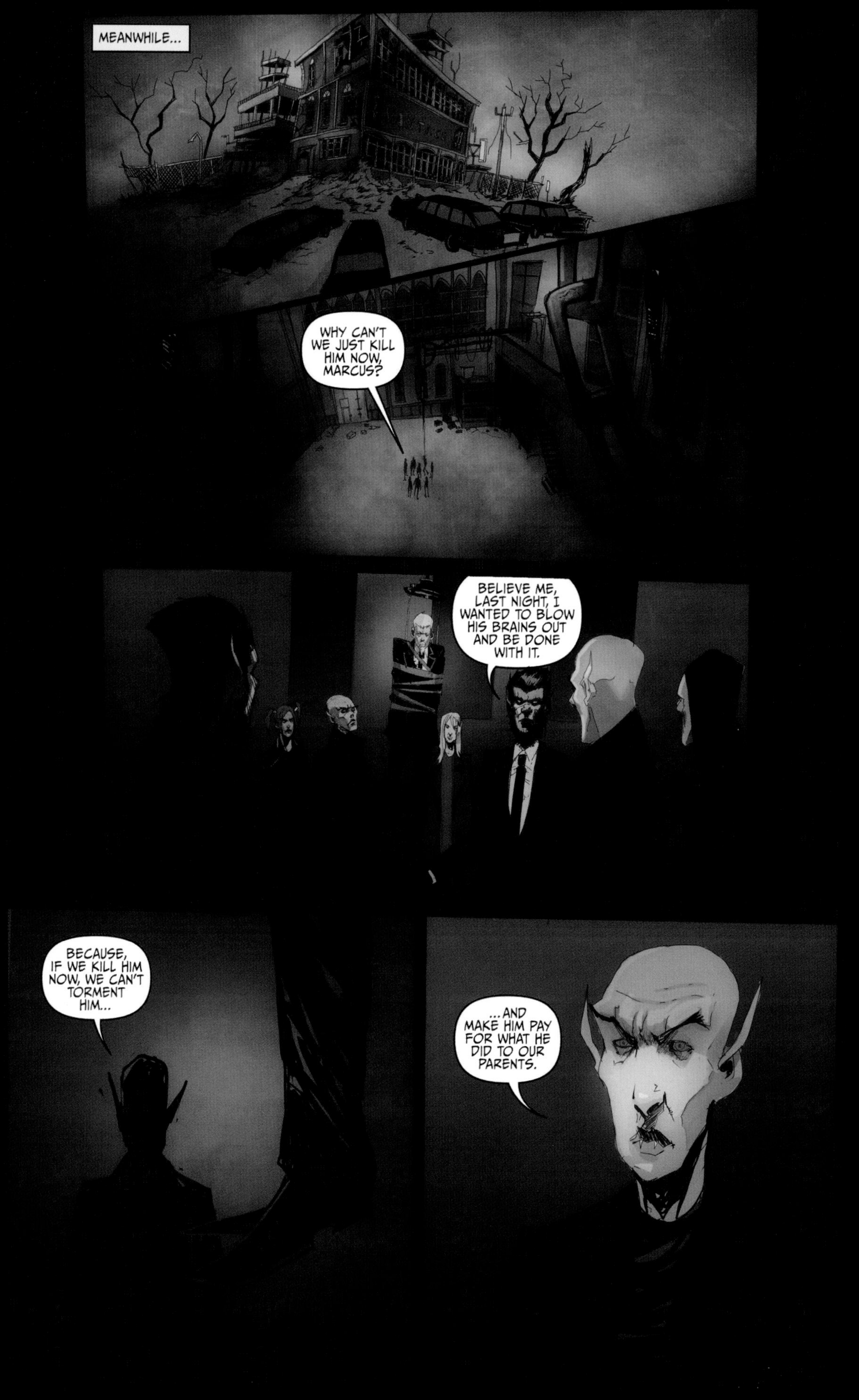
MEANWHILE...
WHY CAN'T WE JUST KILL HIM NOW, MARCUS?
BELIEVE ME, LAST NIGHT, I WANTED TO BLOW HIS BRAINS OUT AND BE DONE WITH IT.
BECAUSE, IF WE KILL HIM NOW, WE CAN'T TORMENT HIM...
...AND MAKE HIM PAY FOR WHAT HE DID TO OUR PARENTS.

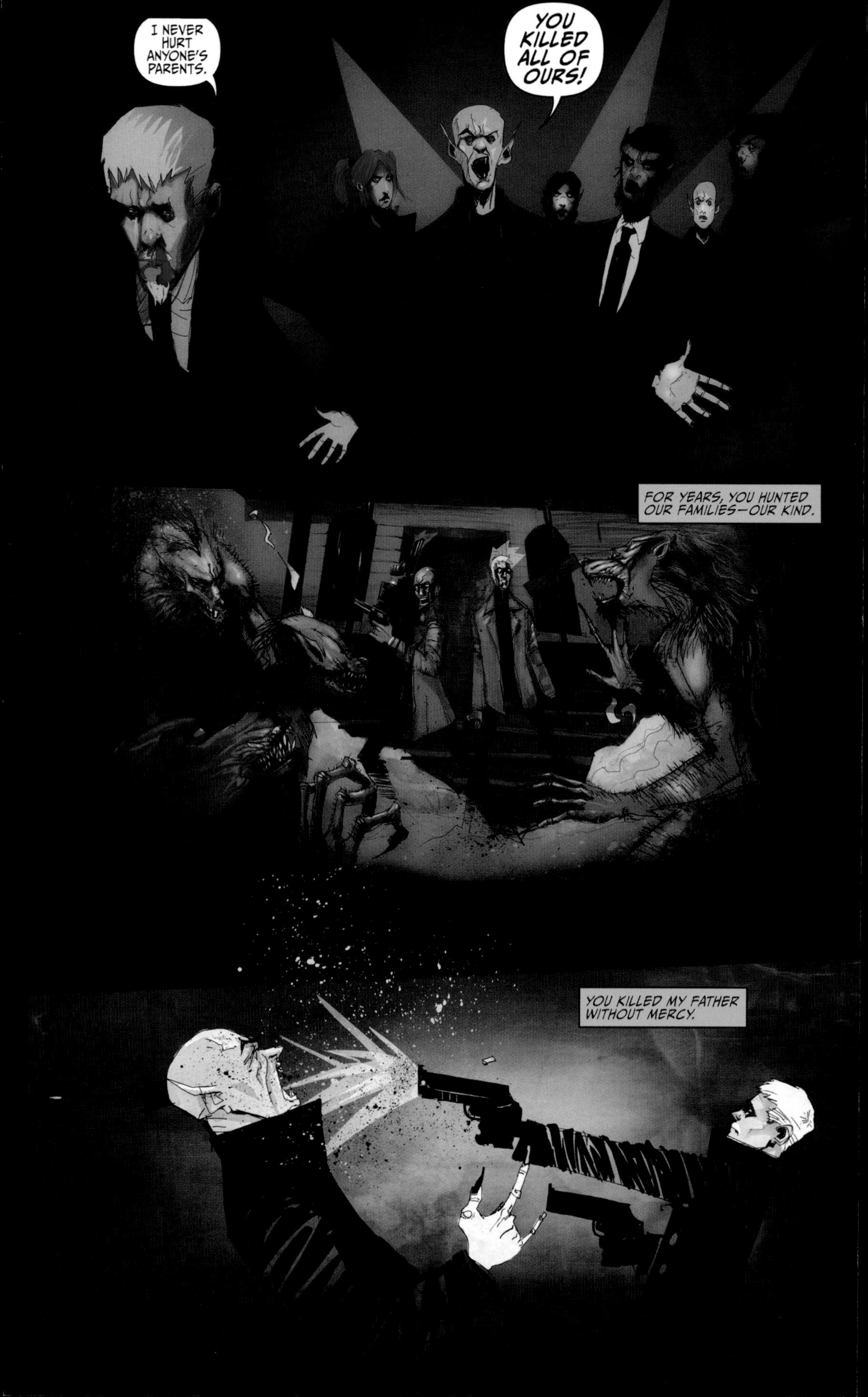
I NEVER HURT ANYONE'S PARENTS.
YOU KILLED ALL OF OURS!
FOR YEARS, YOU HUNTED OUR FAMILIES—OUR KIND.
YOU KILLED MY FATHER WITHOUT MERCY.

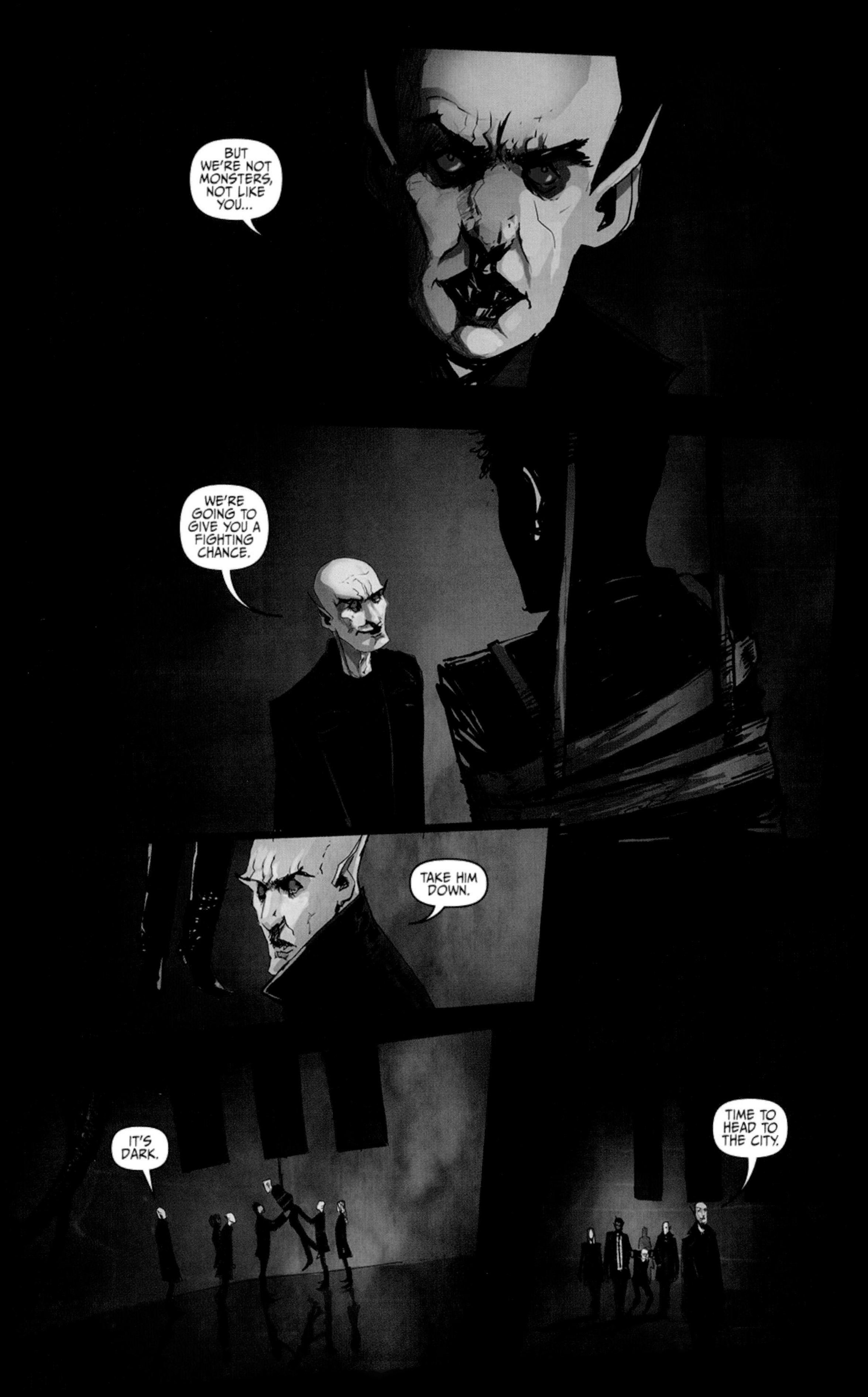
BUT WE'RE NOT MONSTERS, NOT LIKE YOU...
WE'RE GOING TO GIVE YOU A FIGHTING CHANCE.
TAKE HIM DOWN.
IT'S DARK.
TIME TO HEAD TO THE CITY.

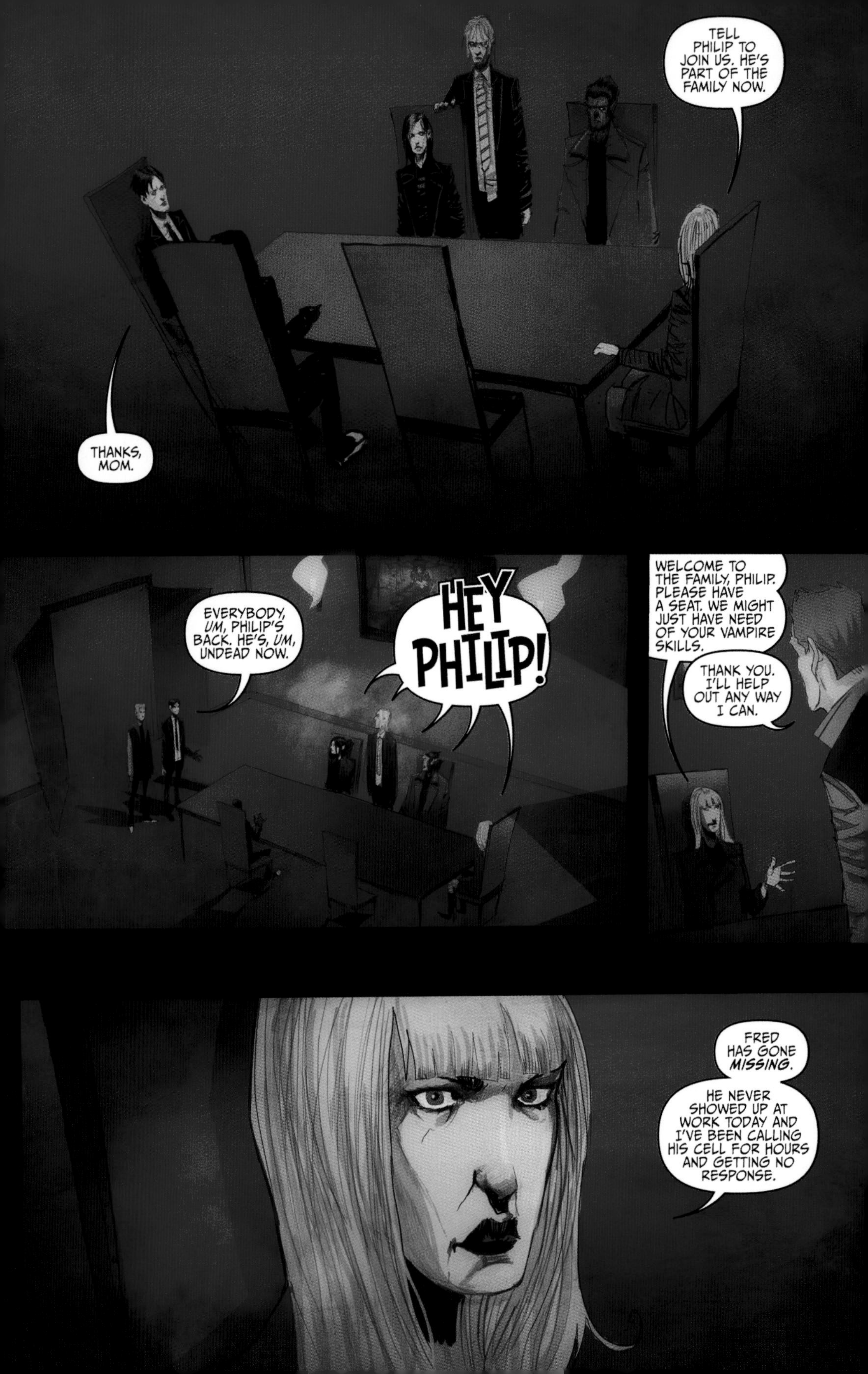
TELL PHILIP TO JOIN US. HE'S PART OF THE FAMILY NOW.
THANKS, MOM.
EVERYBODY, *UM*, PHILIP'S BACK. HE'S, *UM*, UNDEAD NOW.
HEY PHILIP!
WELCOME TO THE FAMILY, PHILIP. PLEASE HAVE A SEAT. WE MIGHT JUST HAVE NEED OF YOUR VAMPIRE SKILLS.
THANK YOU. I'LL HELP OUT ANY WAY I CAN.
FRED HAS GONE *MISSING*.
HE NEVER SHOWED UP AT WORK TODAY AND I'VE BEEN CALLING HIS CELL FOR HOURS AND GETTING NO RESPONSE.

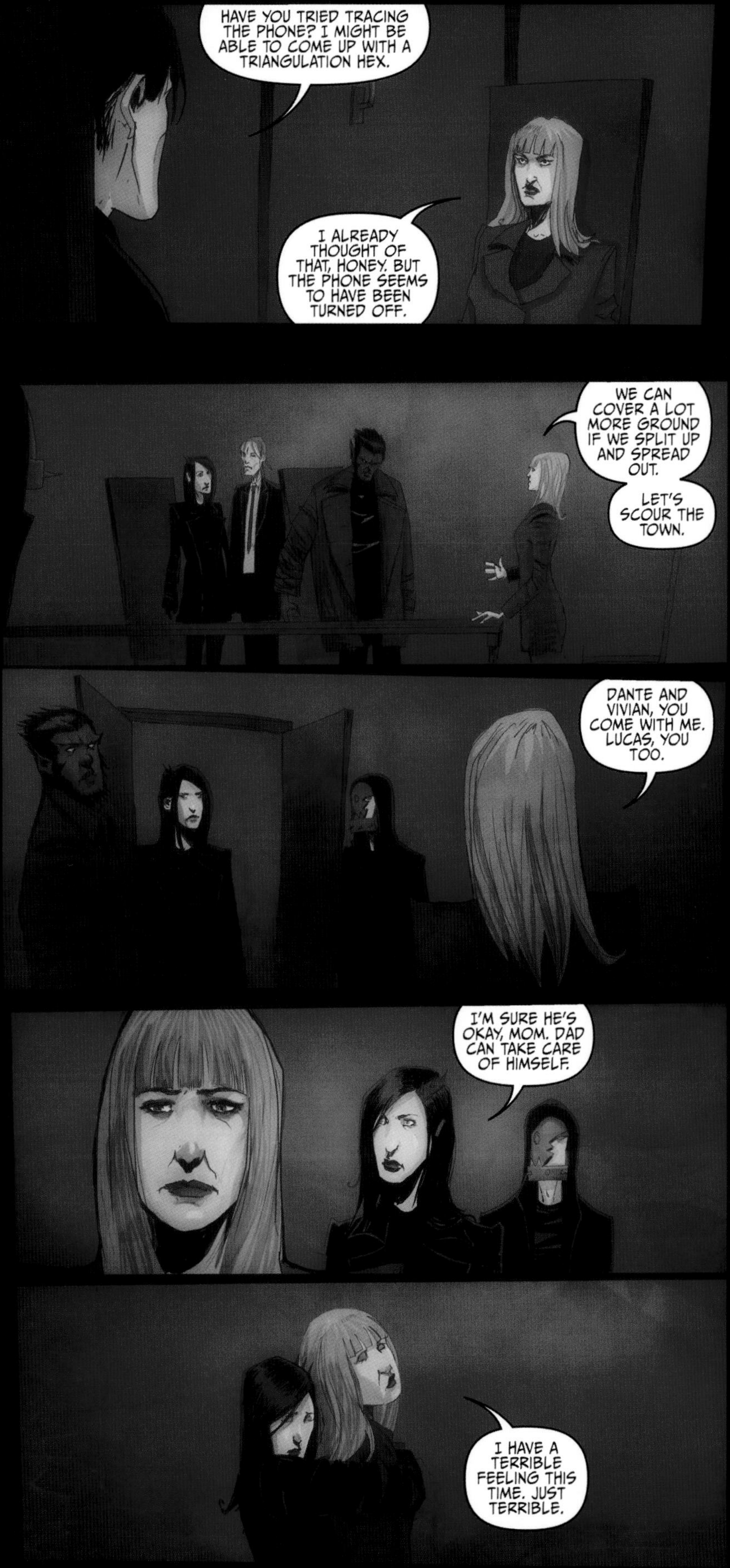
HAVE YOU TRIED TRACING THE PHONE? I MIGHT BE ABLE TO COME UP WITH A TRIANGULATION HEX.
I ALREADY THOUGHT OF THAT, HONEY. BUT THE PHONE SEEMS TO HAVE BEEN TURNED OFF.
WE CAN COVER A LOT MORE GROUND IF WE SPLIT UP AND SPREAD OUT.
LET'S SCOUR THE TOWN.
DANTE AND VIVIAN, YOU COME WITH ME. LUCAS, YOU TOO.
I'M SURE HE'S OKAY, MOM. DAD CAN TAKE CARE OF HIMSELF.
I HAVE A TERRIBLE FEELING THIS TIME. JUST TERRIBLE.

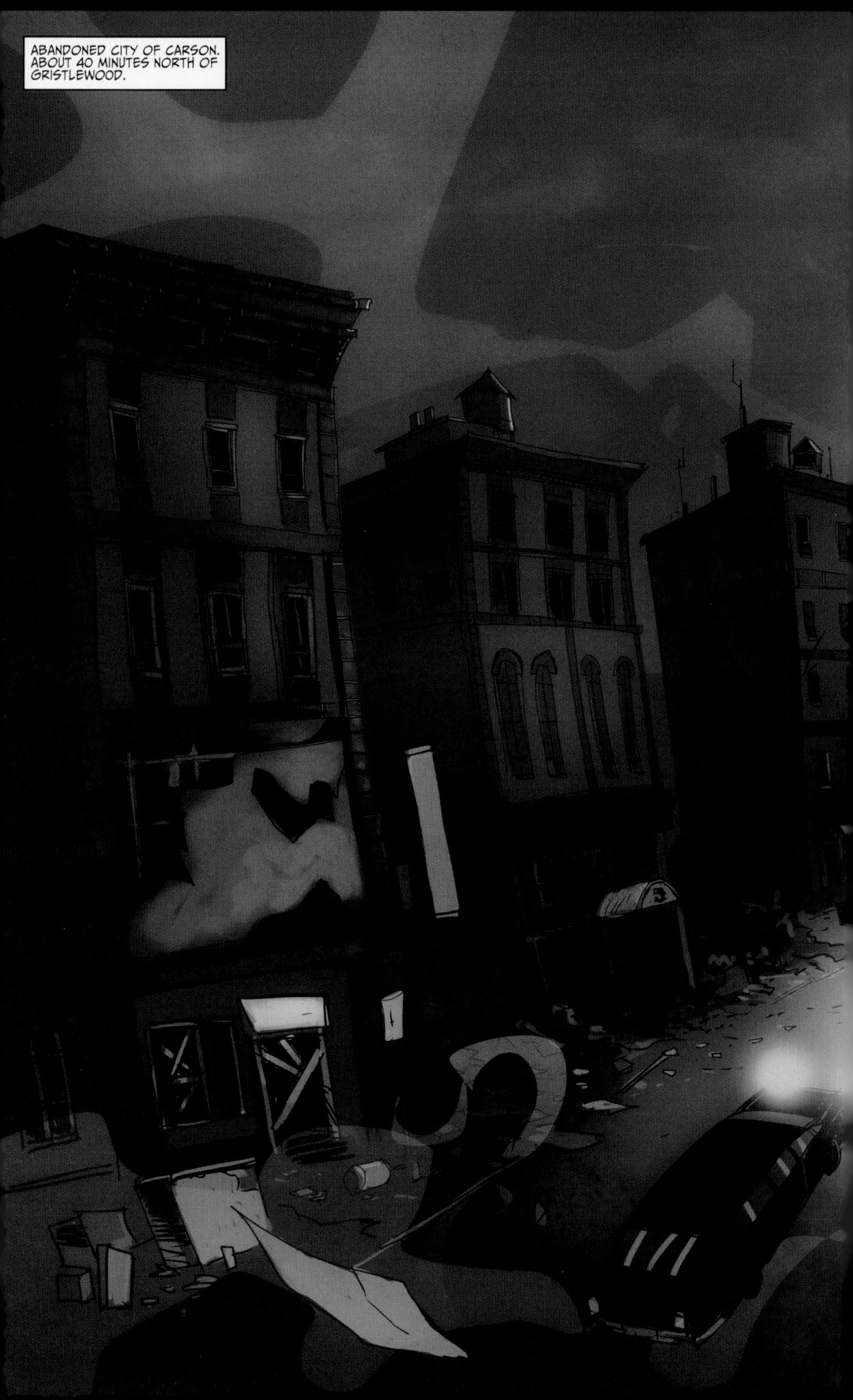
ABANDONED CITY OF CARSON. ABOUT 40 MINUTES NORTH OF GRISTLEWOOD.

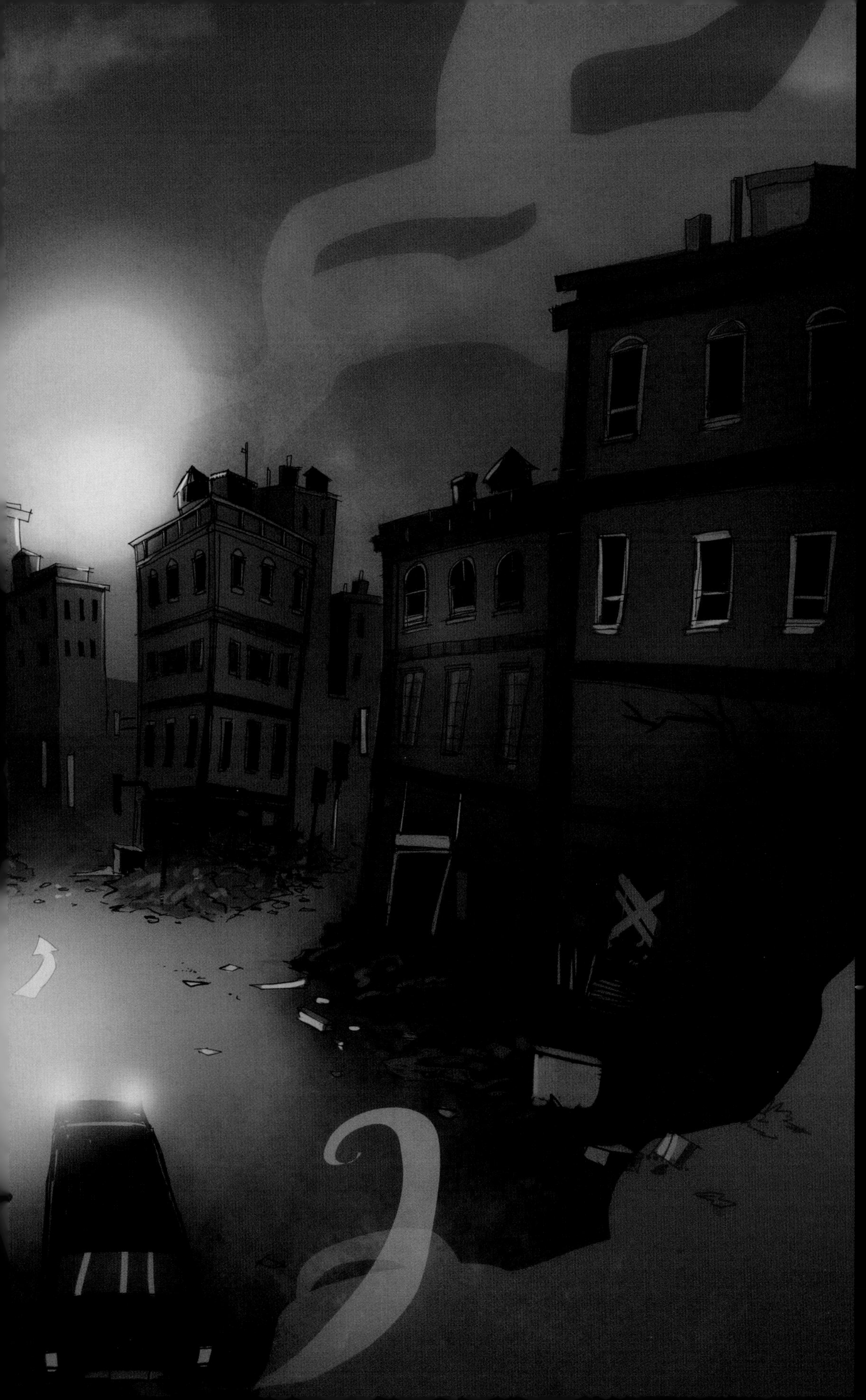

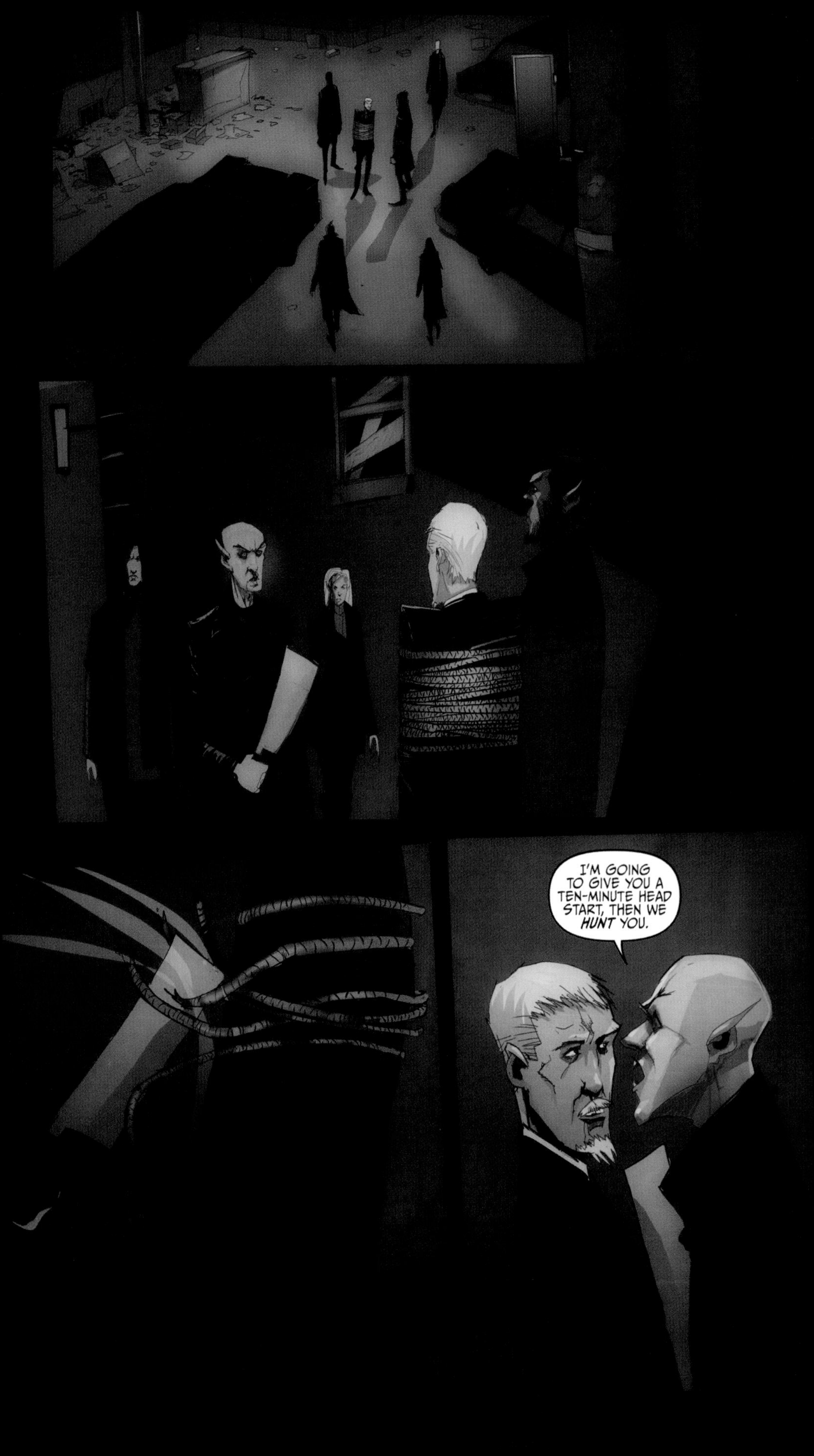
I'M GOING TO GIVE YOU A TEN-MINUTE HEAD START, THEN WE HUNT YOU.

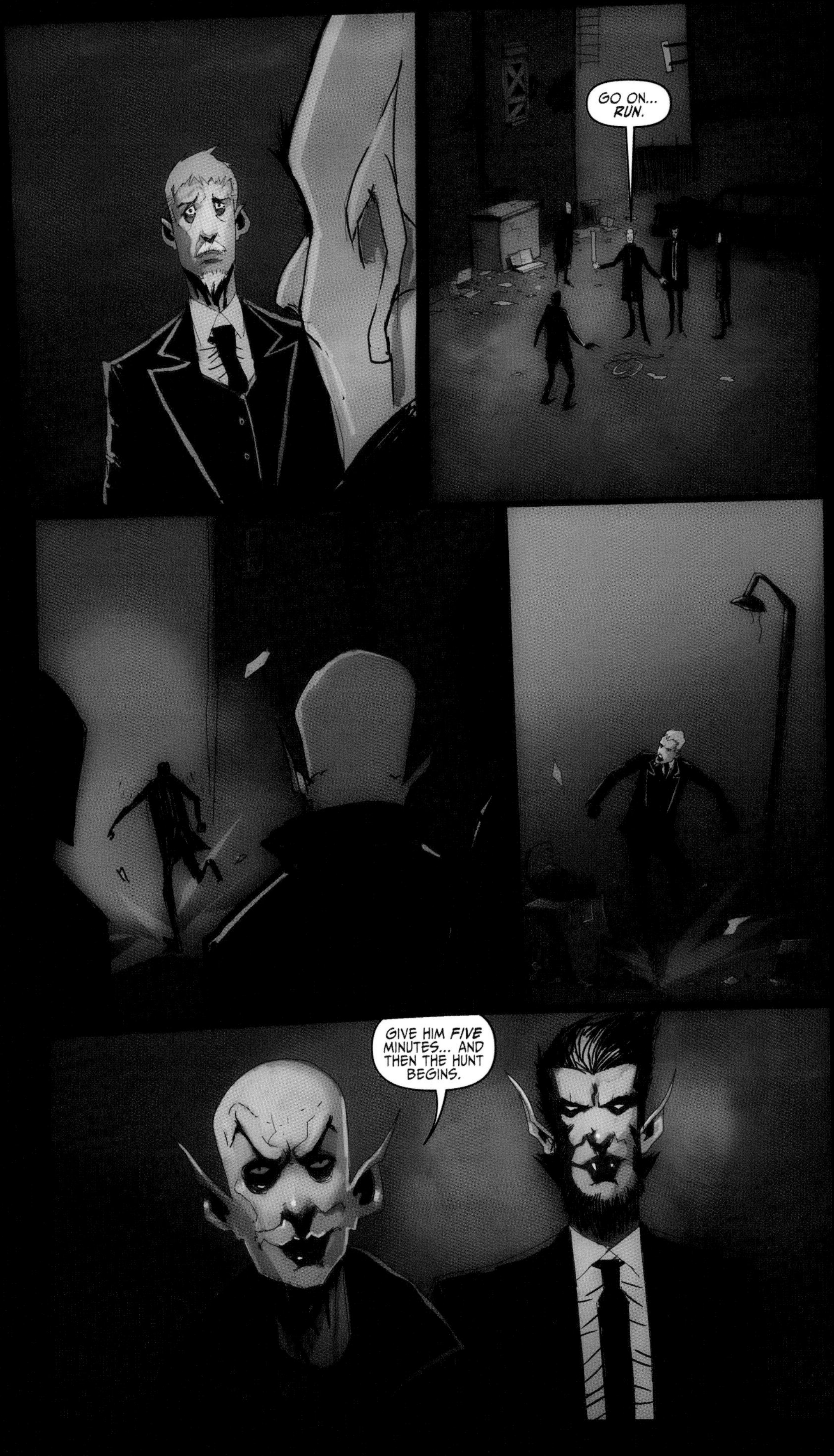
GO ON...
RUN.
GIVE HIM FIVE MINUTES... AND THEN THE HUNT BEGINS.

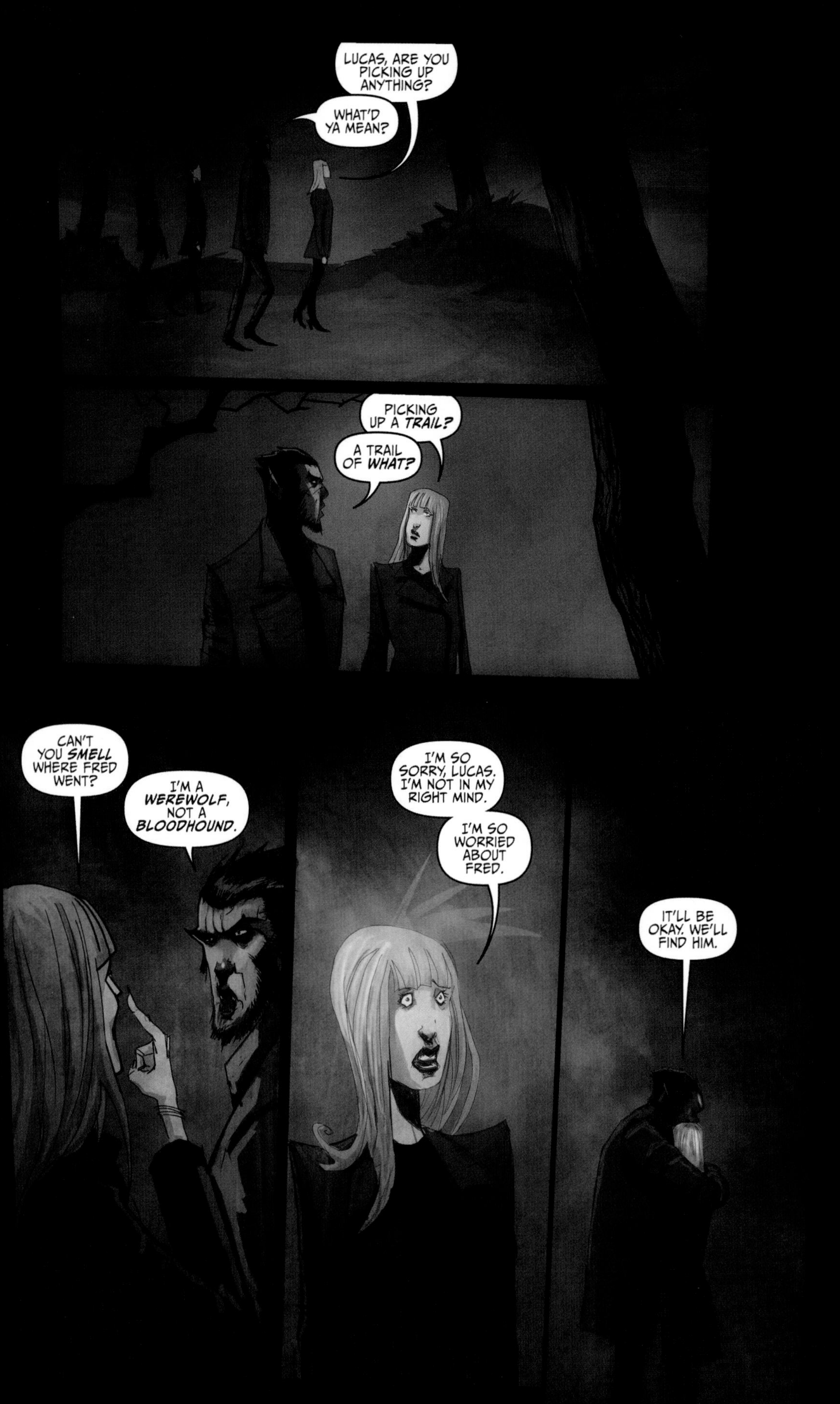
LUCAS, ARE YOU PICKING UP ANYTHING?
WHAT'D YA MEAN?
PICKING UP A *TRAIL?*
A TRAIL OF *WHAT?*
CAN'T YOU *SMELL* WHERE FRED WENT?
I'M A *WEREWOLF*, NOT A *BLOODHOUND*.
I'M SO SORRY, LUCAS. I'M NOT IN MY RIGHT MIND.
I'M SO WORRIED ABOUT FRED.
IT'LL BE OKAY. WE'LL FIND HIM.

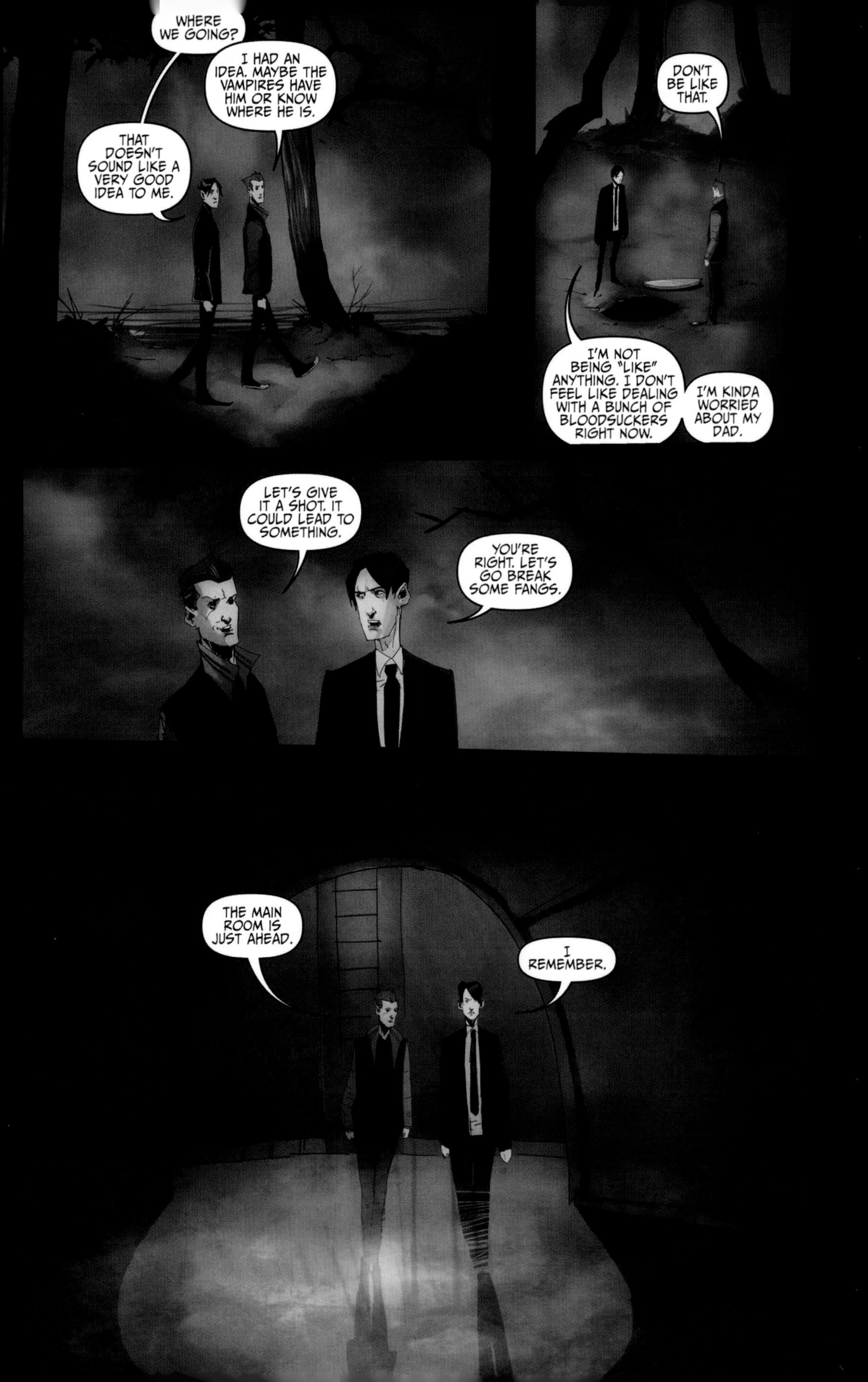
WHERE WE GOING?
I HAD AN IDEA. MAYBE THE VAMPIRES HAVE HIM OR KNOW WHERE HE IS.
THAT DOESN'T SOUND LIKE A VERY GOOD IDEA TO ME.
DON'T BE LIKE THAT.
I'M NOT BEING "LIKE" ANYTHING. I DON'T FEEL LIKE DEALING WITH A BUNCH OF BLOODSUCKERS RIGHT NOW.
I'M KINDA WORRIED ABOUT MY DAD.
LET'S GIVE IT A SHOT. IT COULD LEAD TO SOMETHING.
YOU'RE RIGHT. LET'S GO BREAK SOME FANGS.
THE MAIN ROOM IS JUST AHEAD.
I REMEMBER.

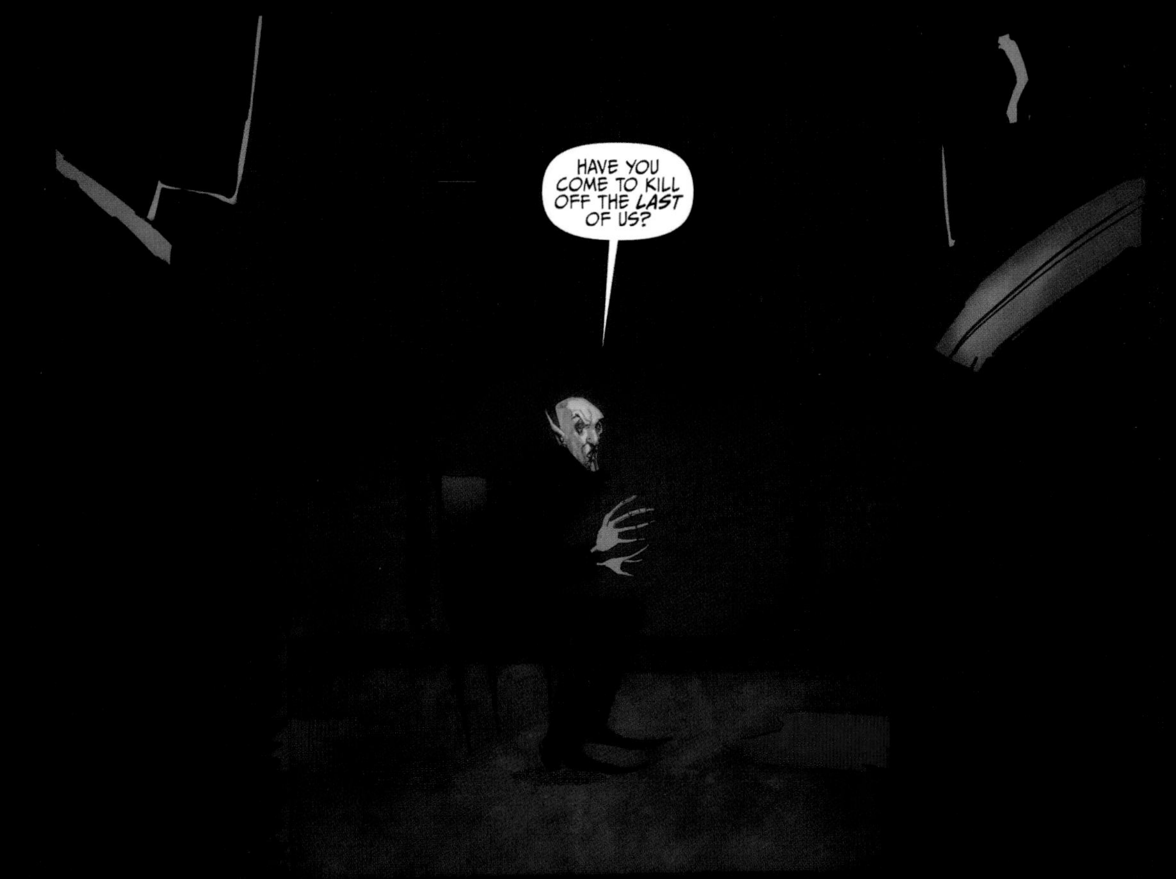
HAVE YOU COME TO KILL OFF THE *LAST* OF US?

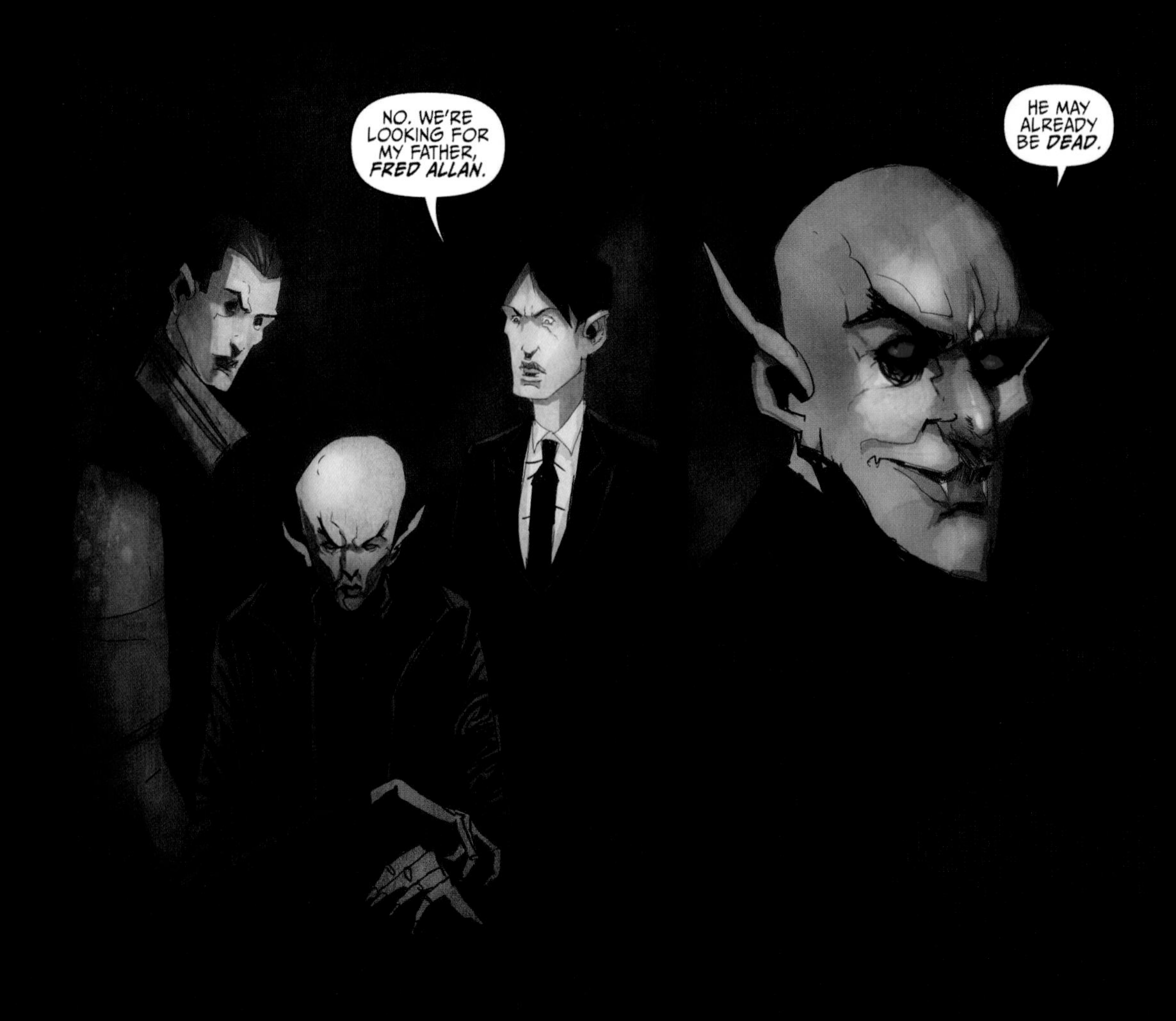
NO. WE'RE LOOKING FOR MY FATHER, ***FRED ALLAN***.
HE MAY ALREADY BE *DEAD*.

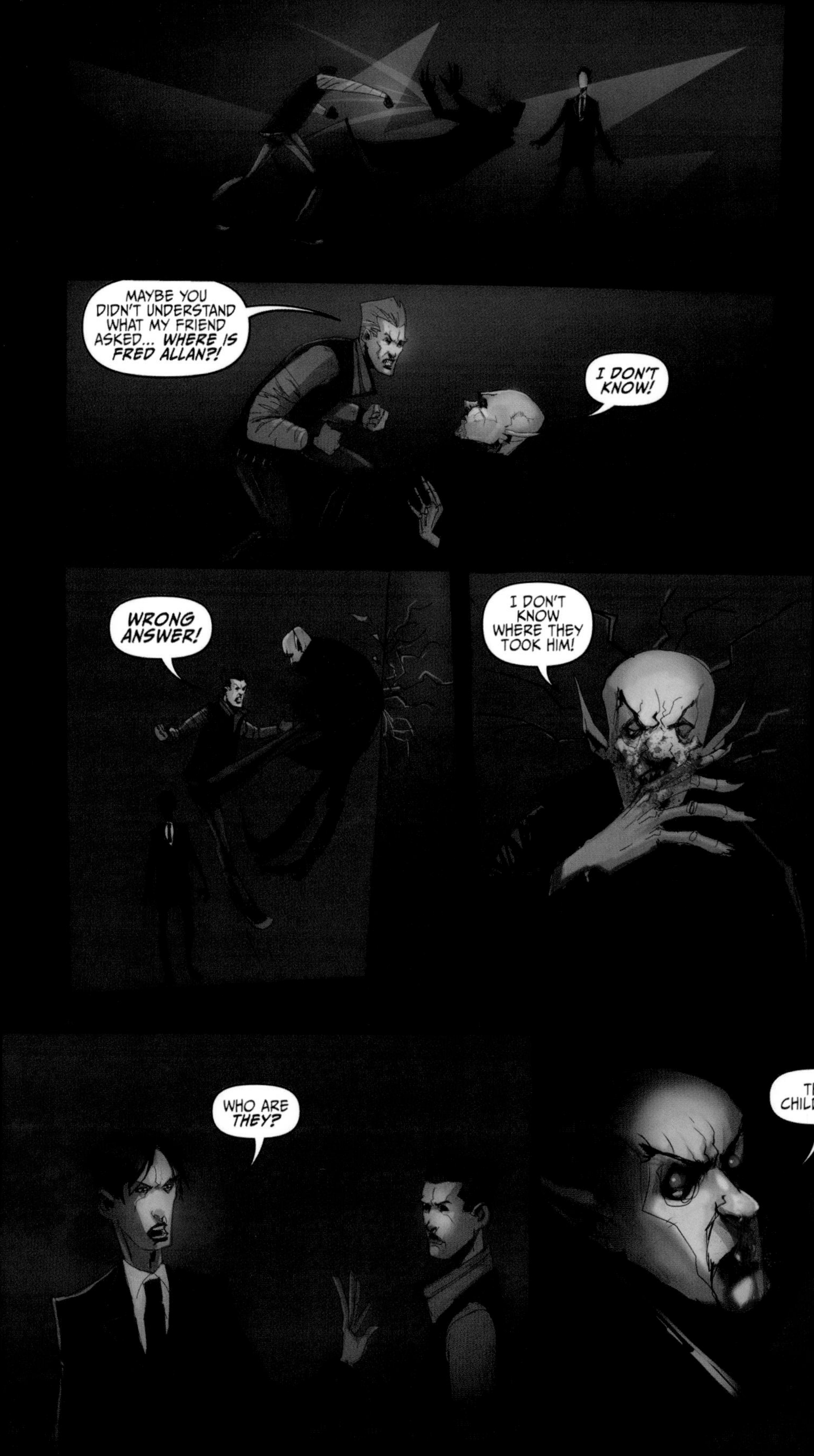
MAYBE YOU DIDN'T UNDERSTAND WHAT MY FRIEND ASKED... WHERE IS FRED ALLAN?!
I DON'T KNOW!
WRONG ANSWER!
I DON'T KNOW WHERE THEY TOOK HIM!
WHO ARE THEY?
THE CHILDREN.

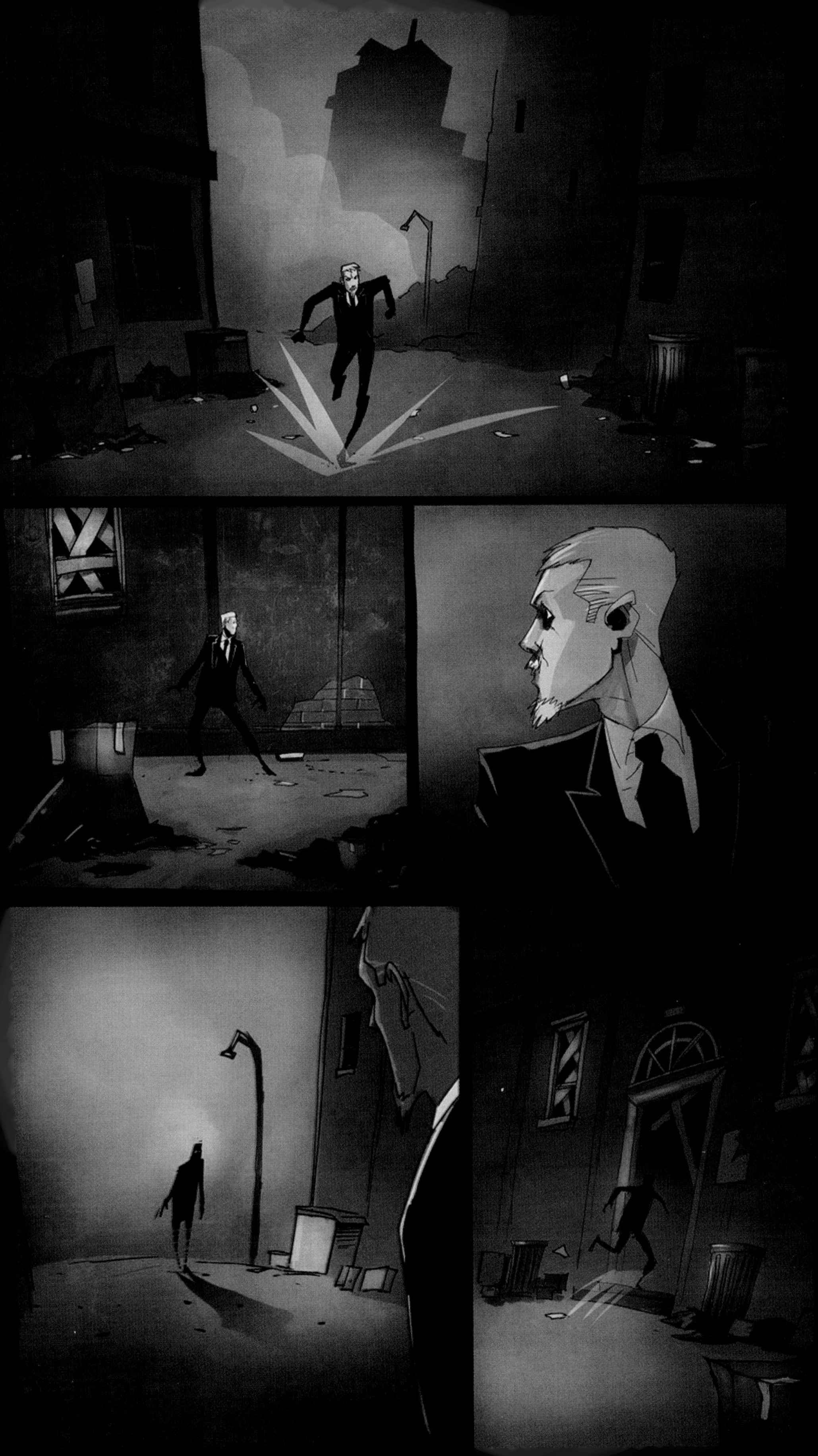

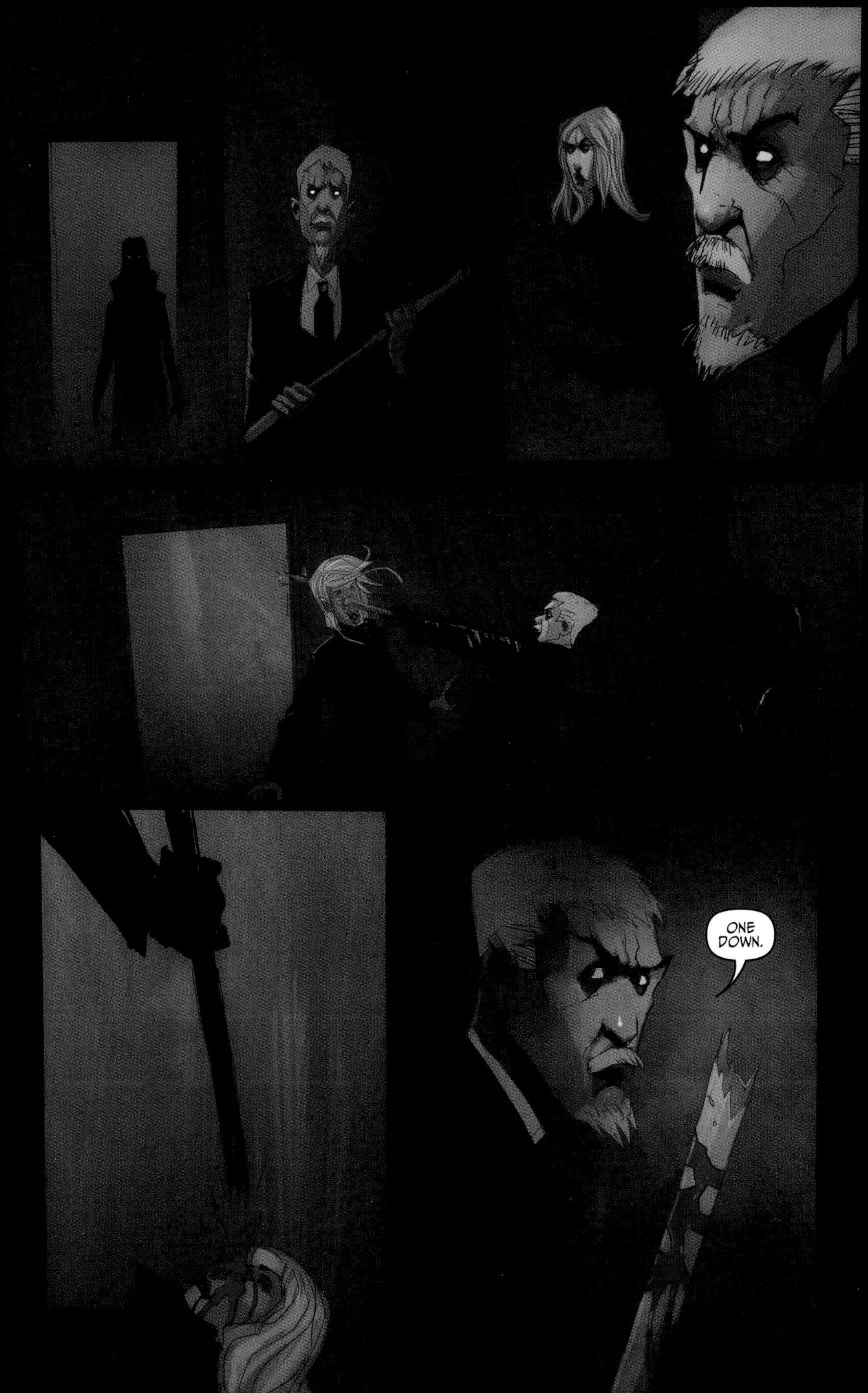
ONE DOWN.

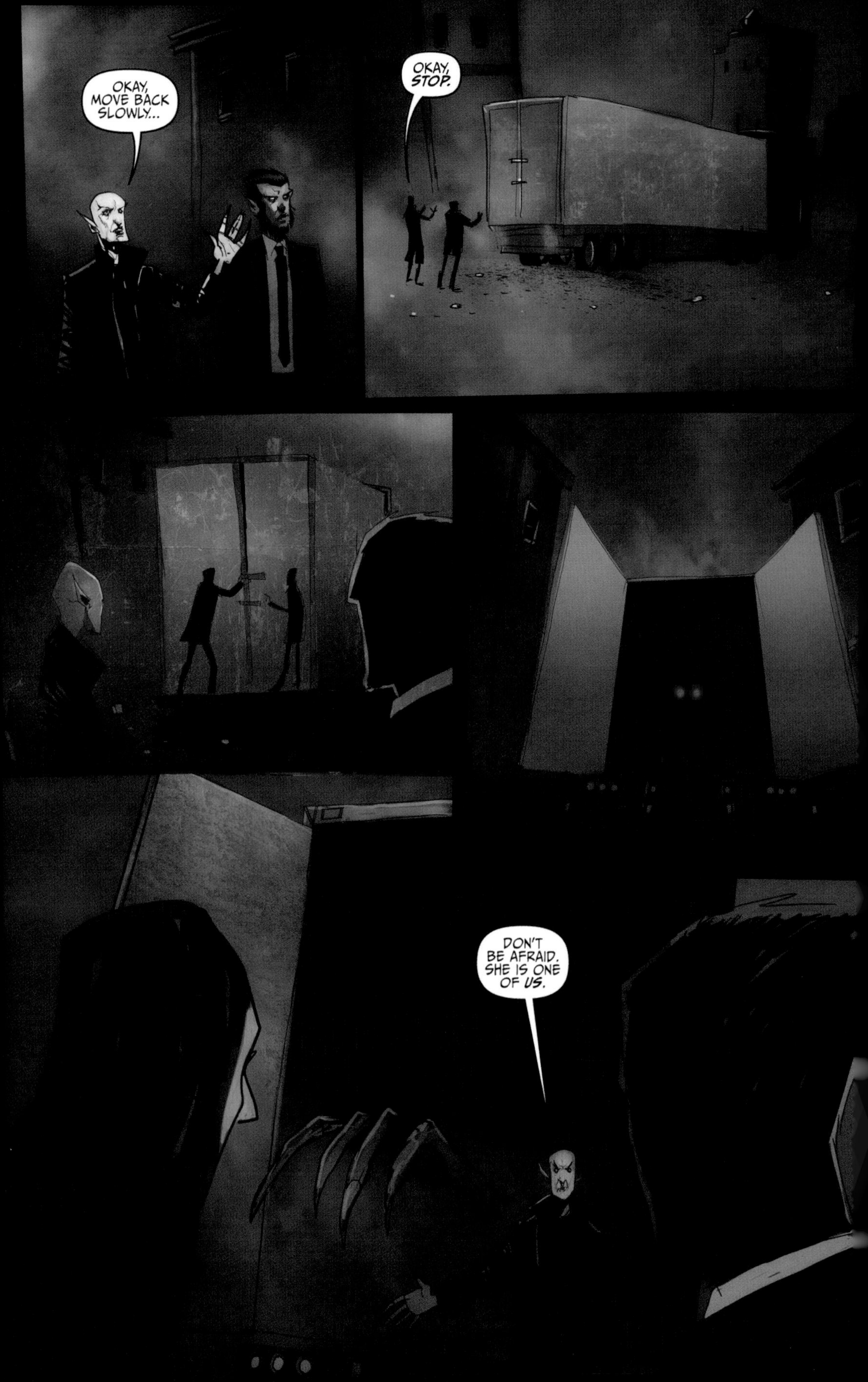
OKAY, MOVE BACK SLOWLY...
OKAY, STOP.
DON'T BE AFRAID. SHE IS ONE OF US.

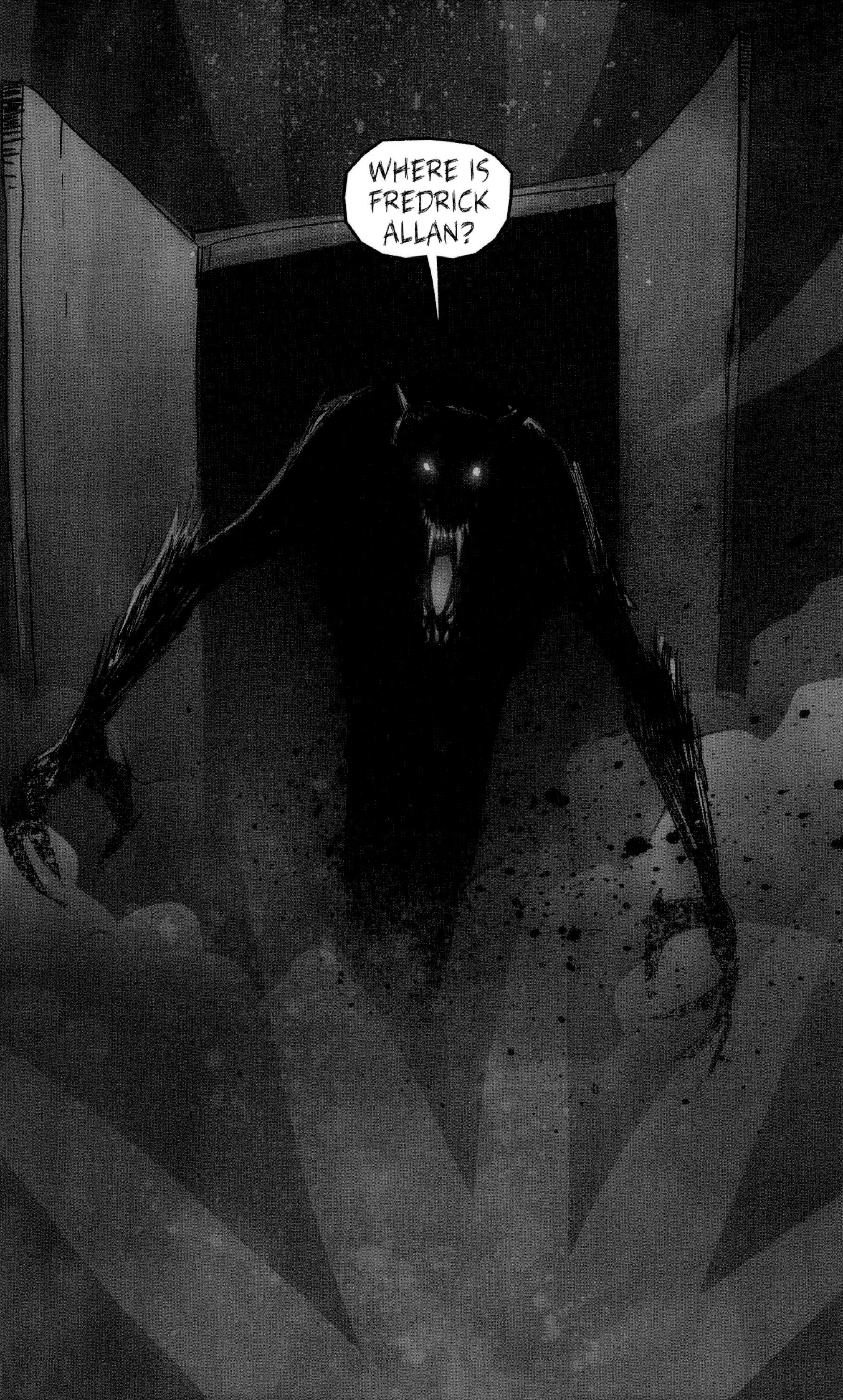
WHERE IS FREDRICK ALLAN?

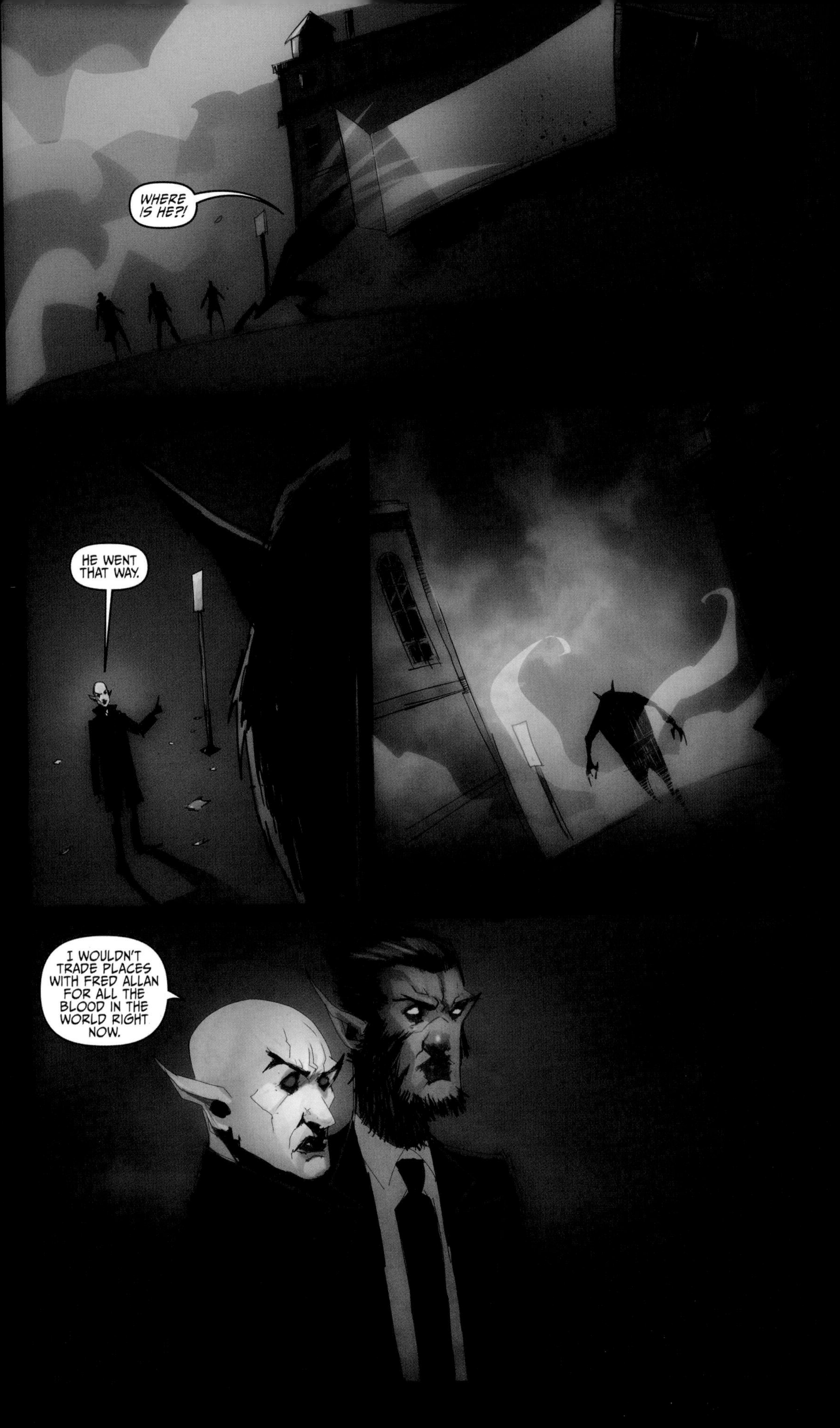
WHERE IS HE?!
HE WENT THAT WAY.
I WOULDN'T TRADE PLACES WITH FRED ALLAN FOR ALL THE BLOOD IN THE WORLD RIGHT NOW.

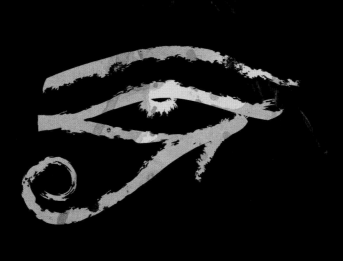

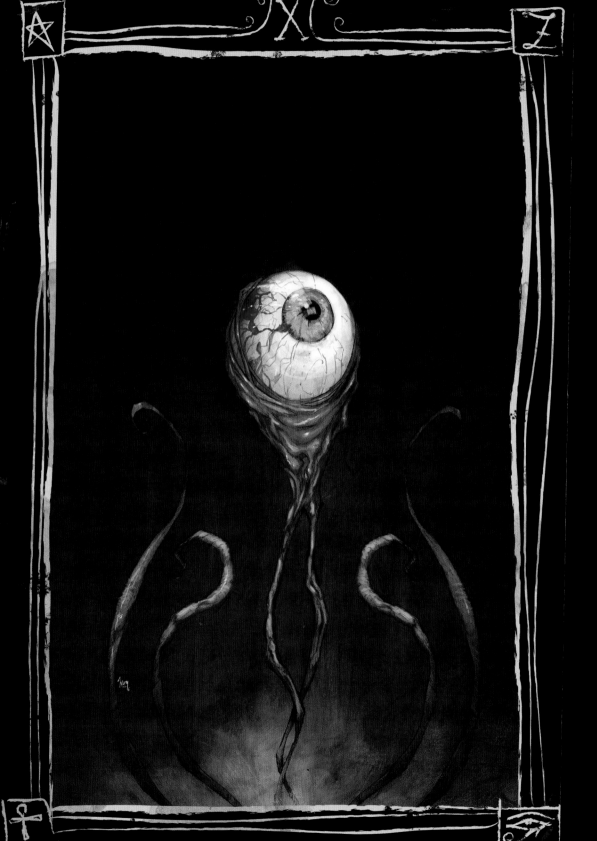

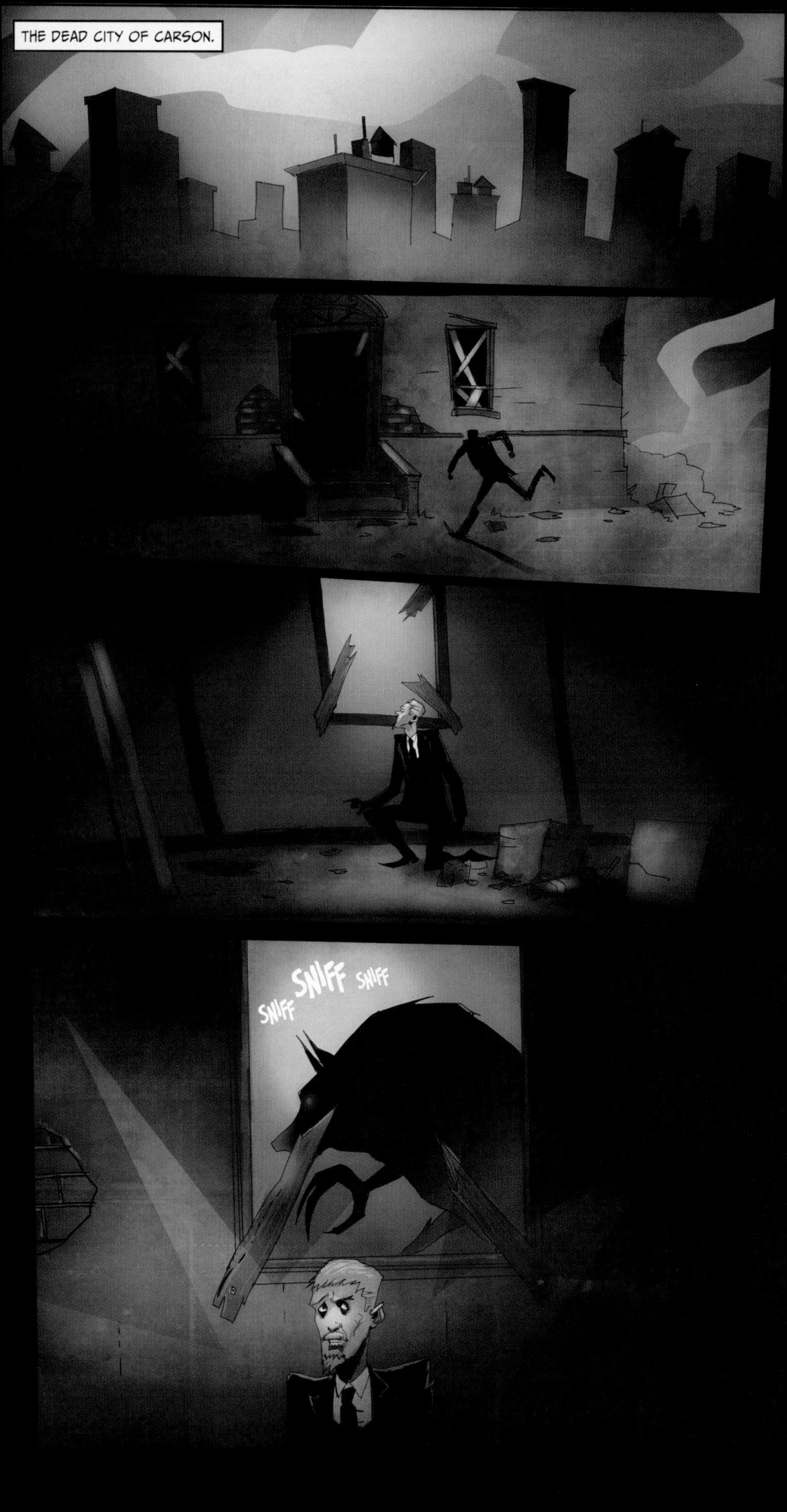
THE DEAD CITY OF CARSON.
SNIFF
SNIFF
SNIFF

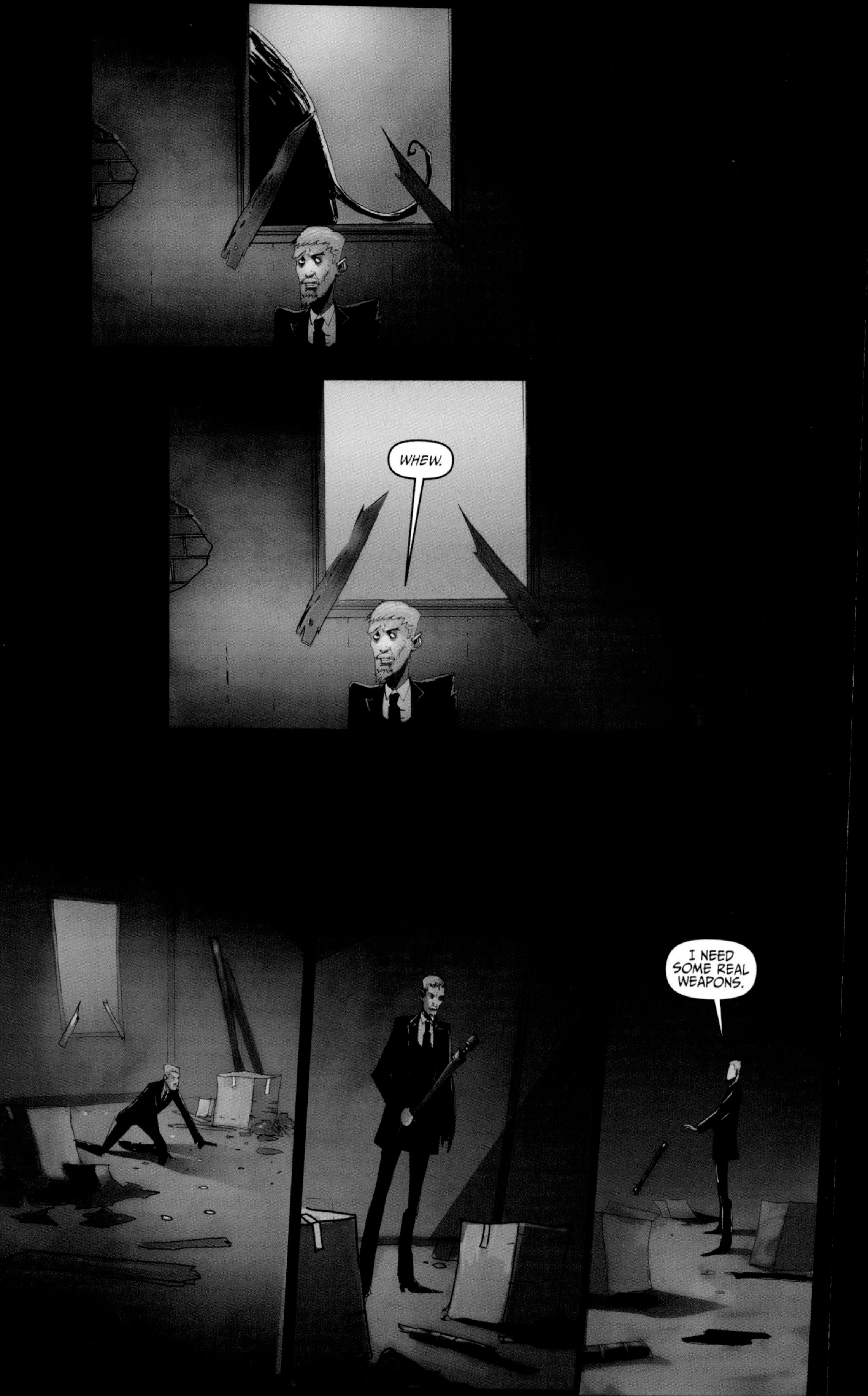
WHEW.
I NEED SOME REAL WEAPONS.

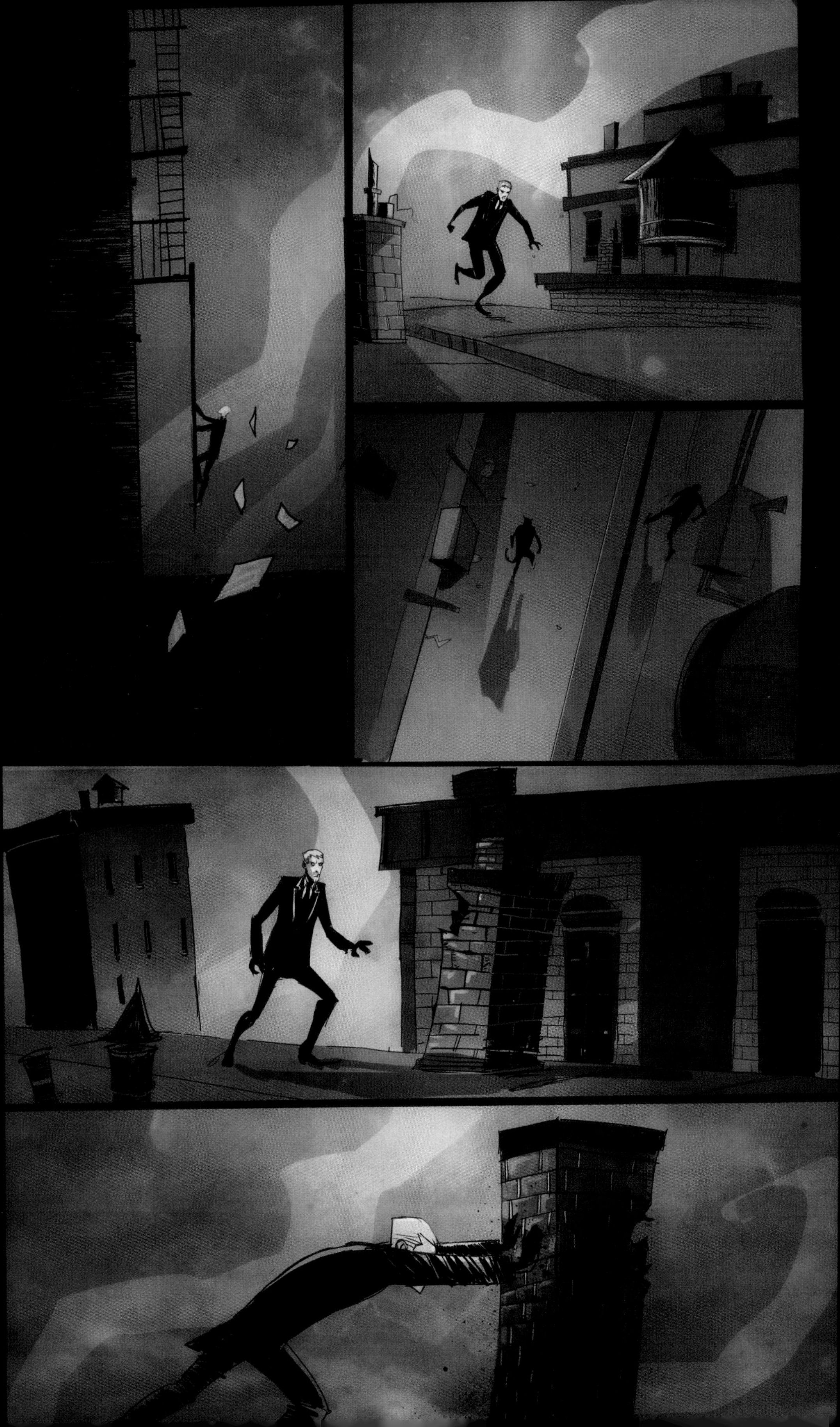

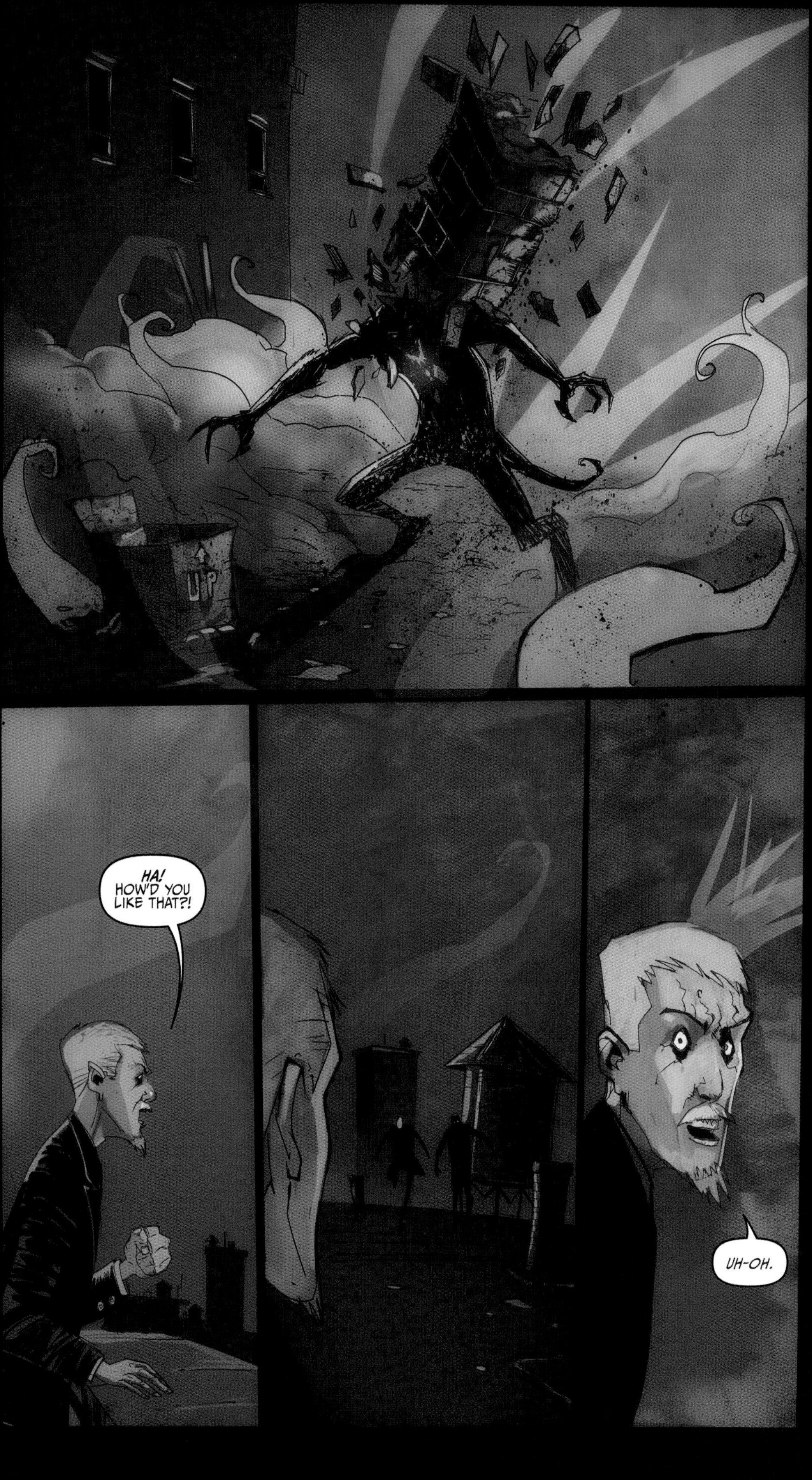
HA!
HOW'D YOU LIKE THAT?!
UH-OH.

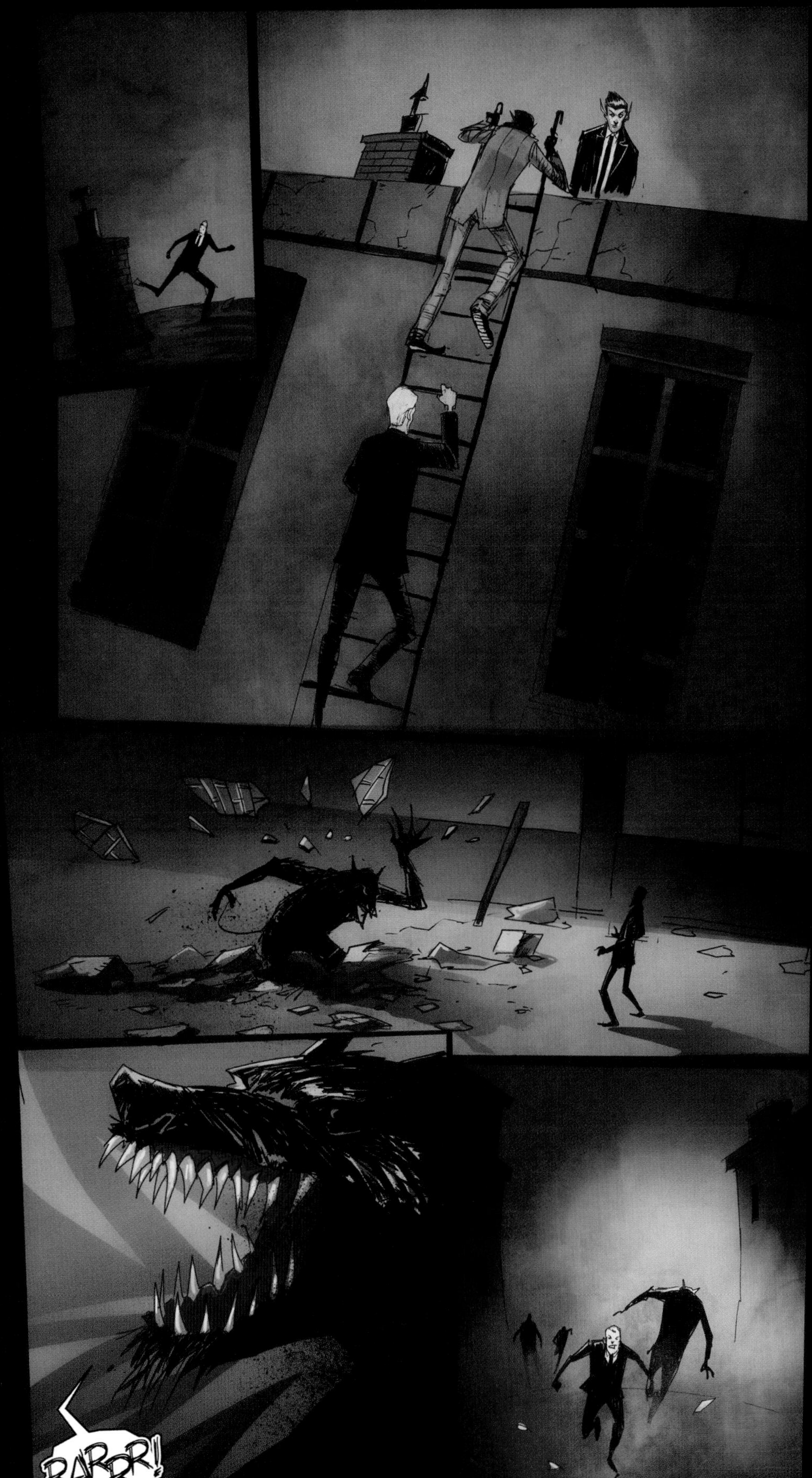
RARRR!

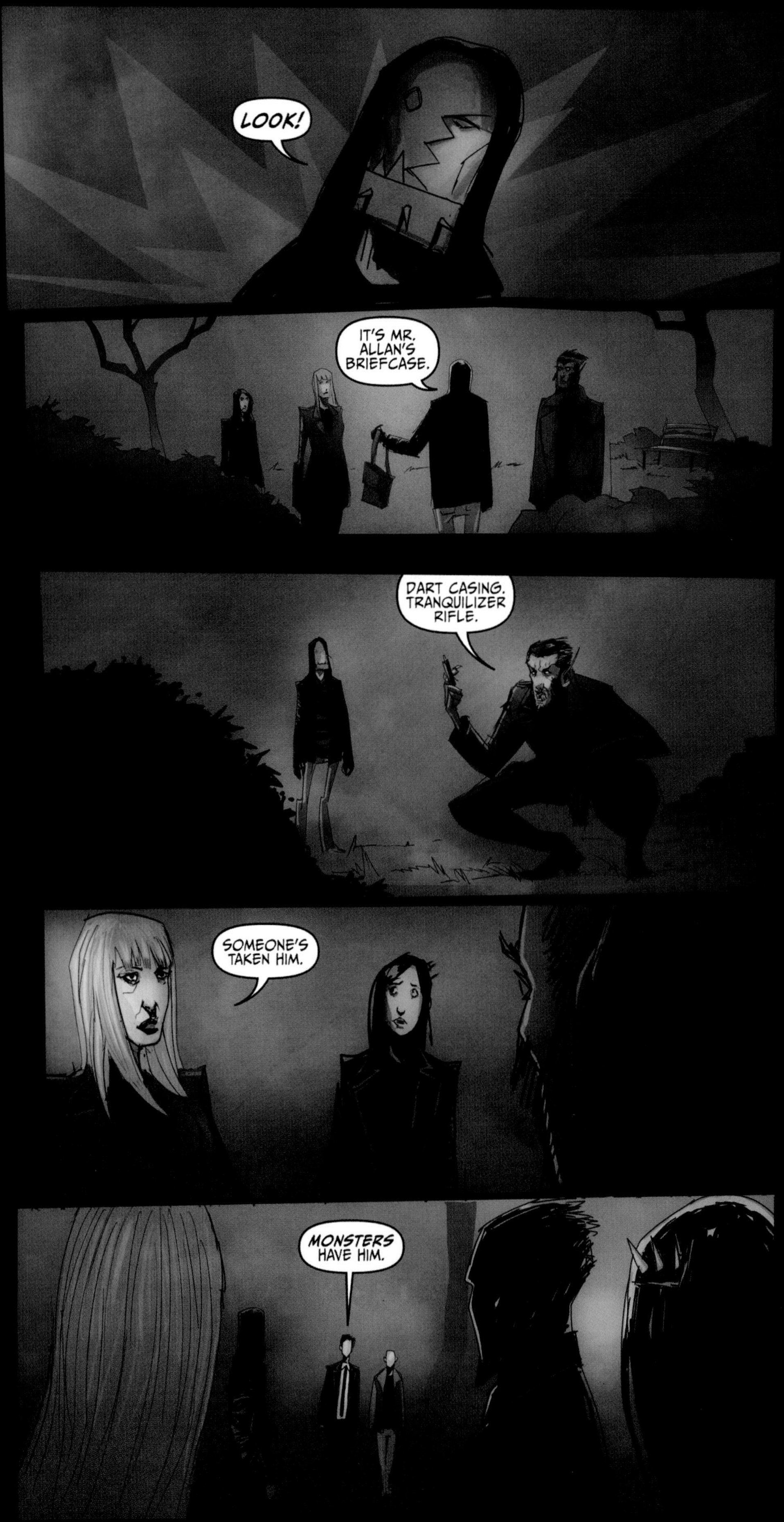
LOOK!
IT'S MR. ALLAN'S BRIEFCASE.
DART CASING. TRANQUILIZER RIFLE.
SOMEONE'S TAKEN HIM.
MONSTERS HAVE HIM.

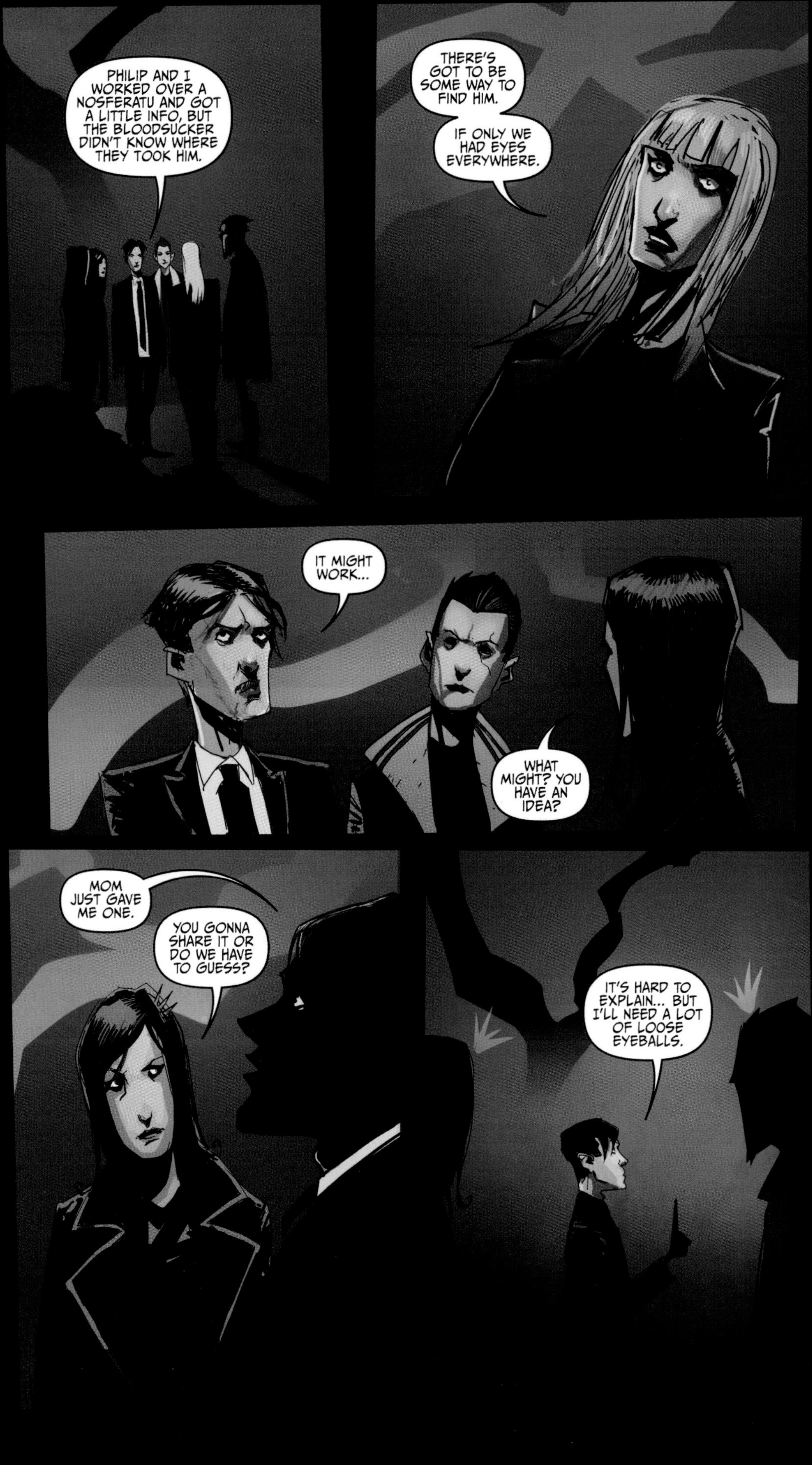
PHILIP AND I WORKED OVER A NOSFERATU AND GOT A LITTLE INFO, BUT THE BLOODSUCKER DIDN'T KNOW WHERE THEY TOOK HIM.
THERE'S GOT TO BE SOME WAY TO FIND HIM.
IF ONLY WE HAD EYES EVERYWHERE.
IT MIGHT WORK...
WHAT MIGHT? YOU HAVE AN IDEA?
MOM JUST GAVE ME ONE.
YOU GONNA SHARE IT OR DO WE HAVE TO GUESS?
IT'S HARD TO EXPLAIN... BUT I'LL NEED A LOT OF LOOSE EYEBALLS.

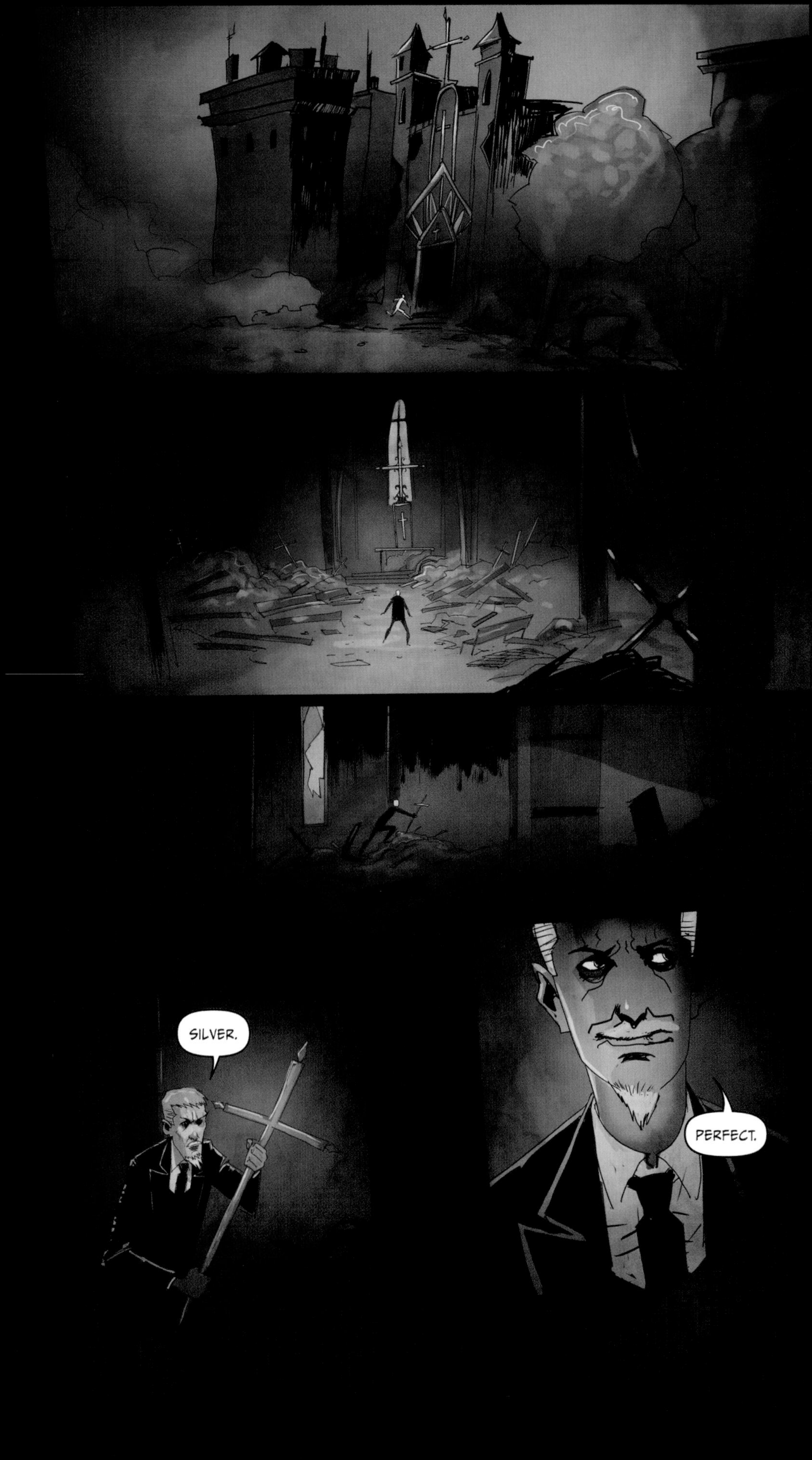
SILVER.
PERFECT.

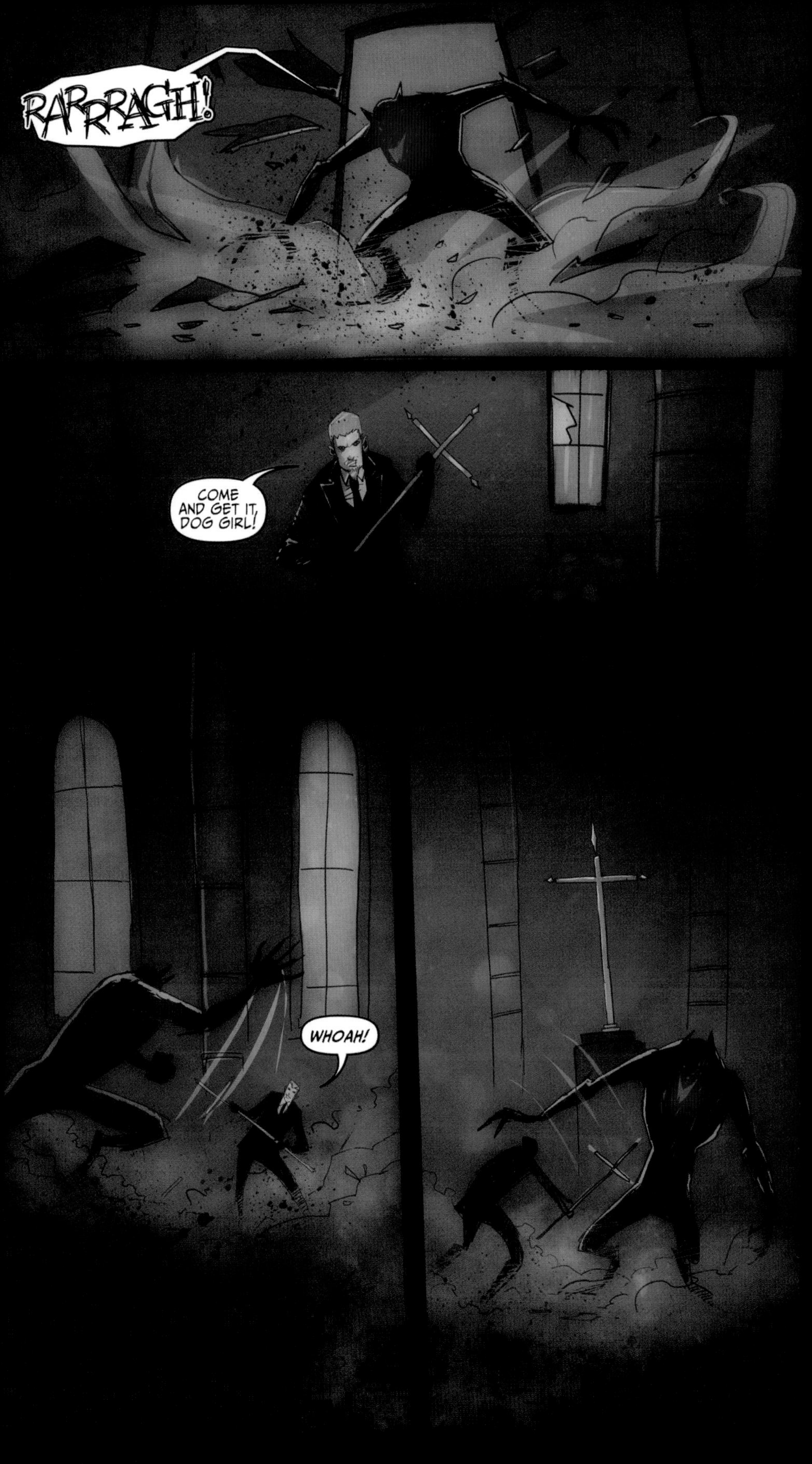
RARRRAGH!
COME AND GET IT, DOG GIRL!
WHOAH!

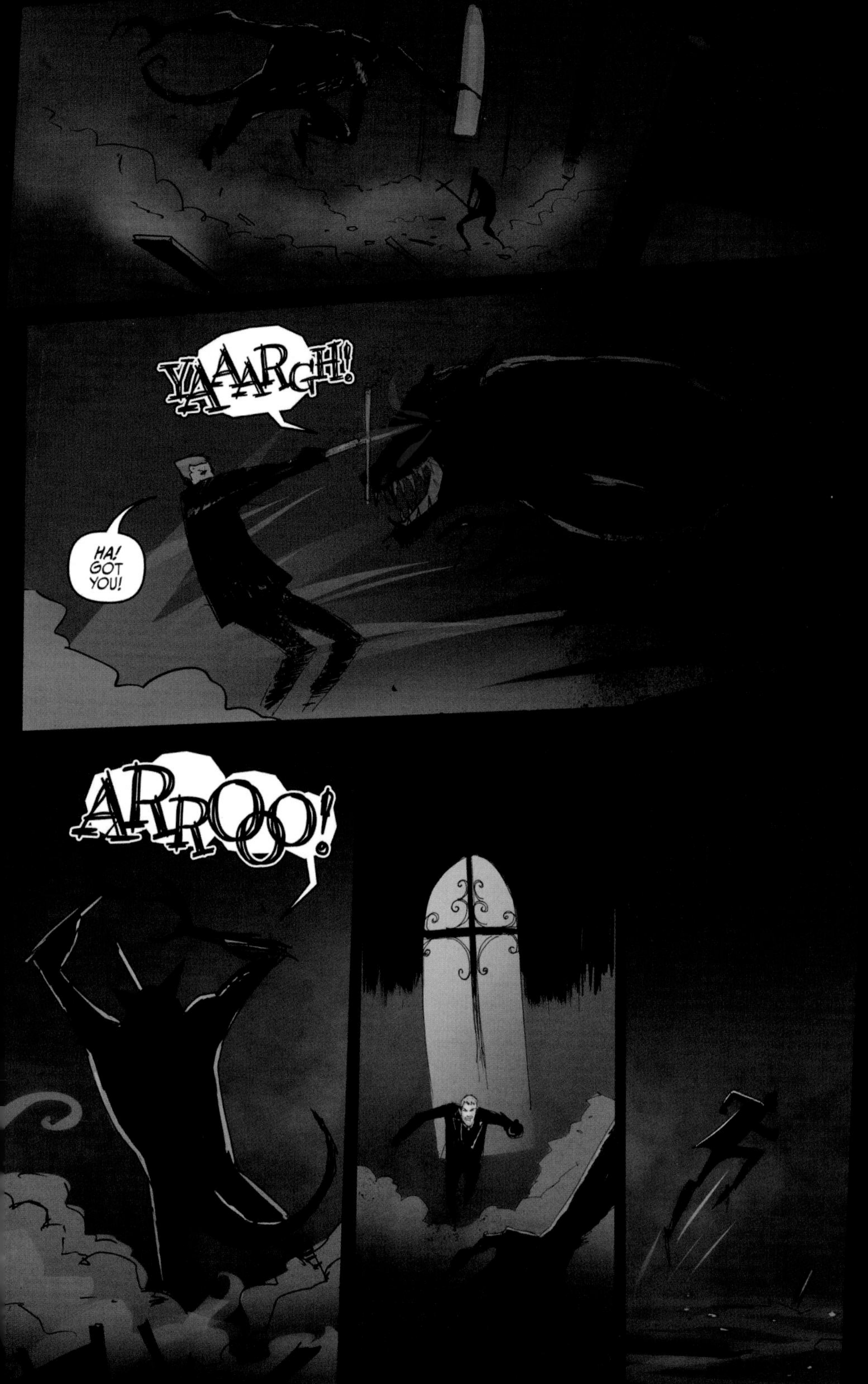
YAAARGH!
HA! GOT YOU!
ARROOO!

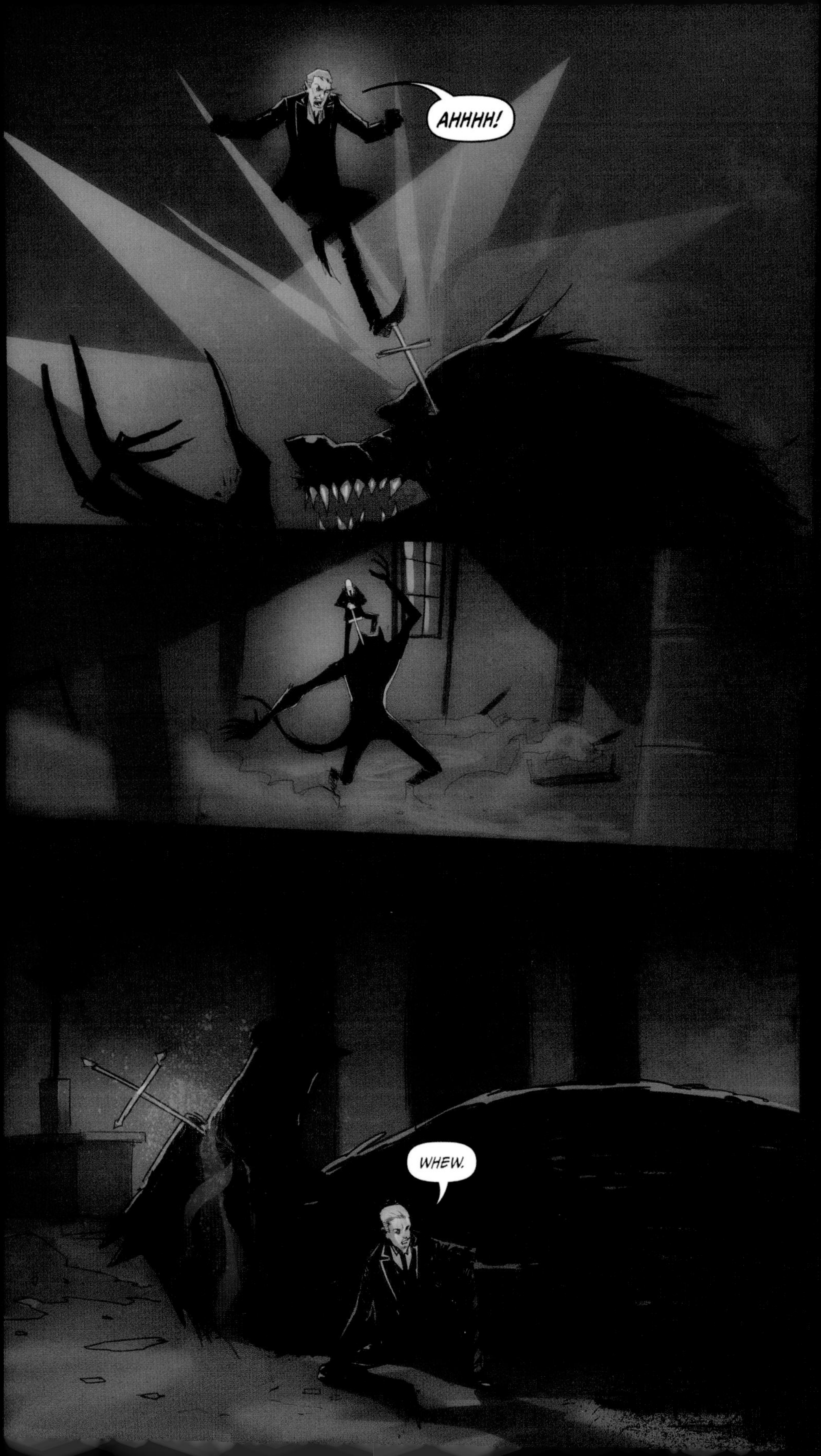
AHHHH!
WHEW.

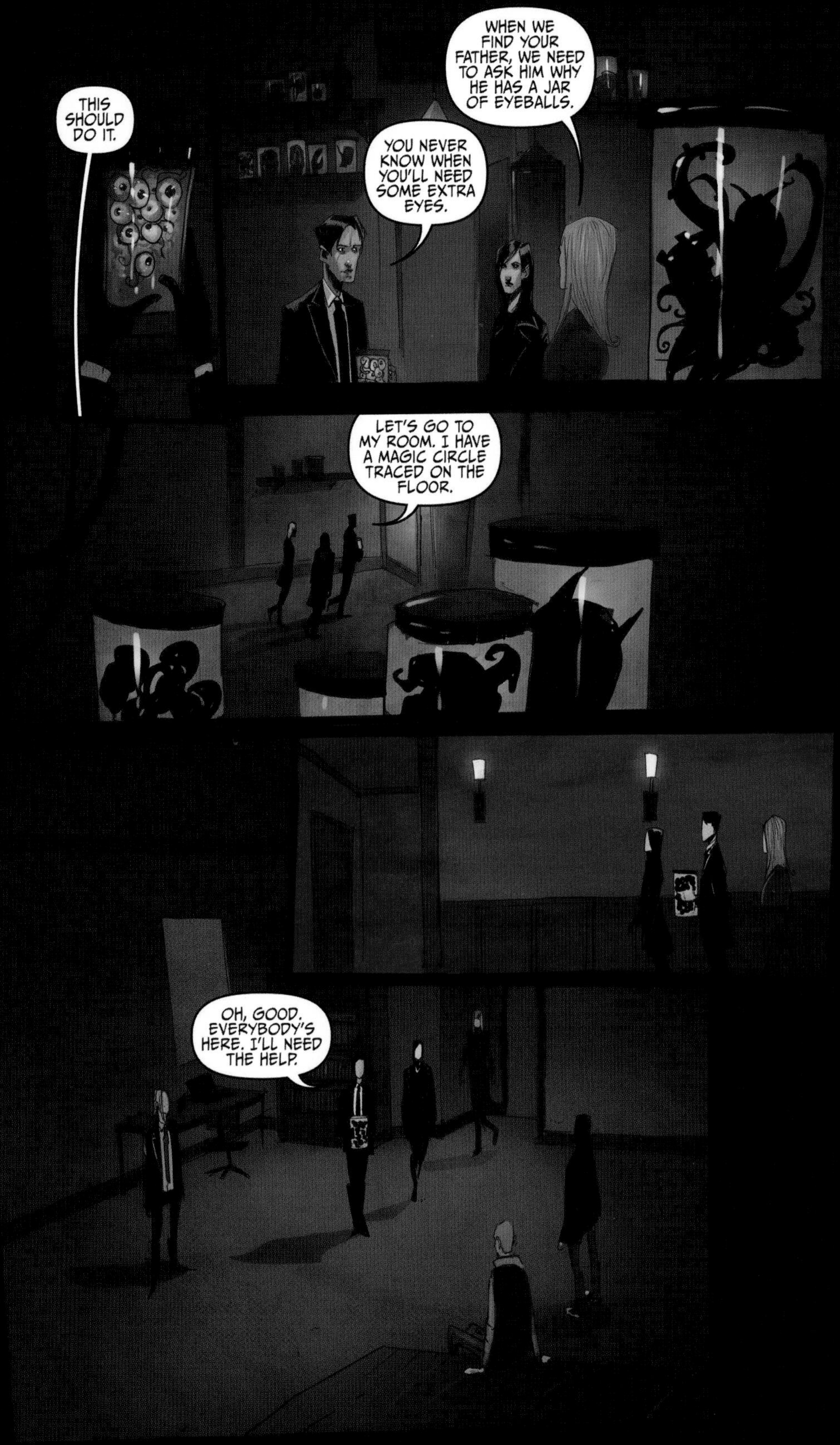
THIS SHOULD DO IT.
WHEN WE FIND YOUR FATHER, WE NEED TO ASK HIM WHY HE HAS A JAR OF EYEBALLS.
YOU NEVER KNOW WHEN YOU'LL NEED SOME EXTRA EYES.
LET'S GO TO MY ROOM. I HAVE A MAGIC CIRCLE TRACED ON THE FLOOR.
OH, GOOD. EVERYBODY'S HERE. I'LL NEED THE HELP.

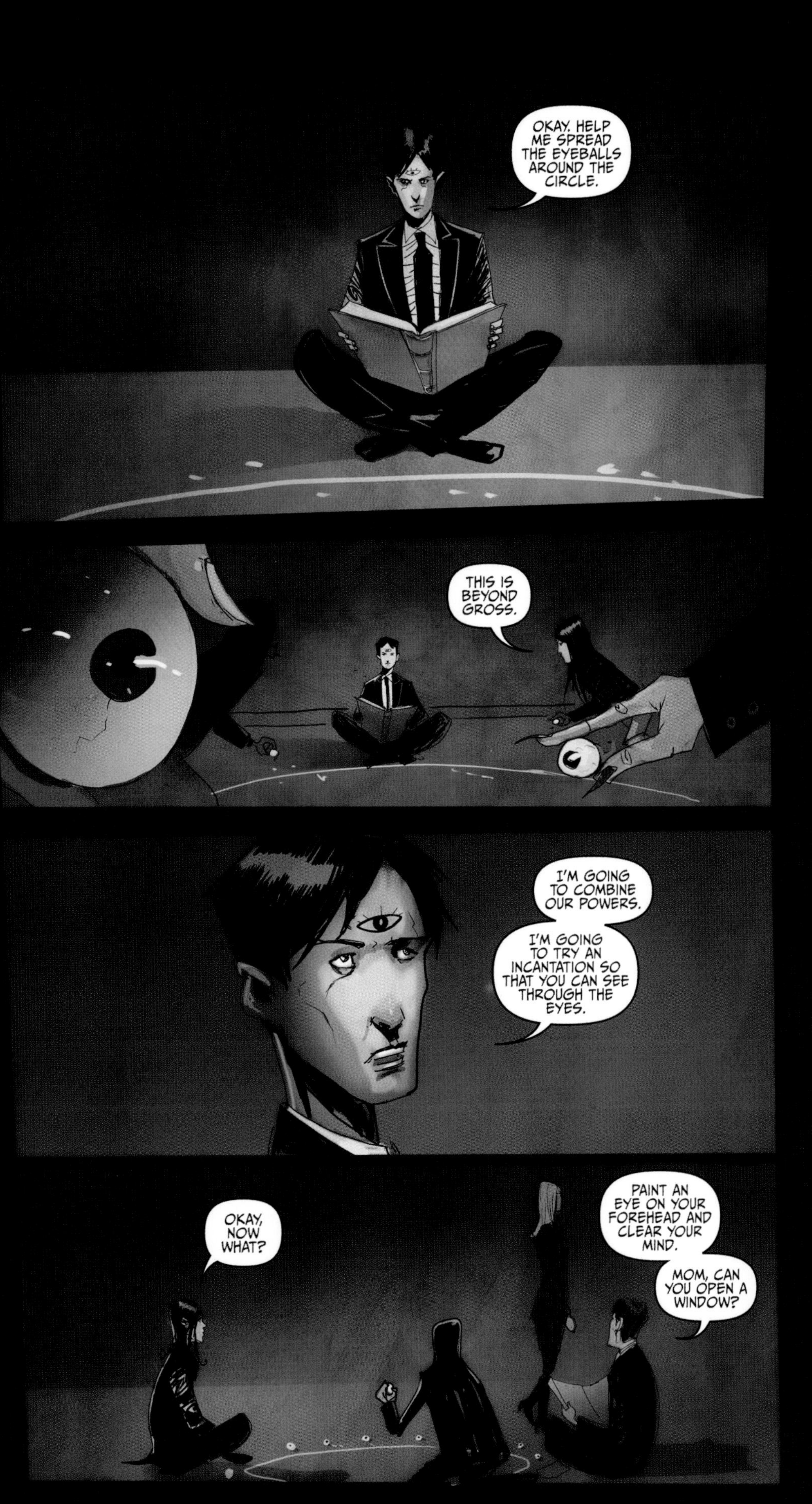
OKAY. HELP ME SPREAD THE EYEBALLS AROUND THE CIRCLE.
THIS IS BEYOND GROSS.
I'M GOING TO COMBINE OUR POWERS.
I'M GOING TO TRY AN INCANTATION SO THAT YOU CAN SEE THROUGH THE EYES.
OKAY, NOW WHAT?
PAINT AN EYE ON YOUR FOREHEAD AND CLEAR YOUR MIND.
MOM, CAN YOU OPEN A WINDOW?

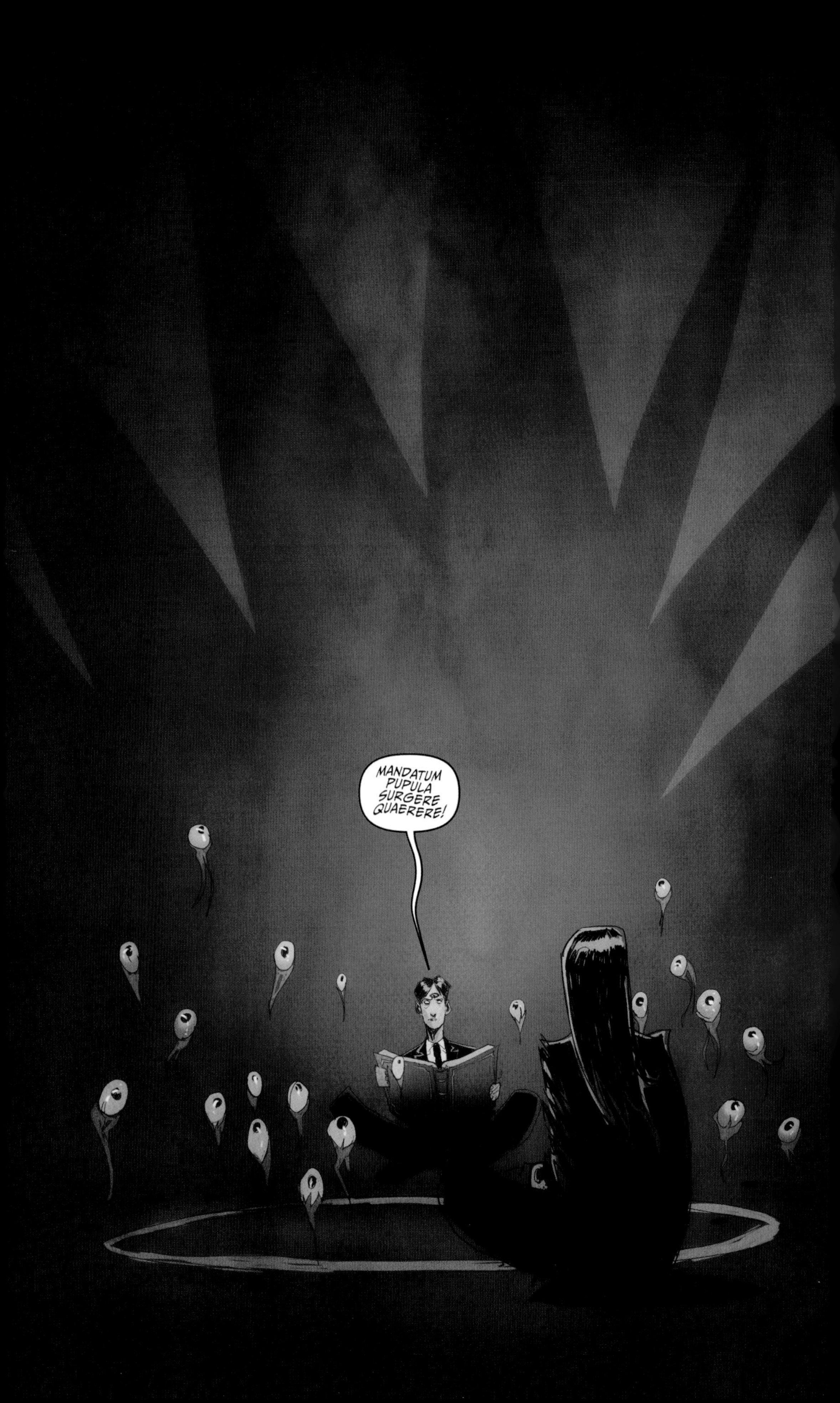
MANDATUM PUPULA SURGERE QUAERERE!

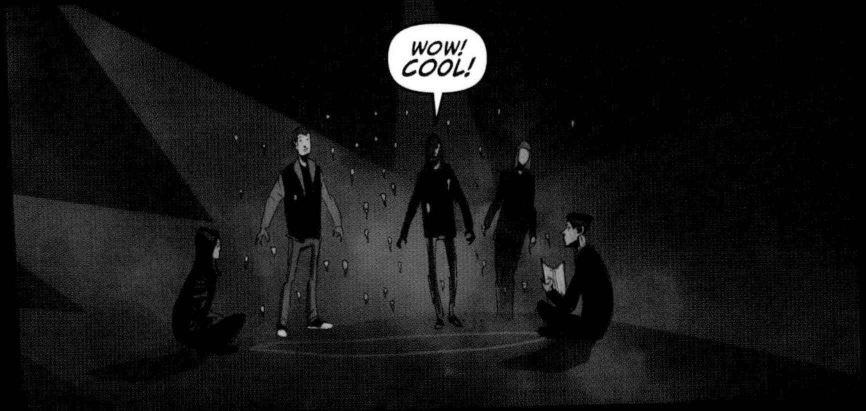
WOW! COOL!

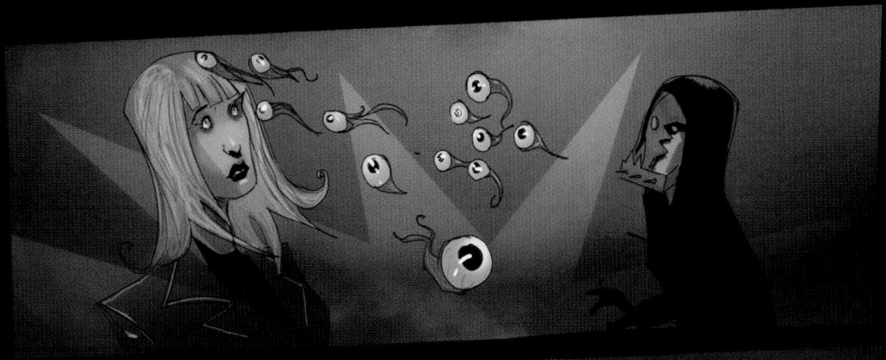

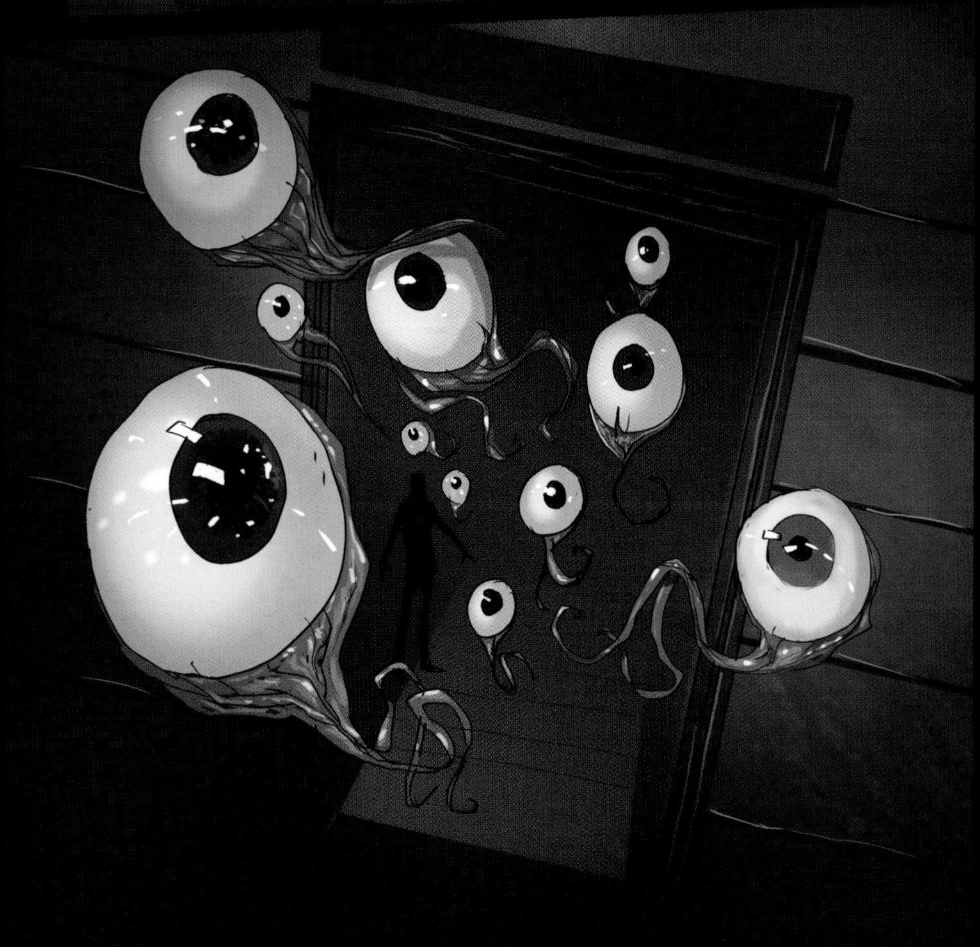

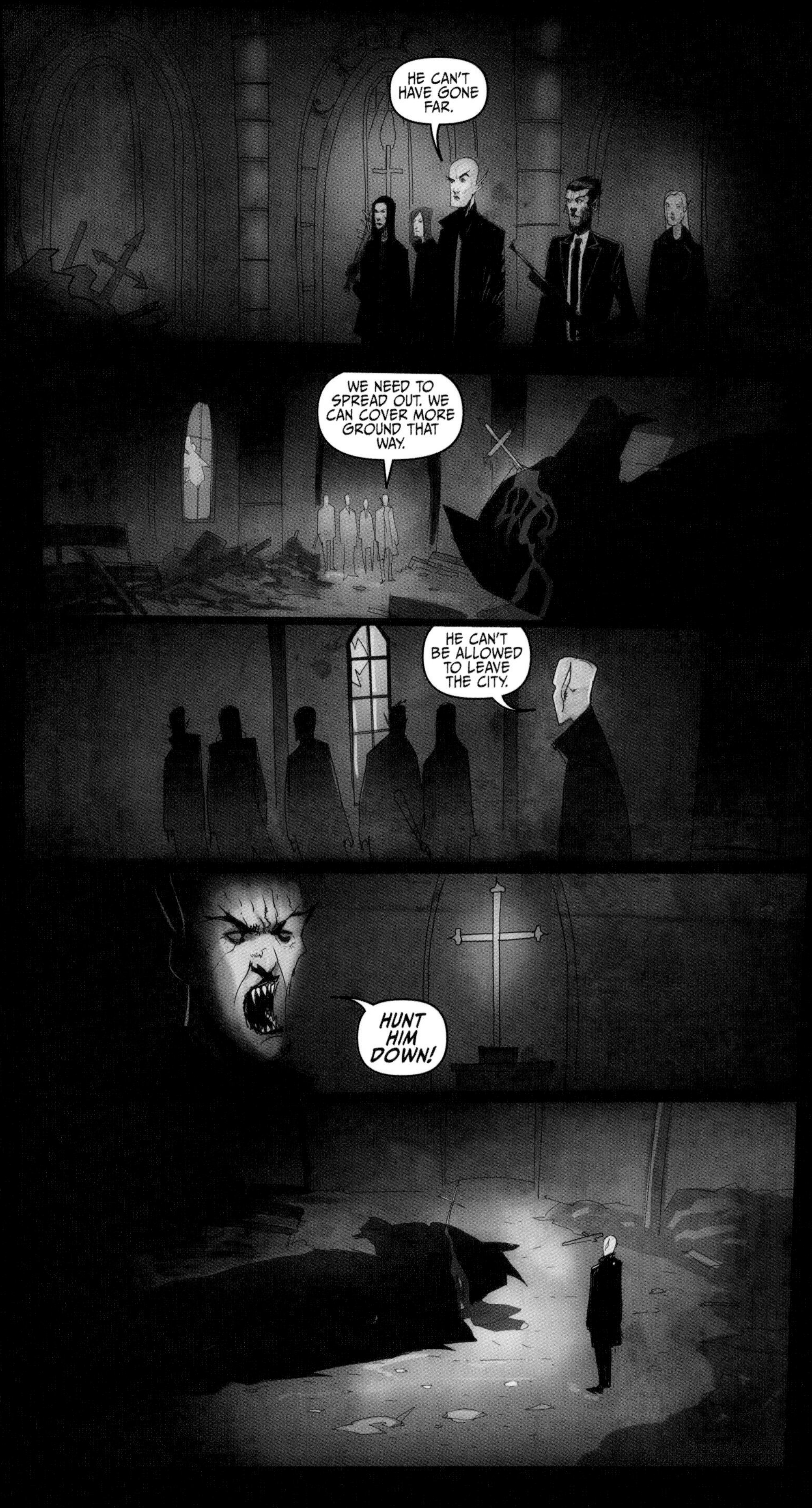
HE CAN'T HAVE GONE FAR.
WE NEED TO SPREAD OUT. WE CAN COVER MORE GROUND THAT WAY.
HE CAN'T BE ALLOWED TO LEAVE THE CITY.
HUNT HIM DOWN!

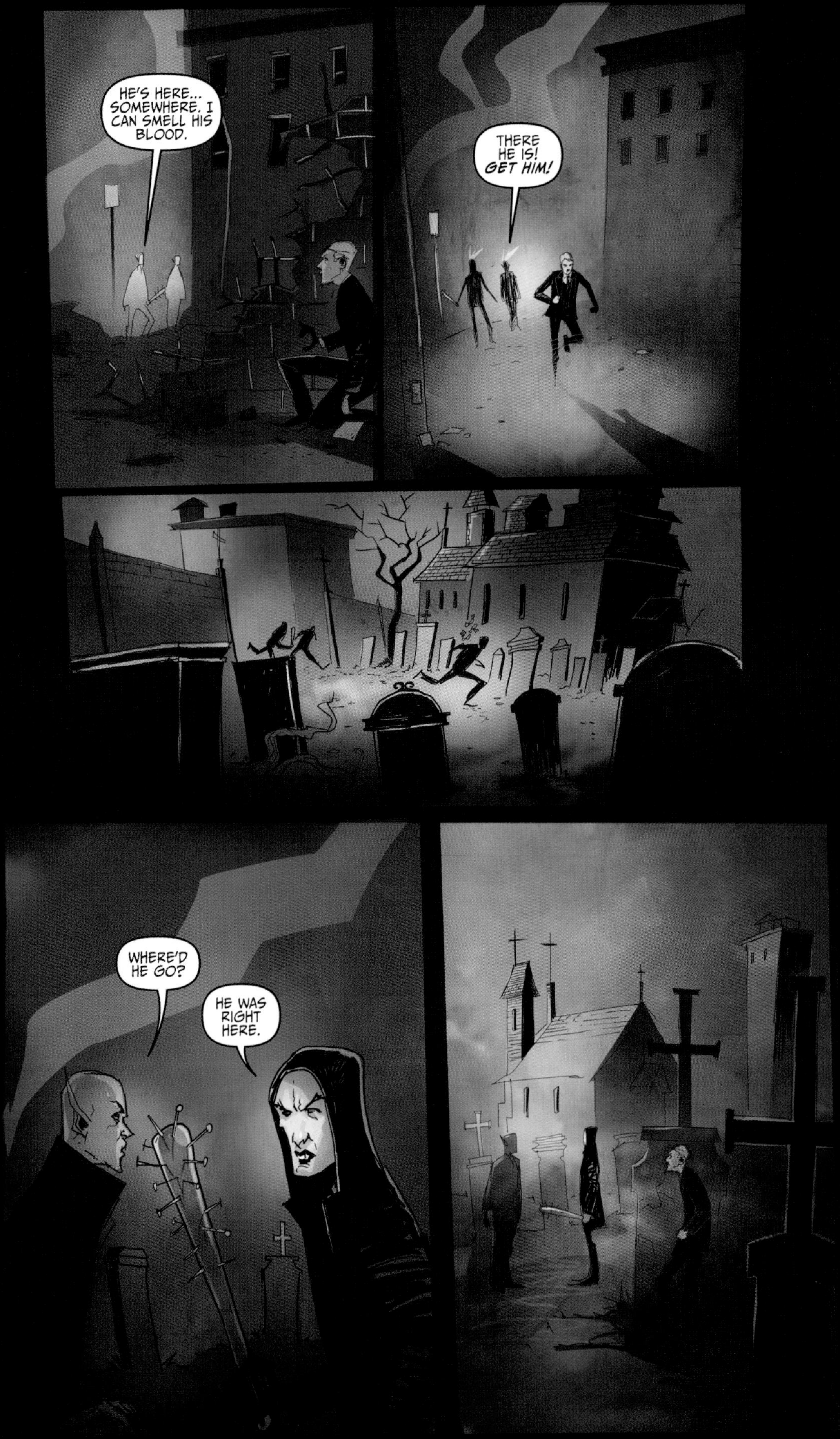
HE'S HERE... SOMEWHERE. I CAN SMELL HIS BLOOD.
THERE HE IS! GET HIM!
WHERE'D HE GO?
HE WAS RIGHT HERE.

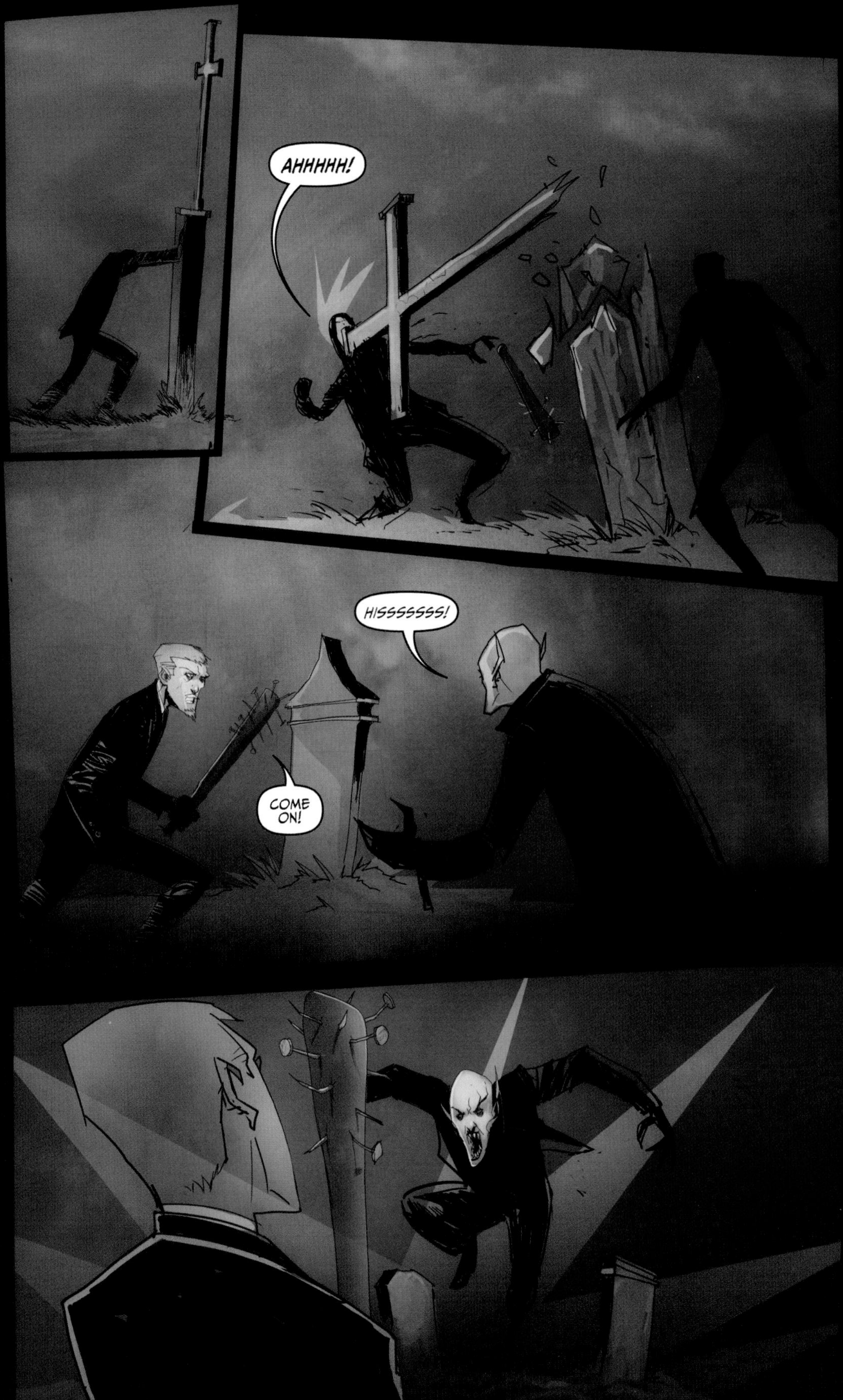
AHHHHH!
HISSSSSSS!
COME ON!

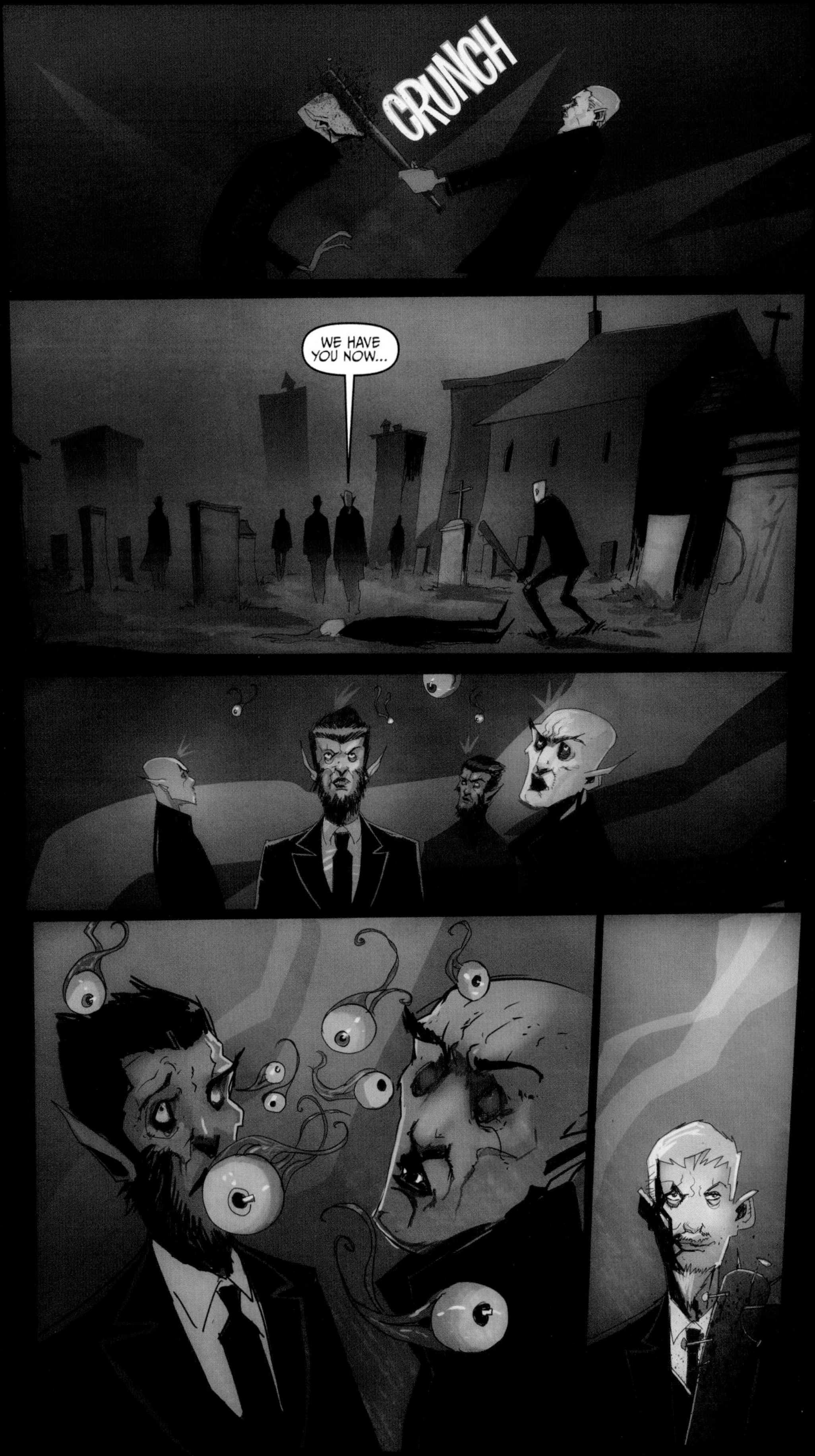
CRUNCH
WE HAVE YOU NOW...

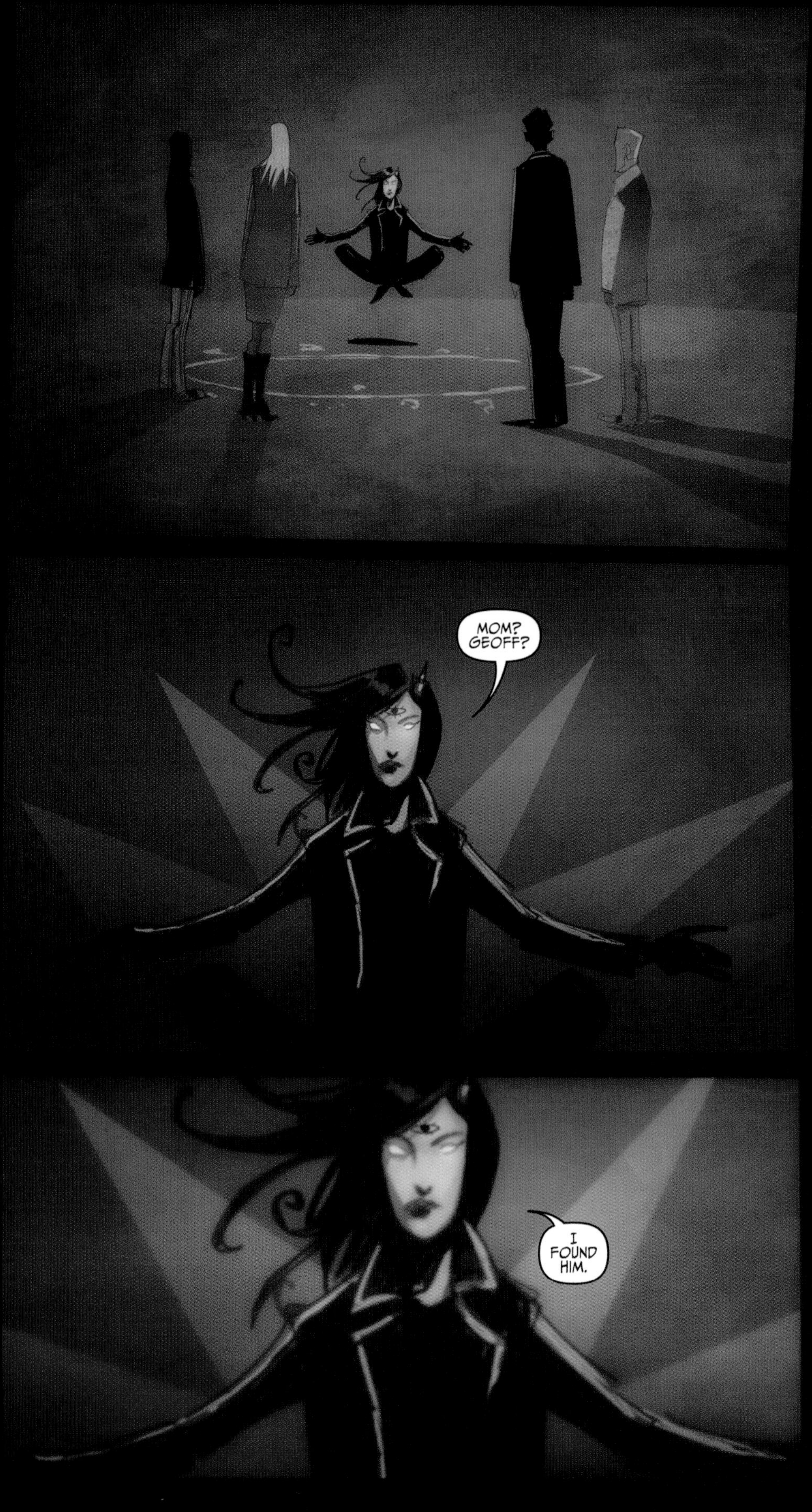

MOM? GEOFF?
I FOUND HIM.

Z

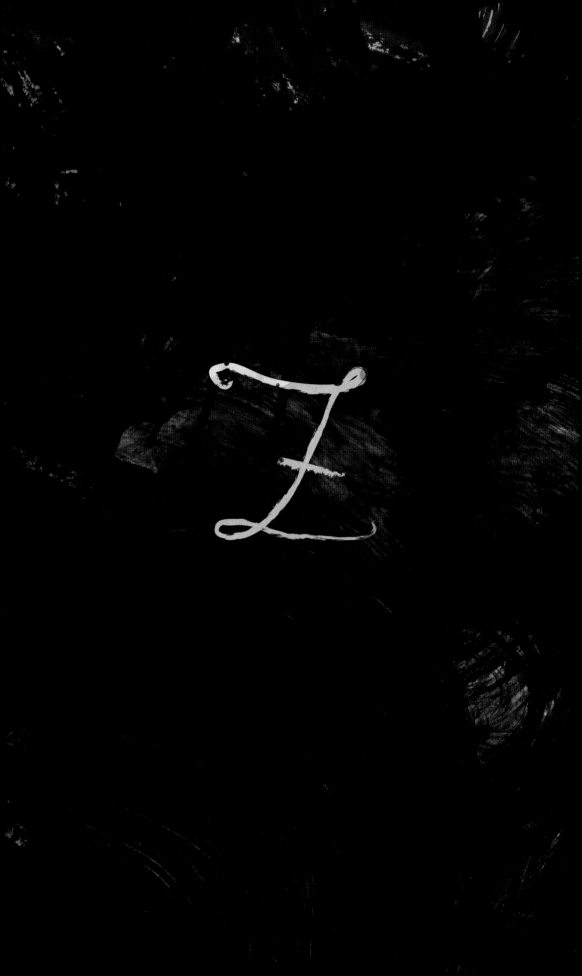

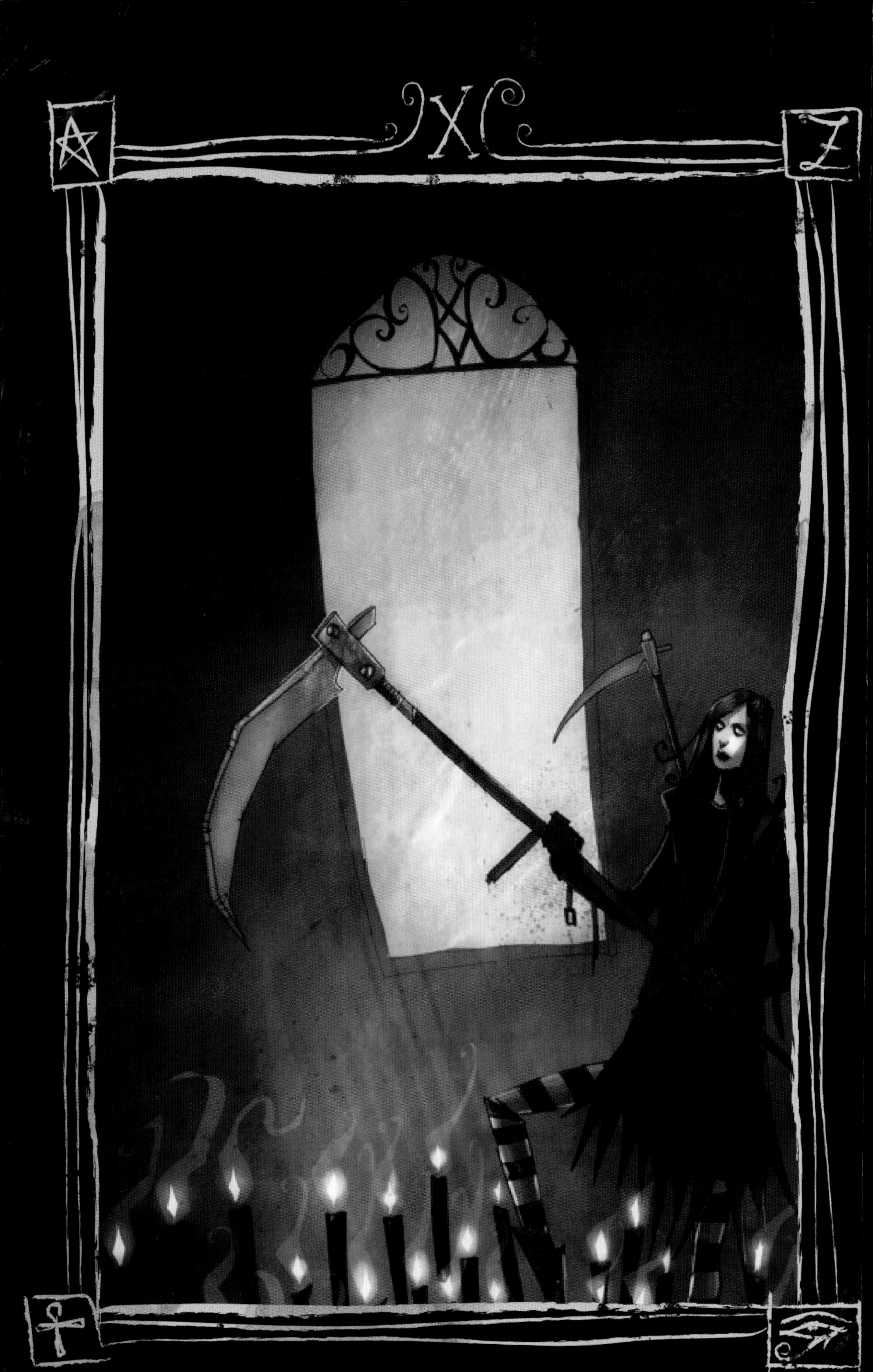
X
Z

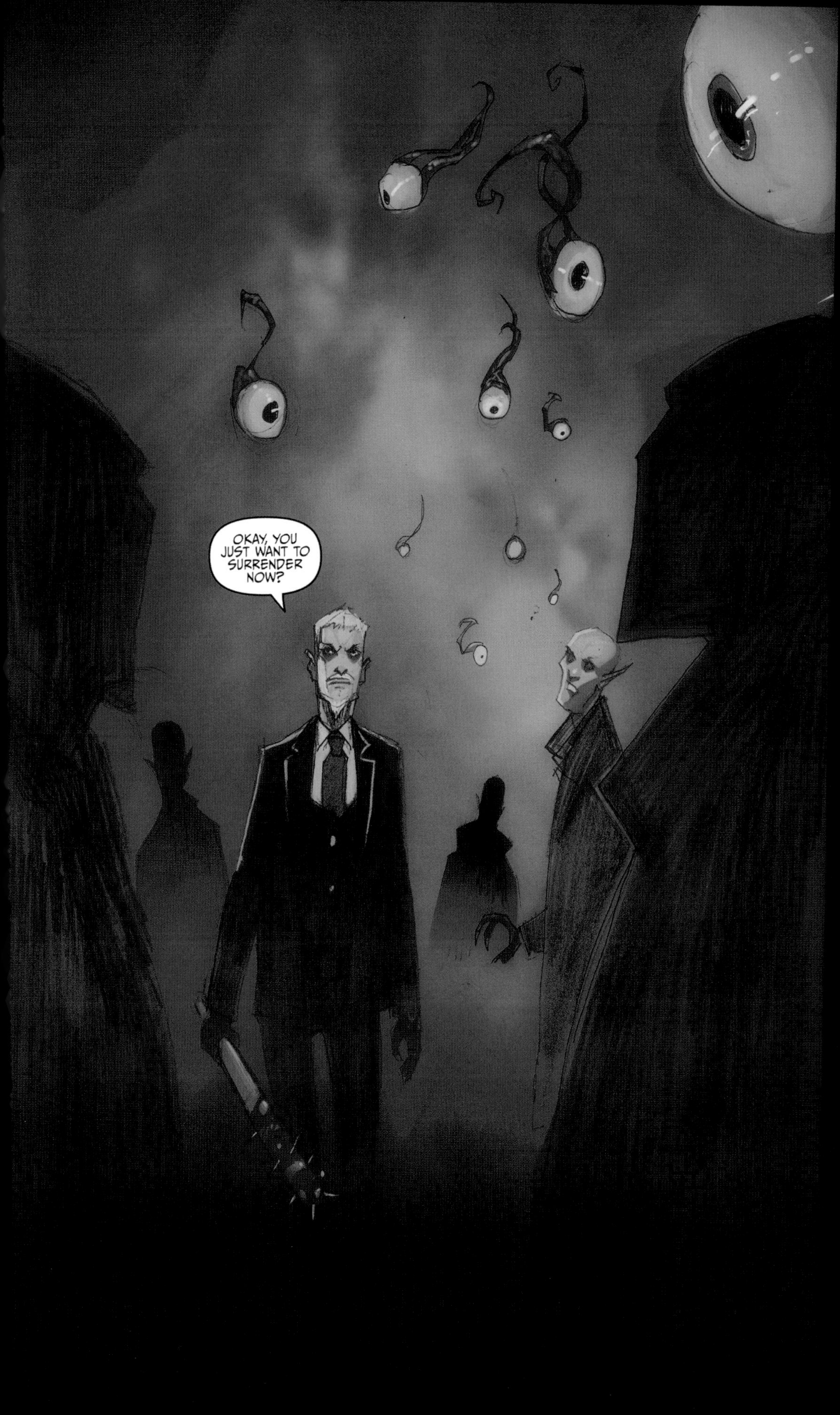
OKAY, YOU JUST WANT TO SURRENDER NOW?

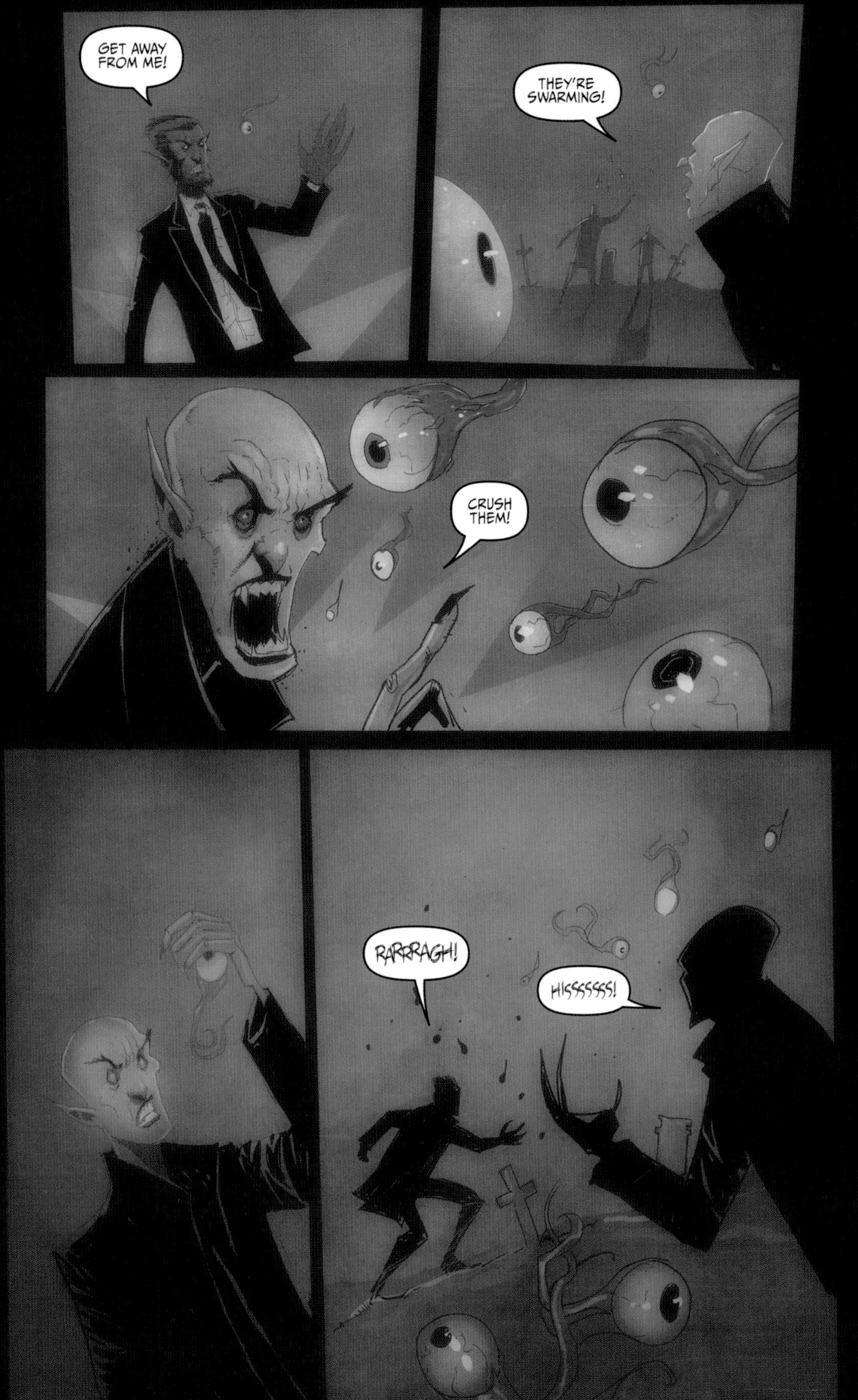
GET AWAY FROM ME!
THEY'RE SWARMING!
CRUSH THEM!
RARRRAGH!
HISSSSSSS!

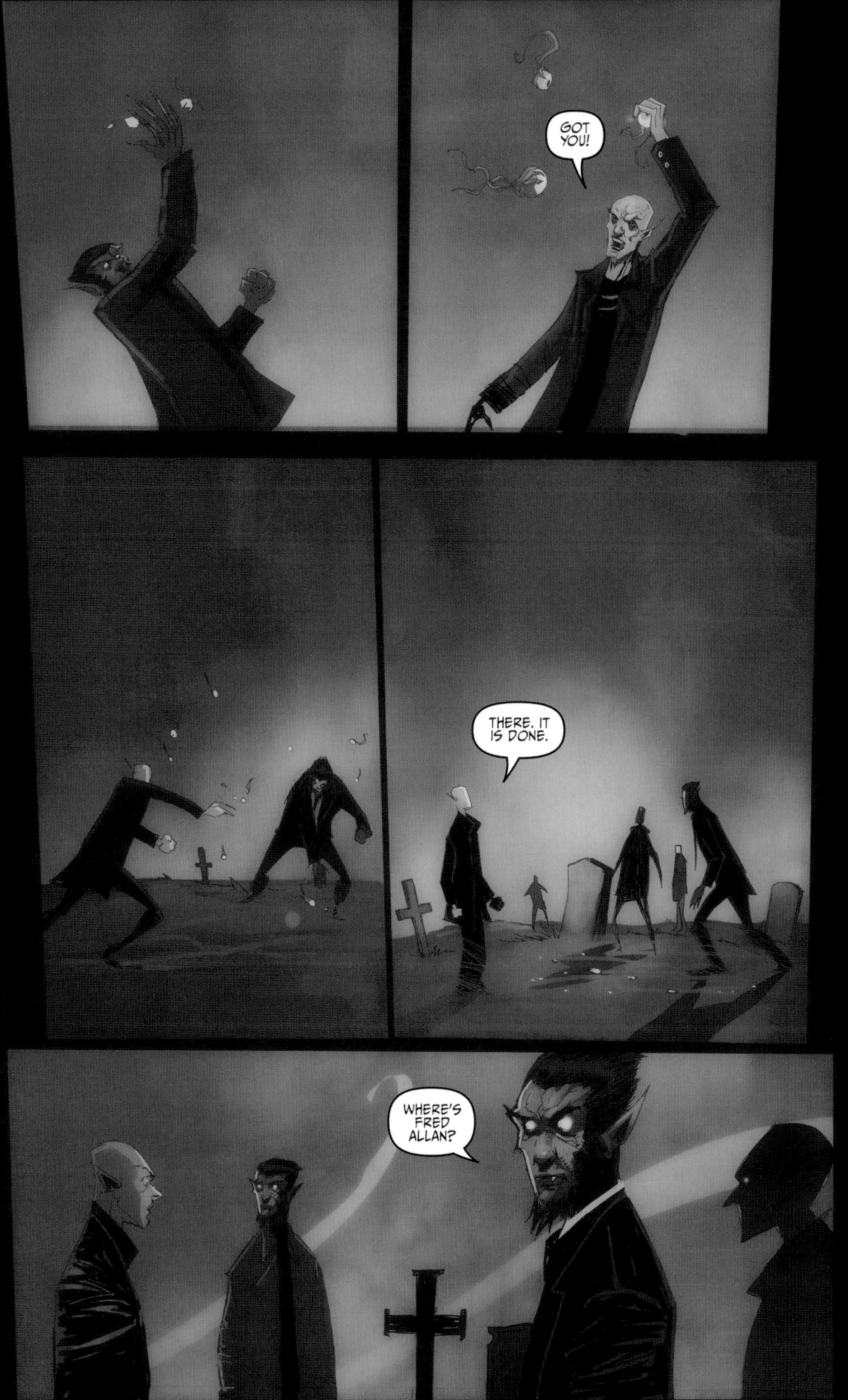
GOT YOU!
THERE. IT IS DONE.
WHERE'S FRED ALLAN?

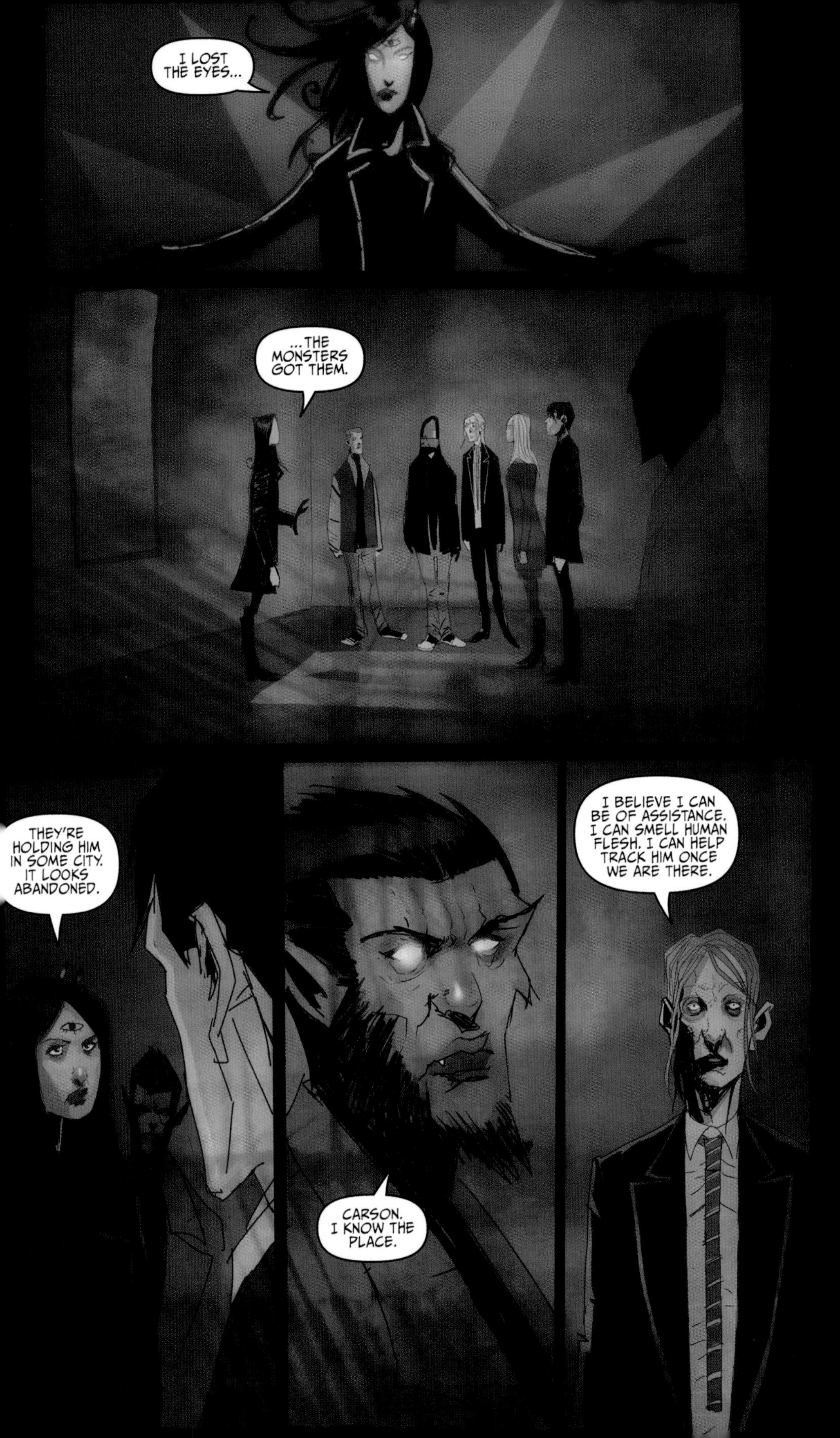
I LOST THE EYES...
...THE MONSTERS GOT THEM.
THEY'RE HOLDING HIM IN SOME CITY. IT LOOKS ABANDONED.
CARSON. I KNOW THE PLACE.
I BELIEVE I CAN BE OF ASSISTANCE. I CAN SMELL HUMAN FLESH. I CAN HELP TRACK HIM ONCE WE ARE THERE.

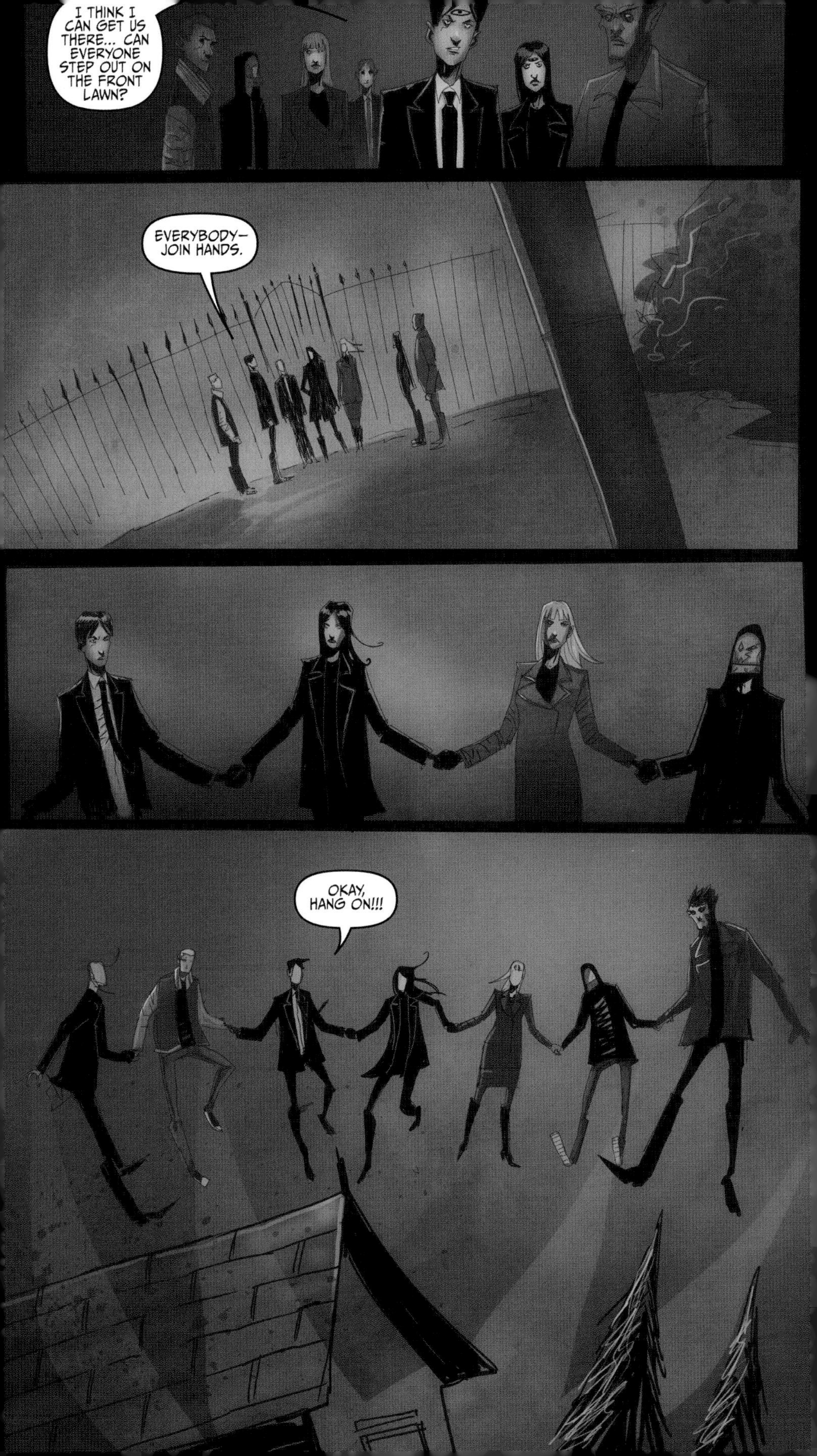
I THINK I CAN GET US THERE... CAN EVERYONE STEP OUT ON THE FRONT LAWN?
EVERYBODY— JOIN HANDS.
OKAY, HANG ON!!!

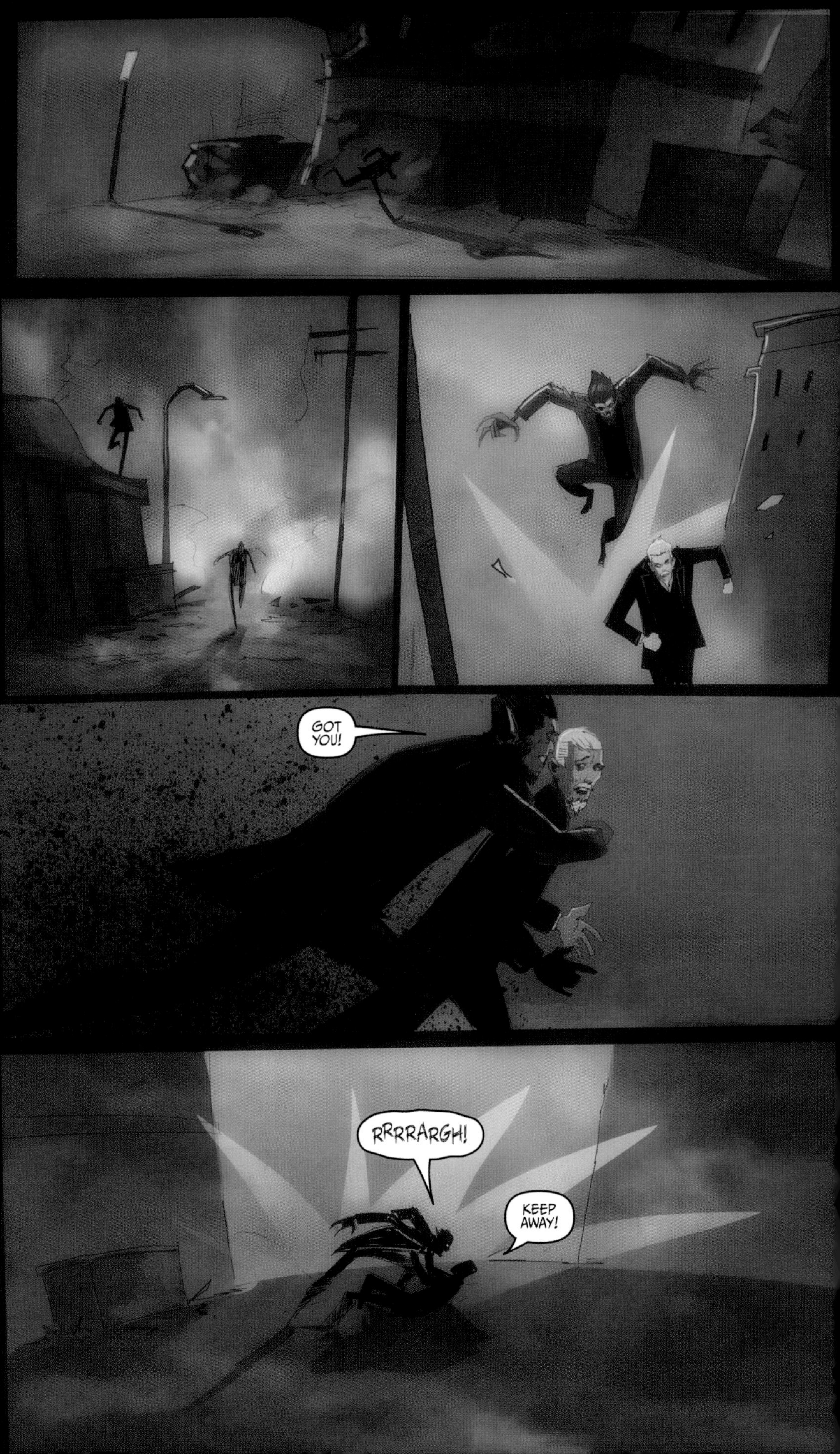
GOT YOU!
RRRRARGH!
KEEP AWAY!

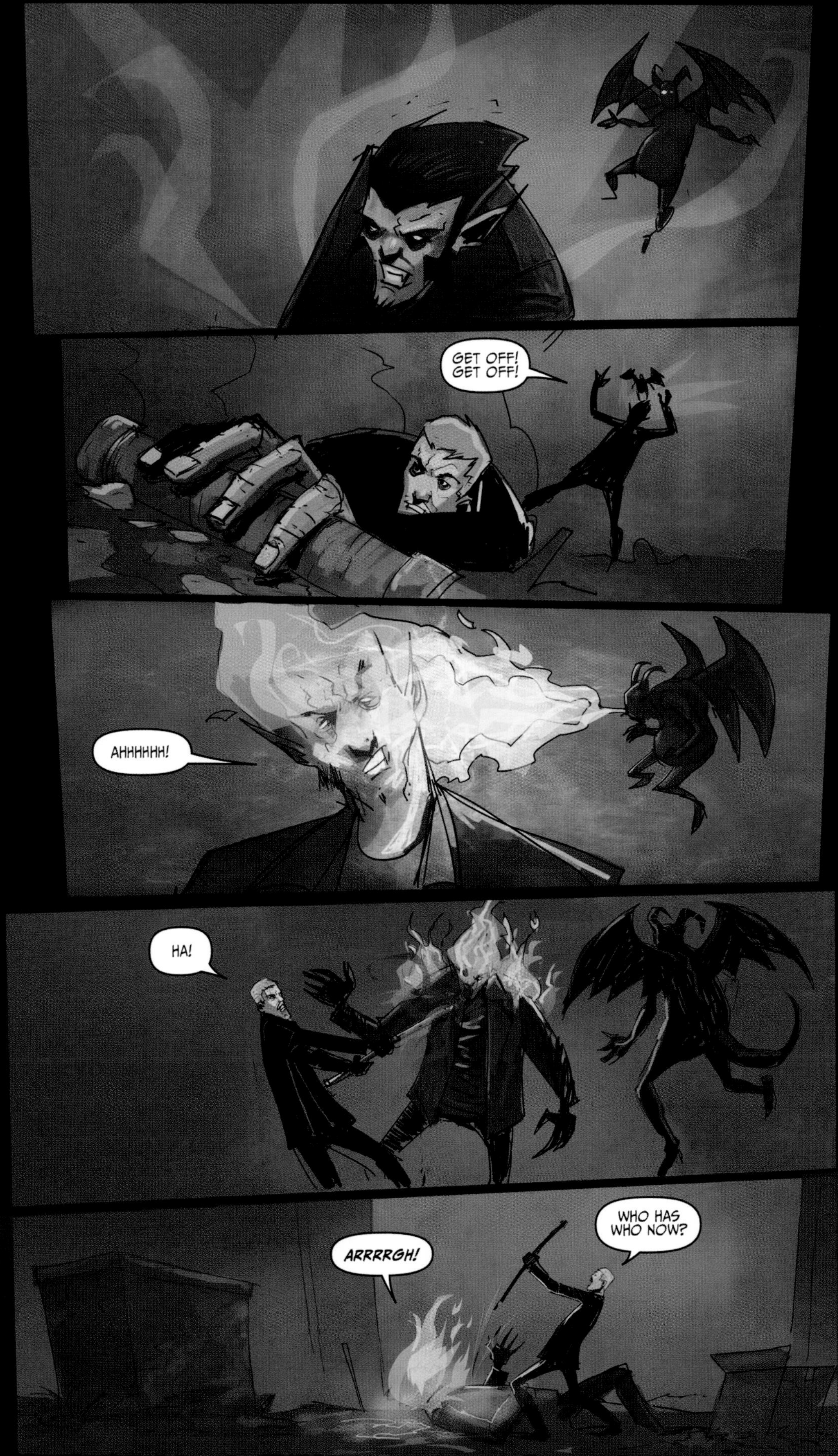
GET OFF! GET OFF!
AHHHHHH!
HA!
ARRRRGH!
WHO HAS WHO NOW?

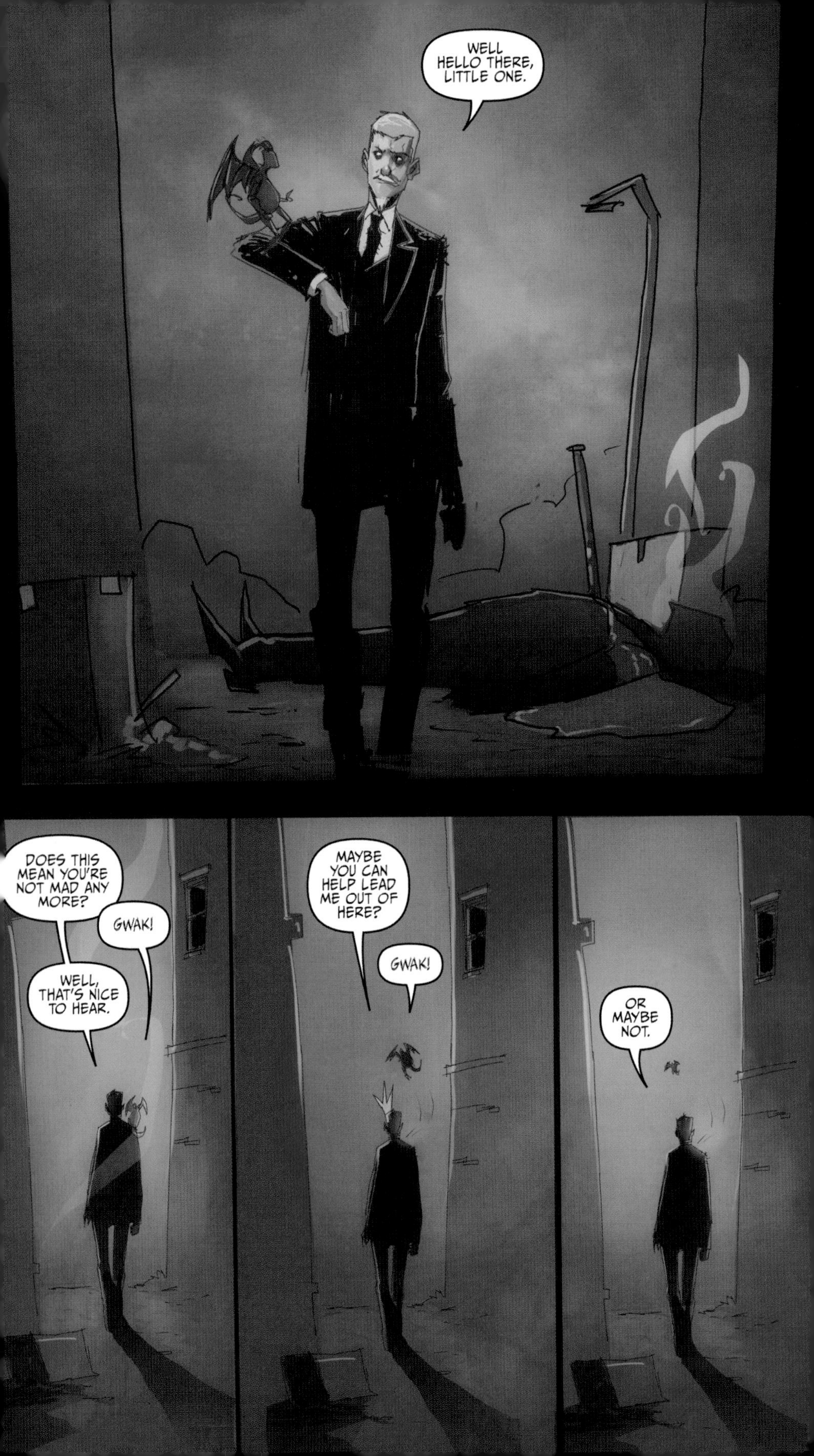
WELL HELLO THERE, LITTLE ONE.
DOES THIS MEAN YOU'RE NOT MAD ANY MORE?
GWAK!
WELL, THAT'S NICE TO HEAR.
MAYBE YOU CAN HELP LEAD ME OUT OF HERE?
GWAK!
OR MAYBE NOT.

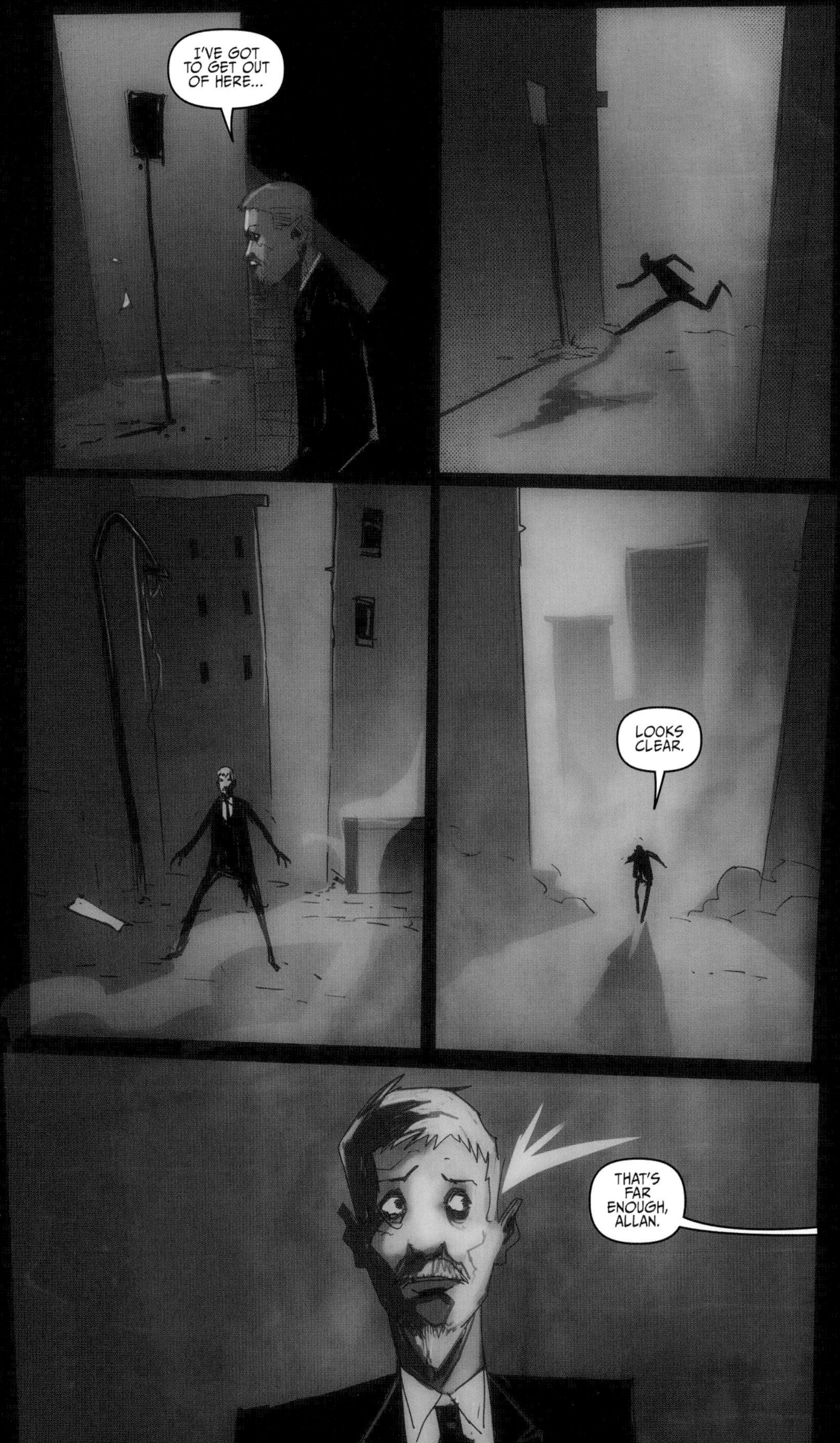
I'VE GOT TO GET OUT OF HERE...
LOOKS CLEAR.
THAT'S FAR ENOUGH, ALLAN.

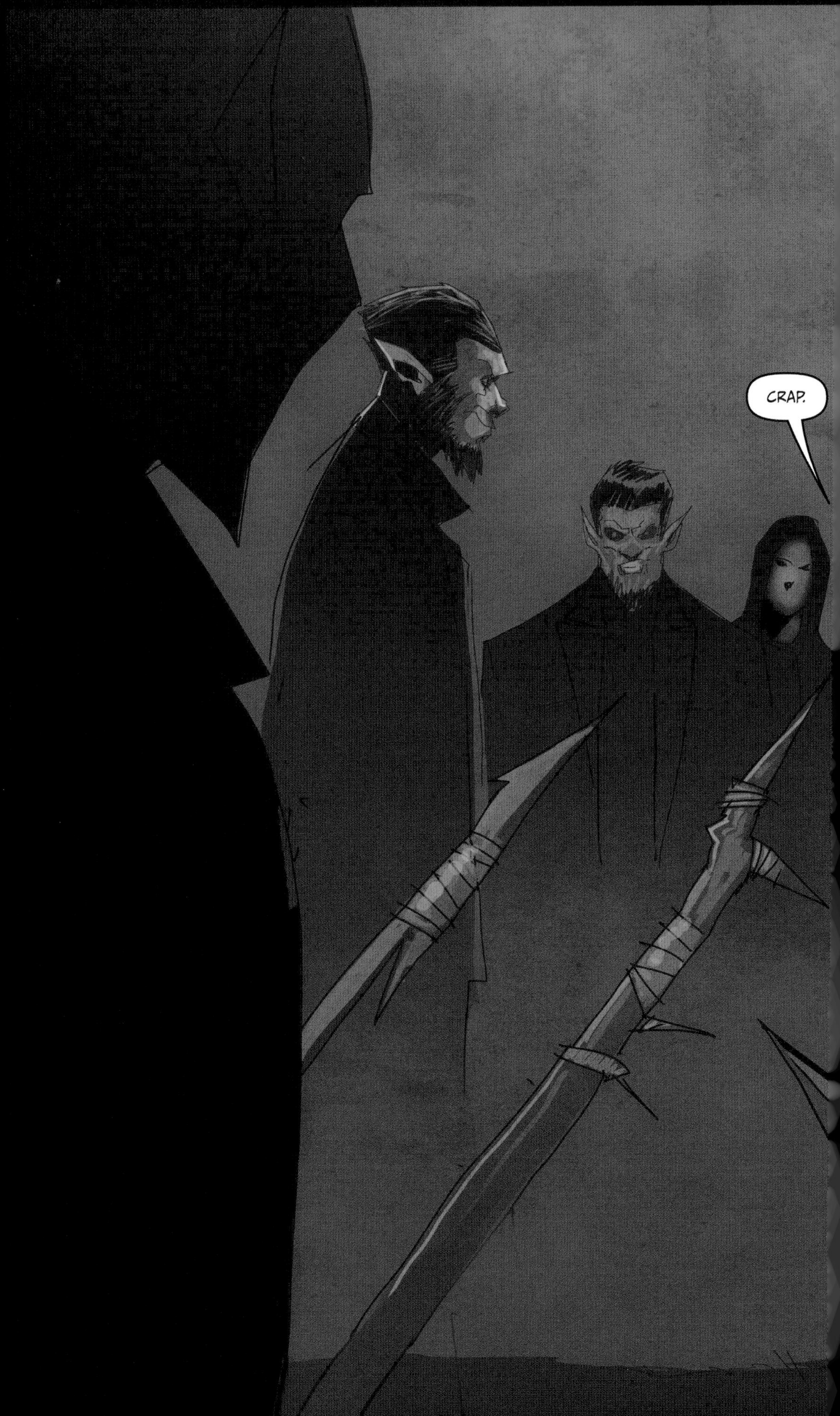
CRAP.

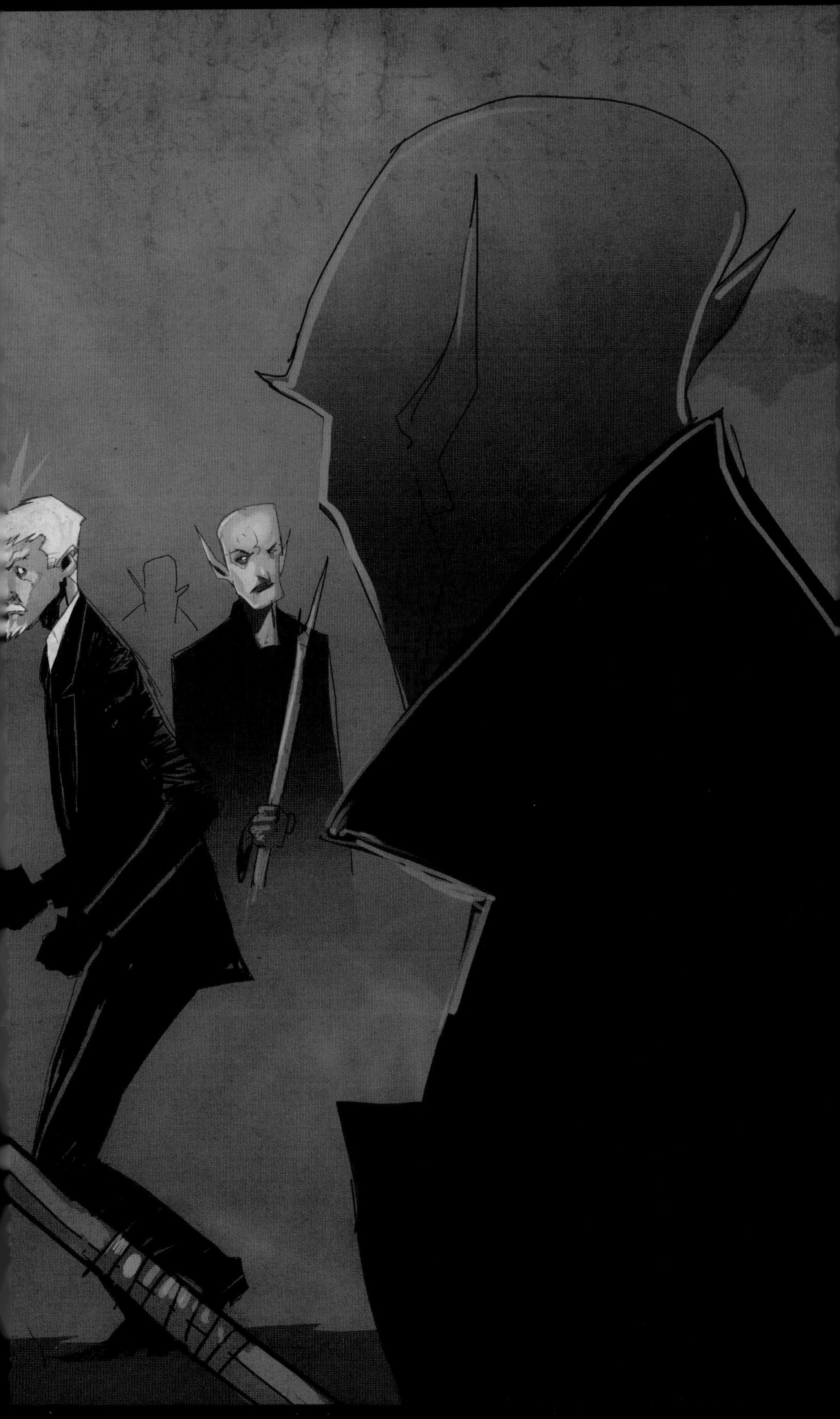

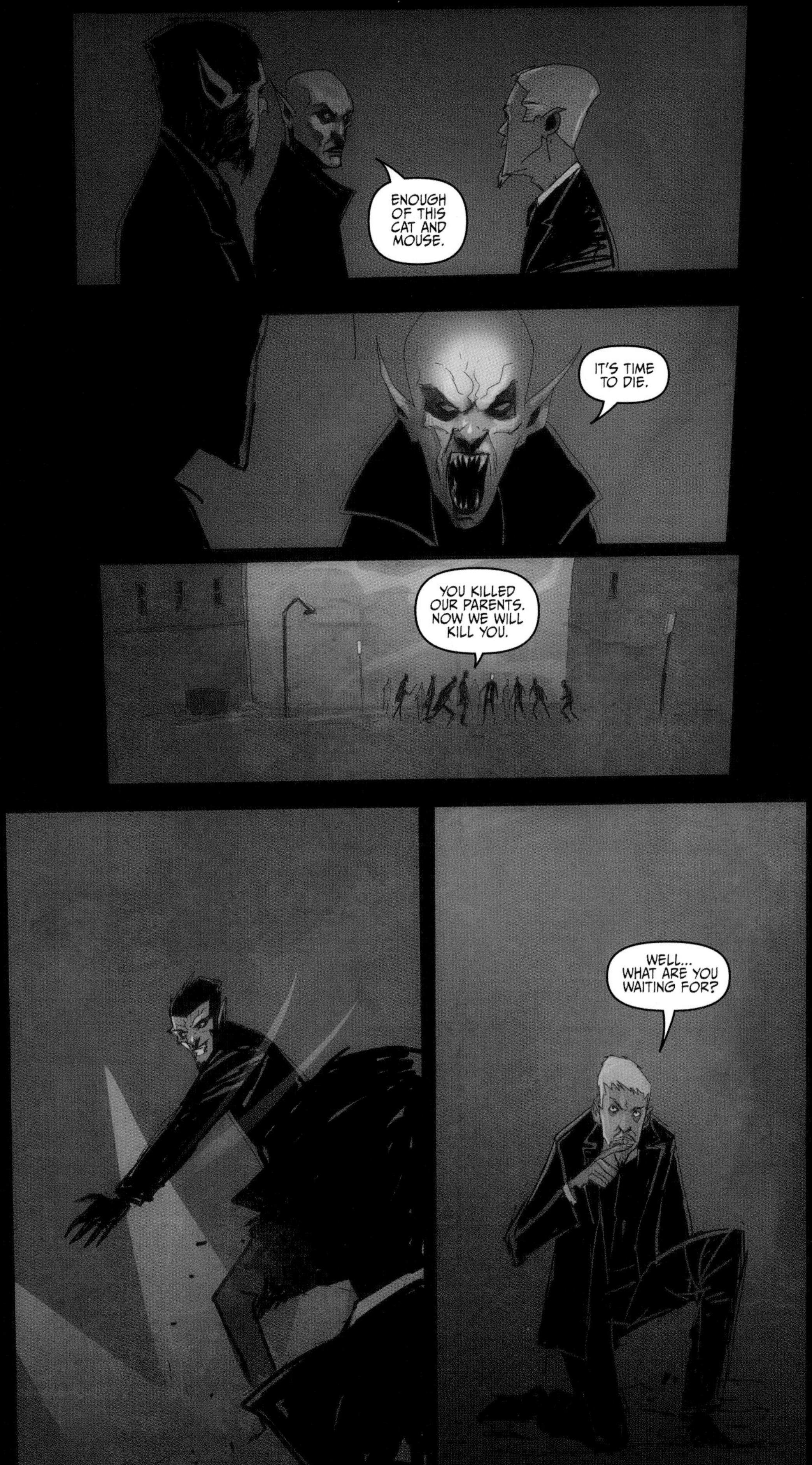
ENOUGH OF THIS CAT AND MOUSE.
IT'S TIME TO DIE.
YOU KILLED OUR PARENTS. NOW WE WILL KILL YOU.
WELL... WHAT ARE YOU WAITING FOR?

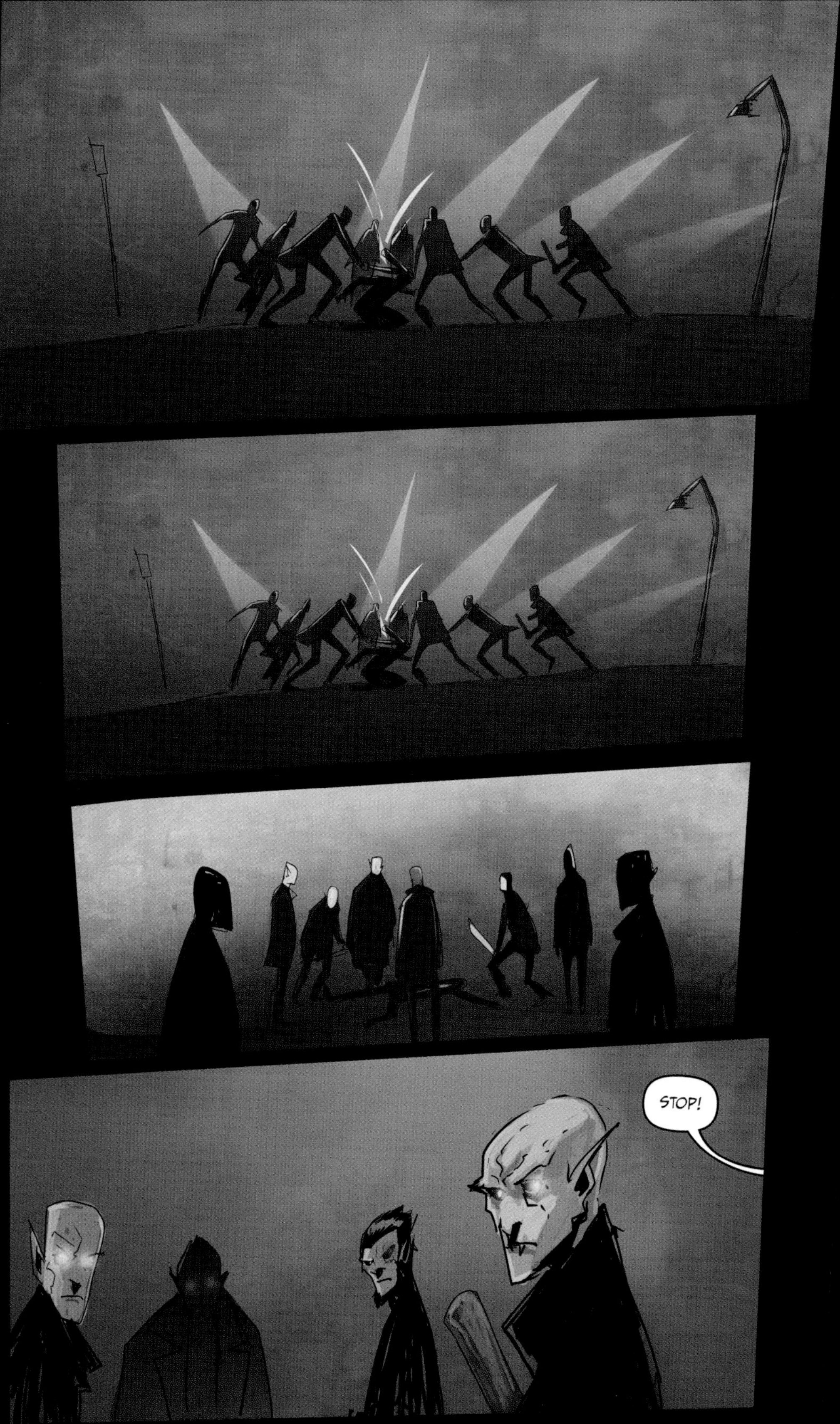
STOP!

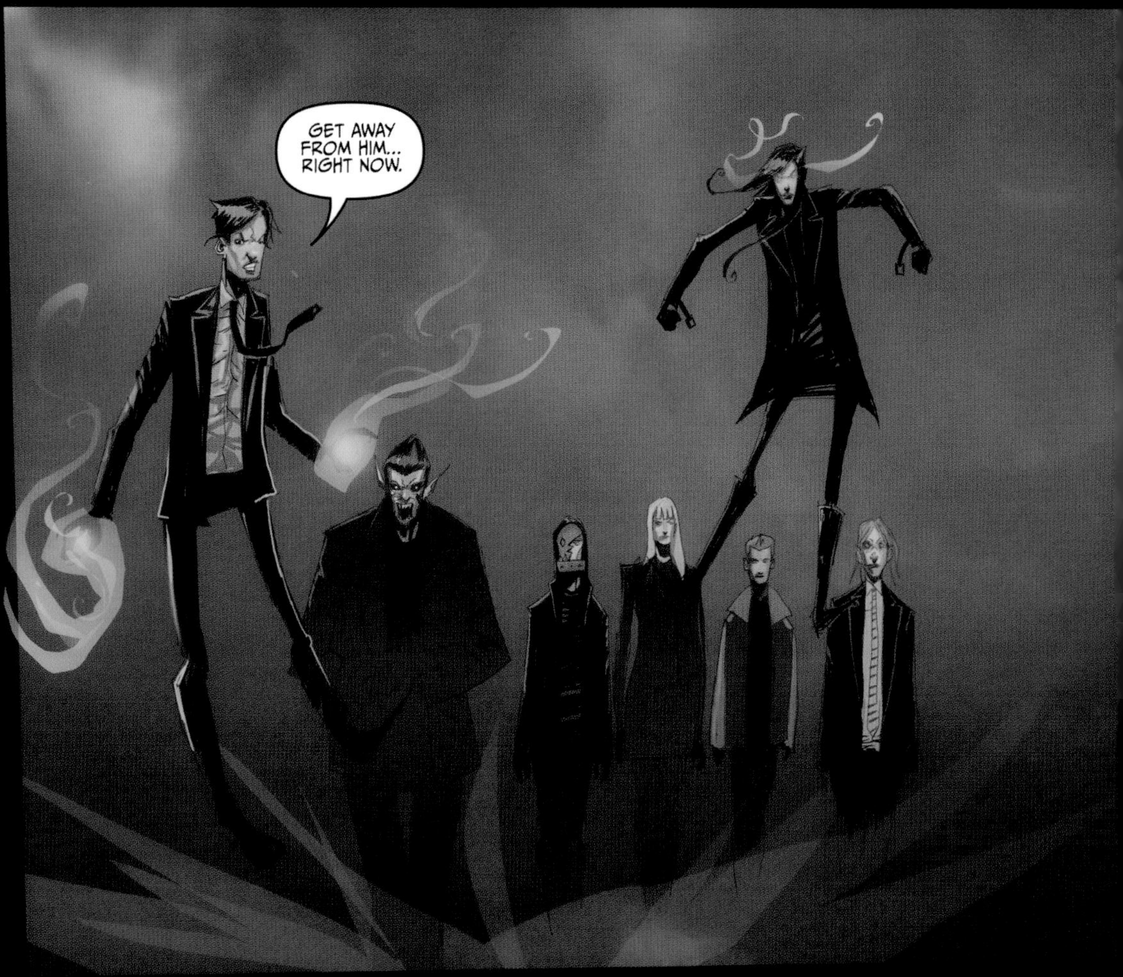
GET AWAY FROM HIM... RIGHT NOW.

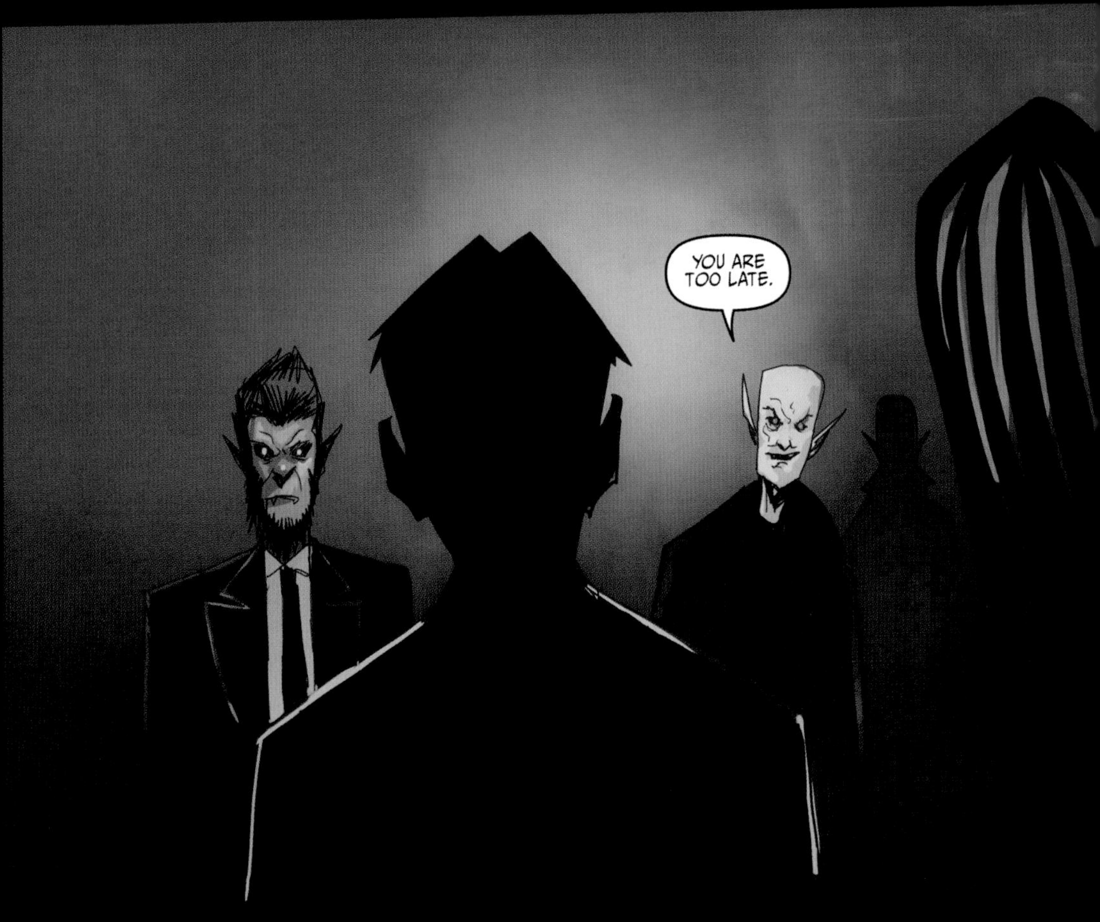
YOU ARE TOO LATE.

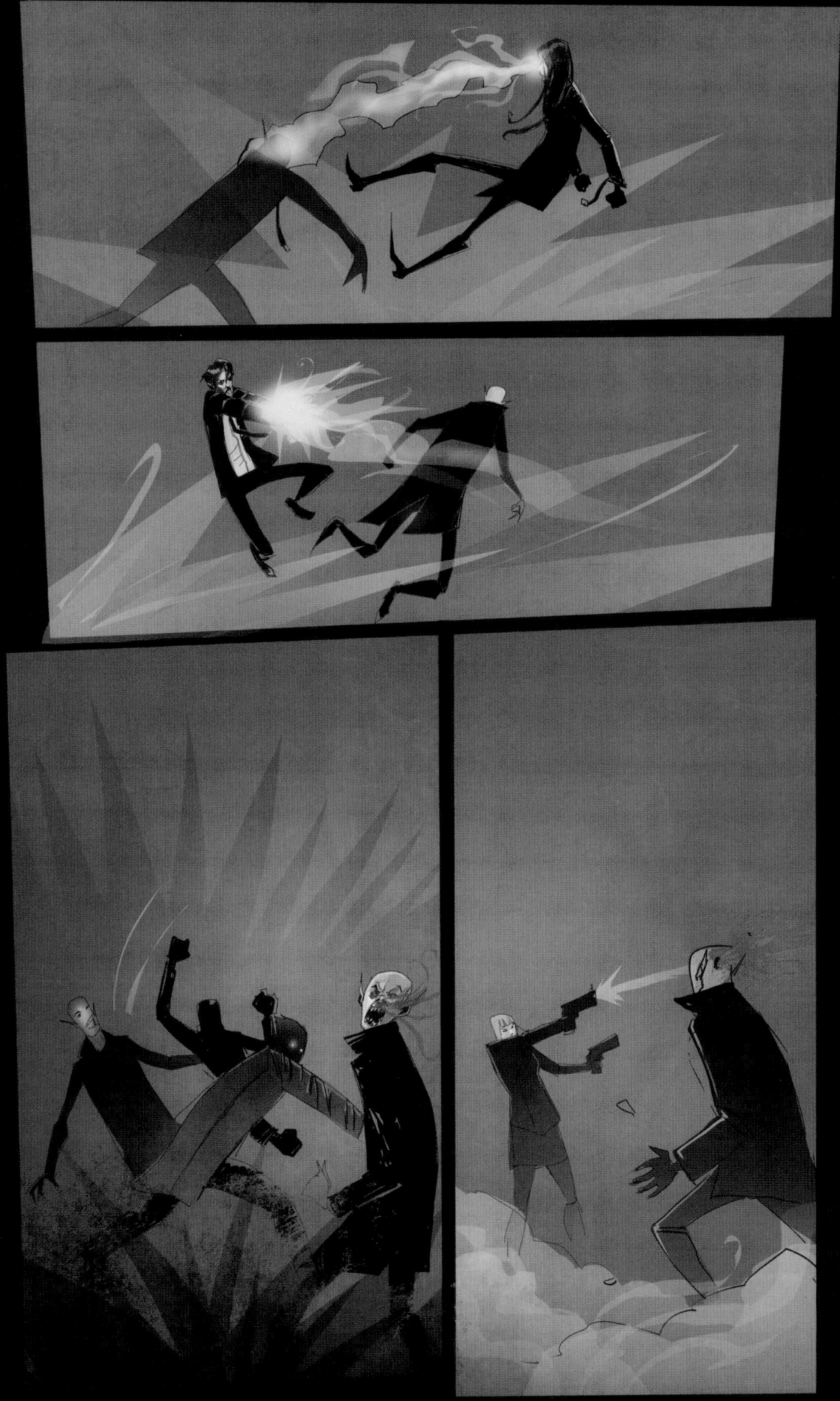

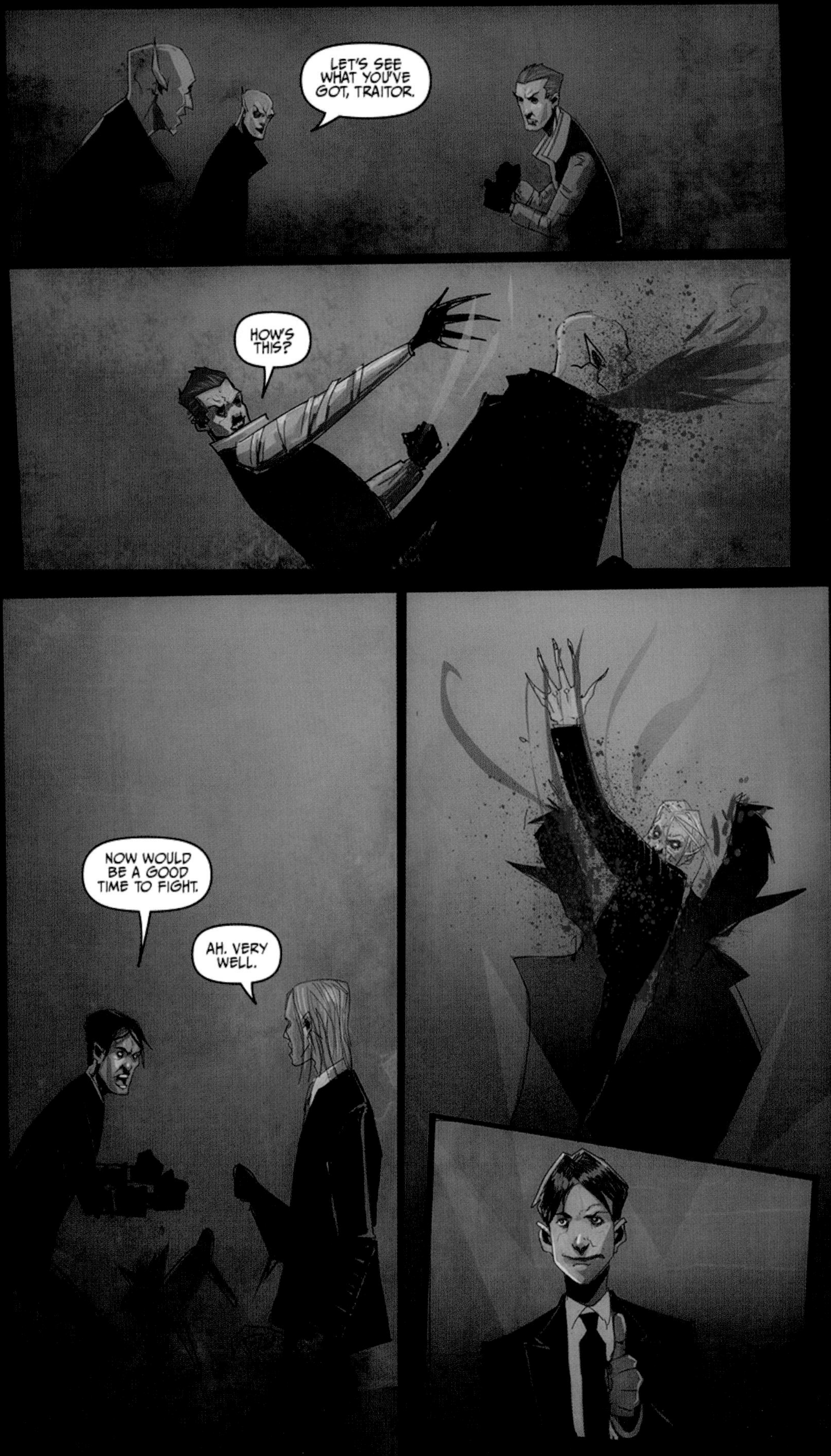
LET'S SEE WHAT YOU'VE GOT, TRAITOR.
HOW'S THIS?
NOW WOULD BE A GOOD TIME TO FIGHT.
AH. VERY WELL.

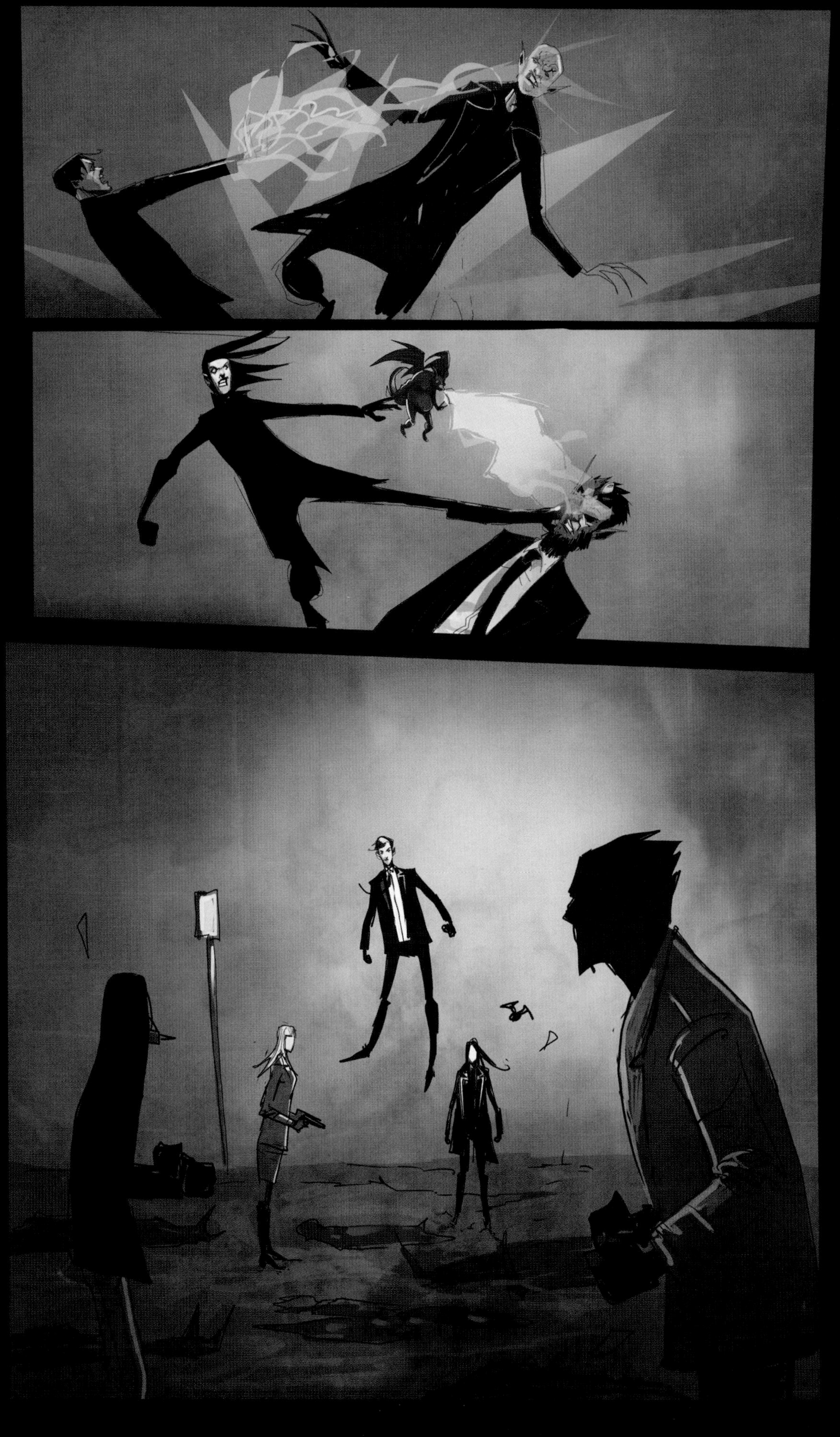

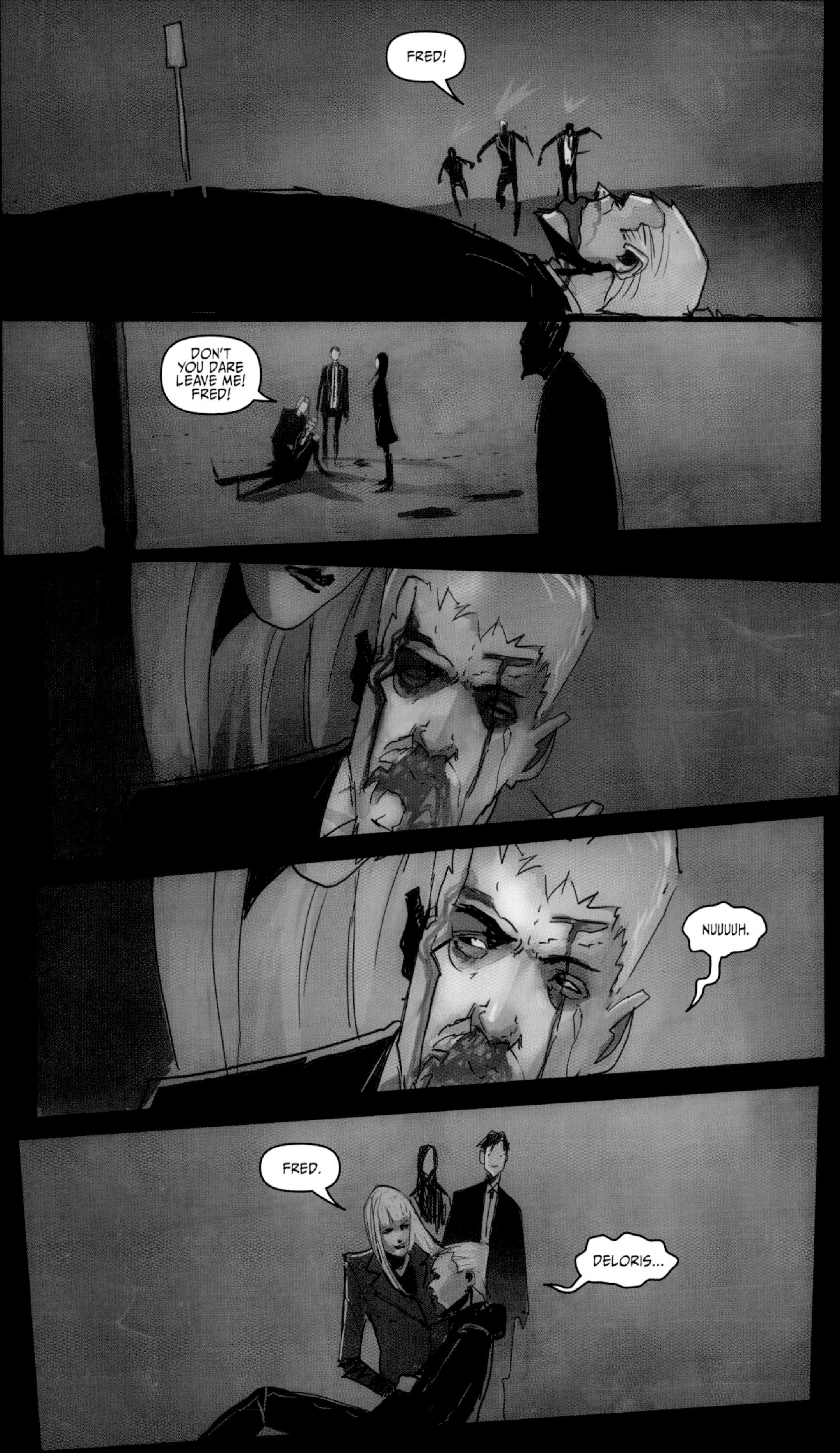
FRED!
DON'T YOU DARE LEAVE ME! FRED!
NUUUUH.
FRED.
DELORIS...

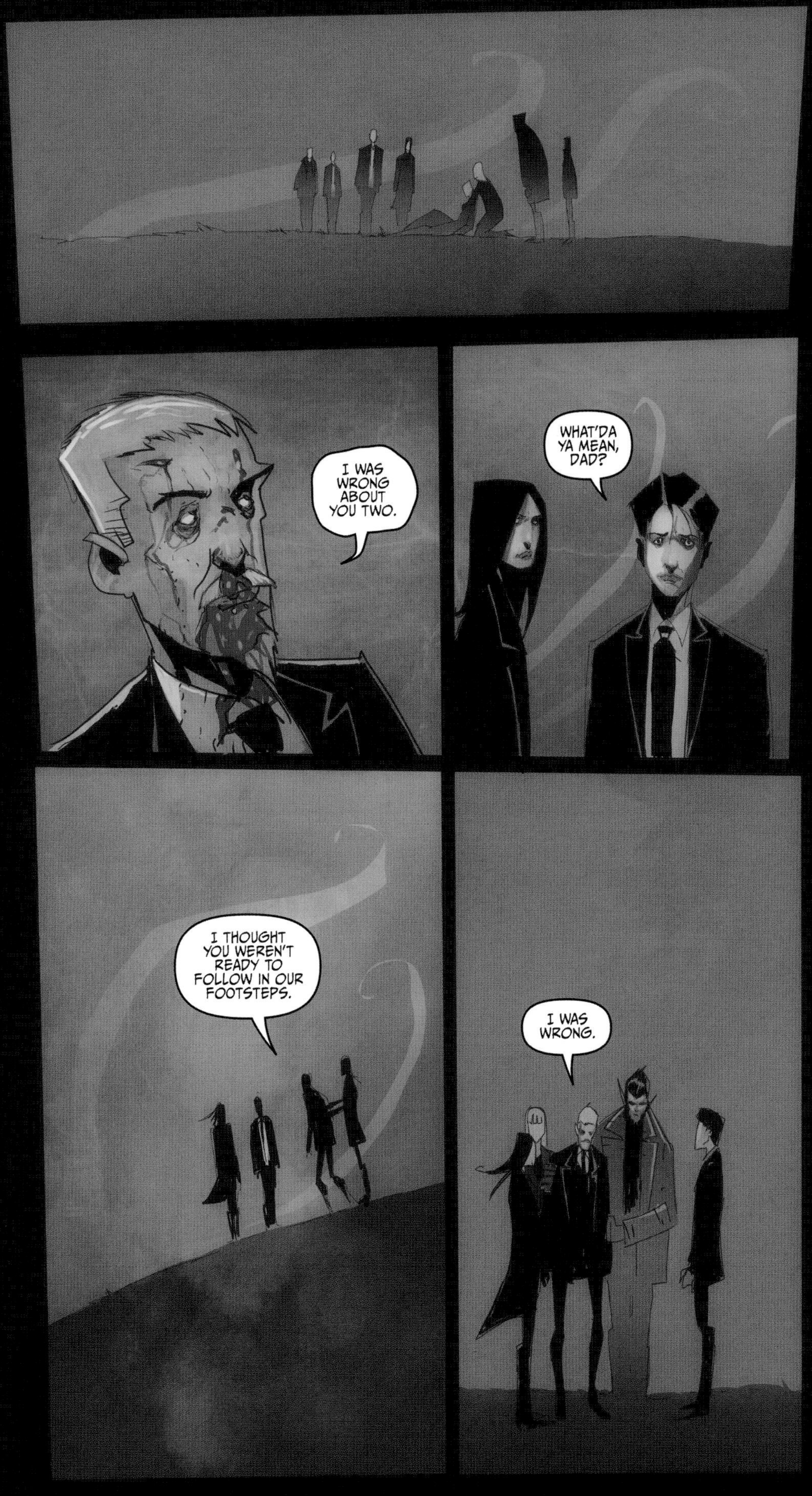

I WAS WRONG ABOUT YOU TWO.
WHAT'DA YA MEAN, DAD?
I THOUGHT YOU WEREN'T READY TO FOLLOW IN OUR FOOTSTEPS.
I WAS WRONG.

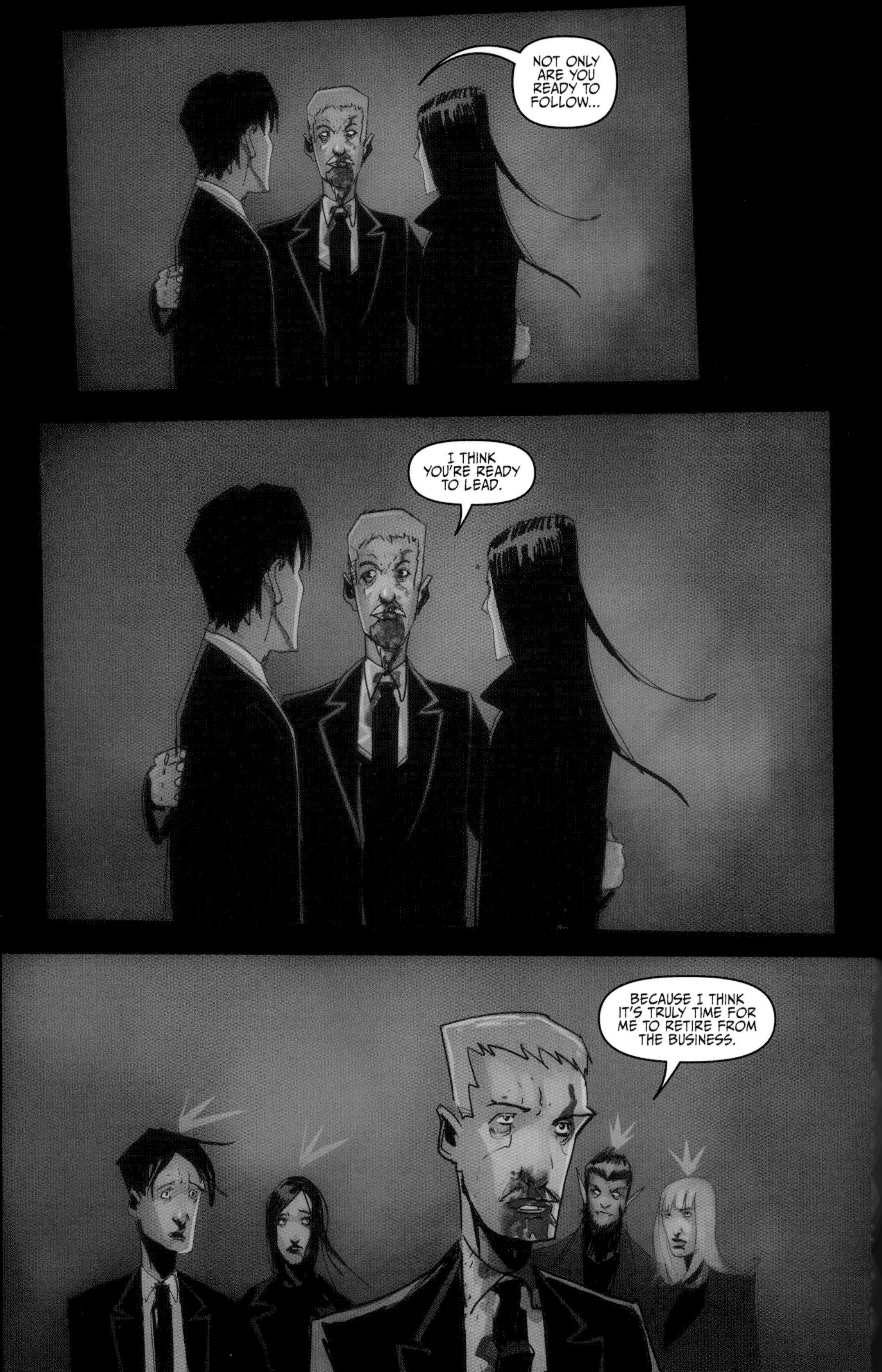
NOT ONLY ARE YOU READY TO FOLLOW...
I THINK YOU'RE READY TO LEAD.
BECAUSE I THINK IT'S TRULY TIME FOR ME TO RETIRE FROM THE BUSINESS.
THE END.

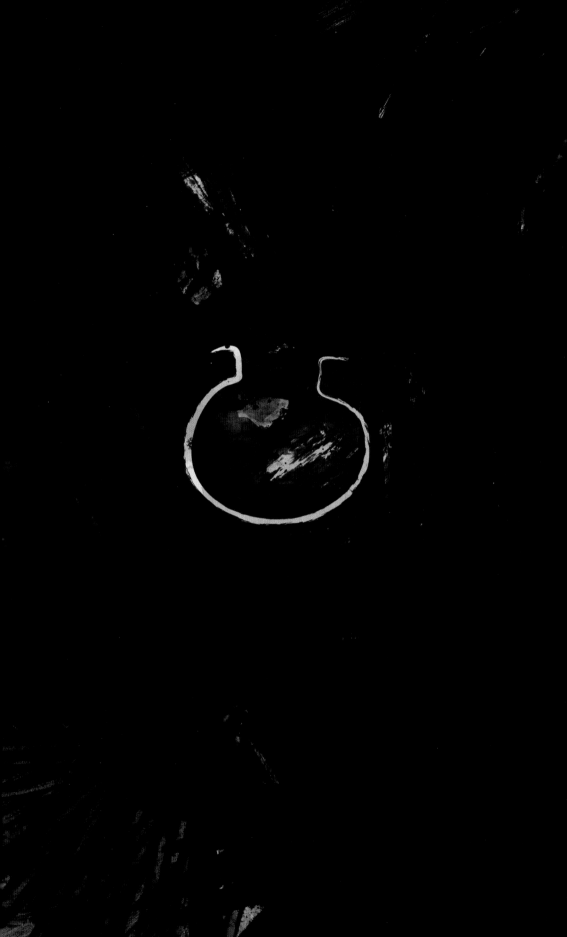

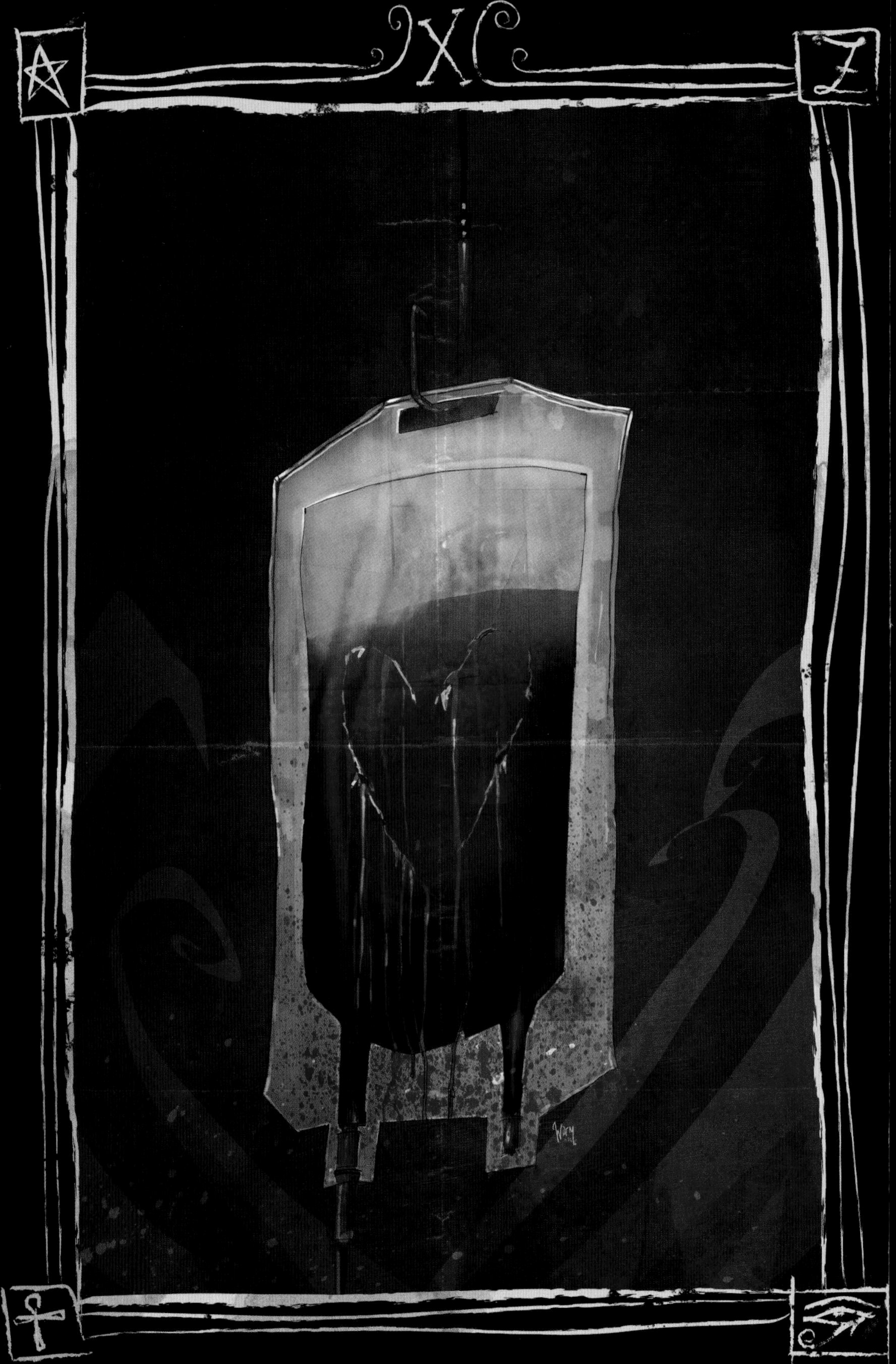
XC

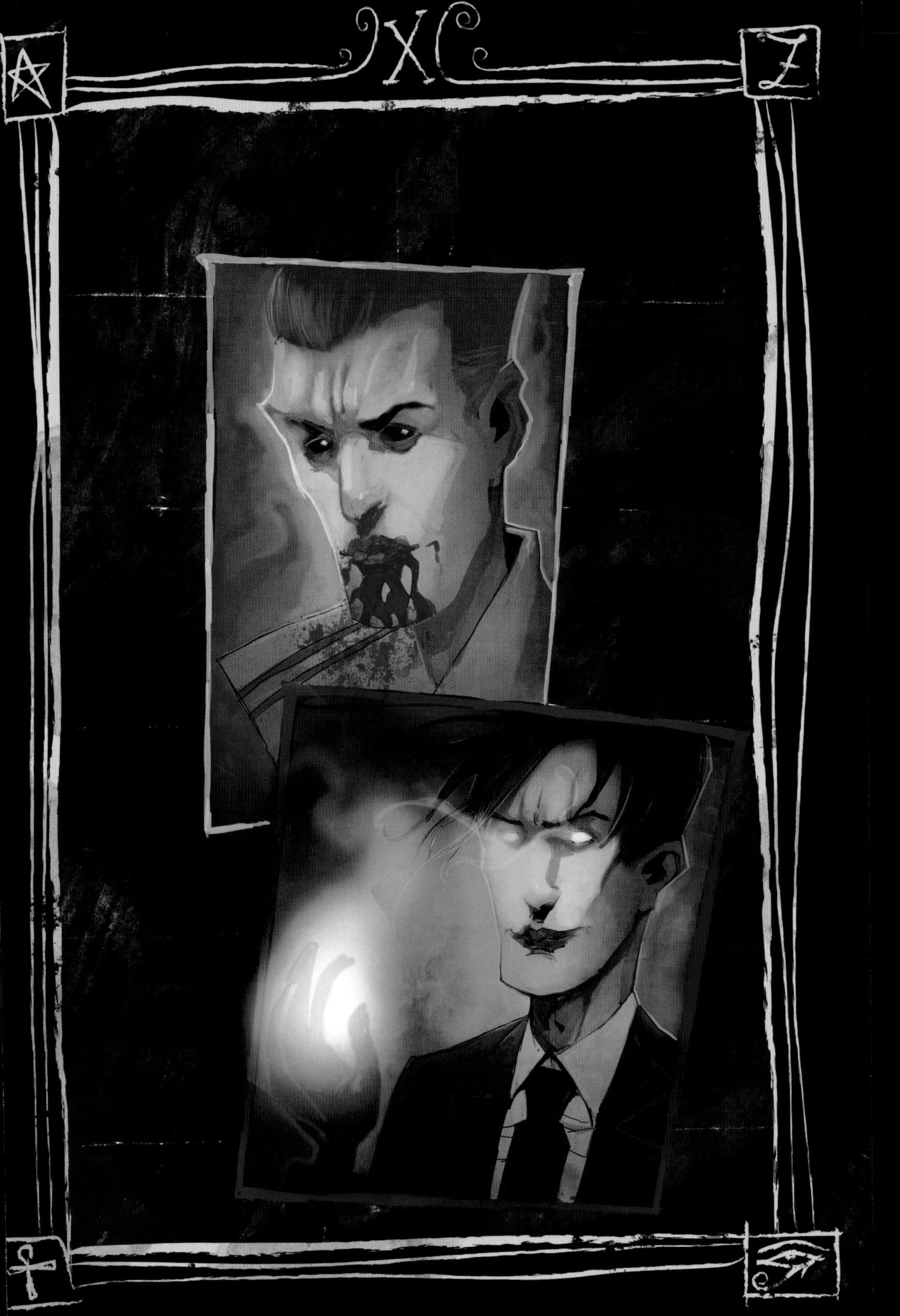
X

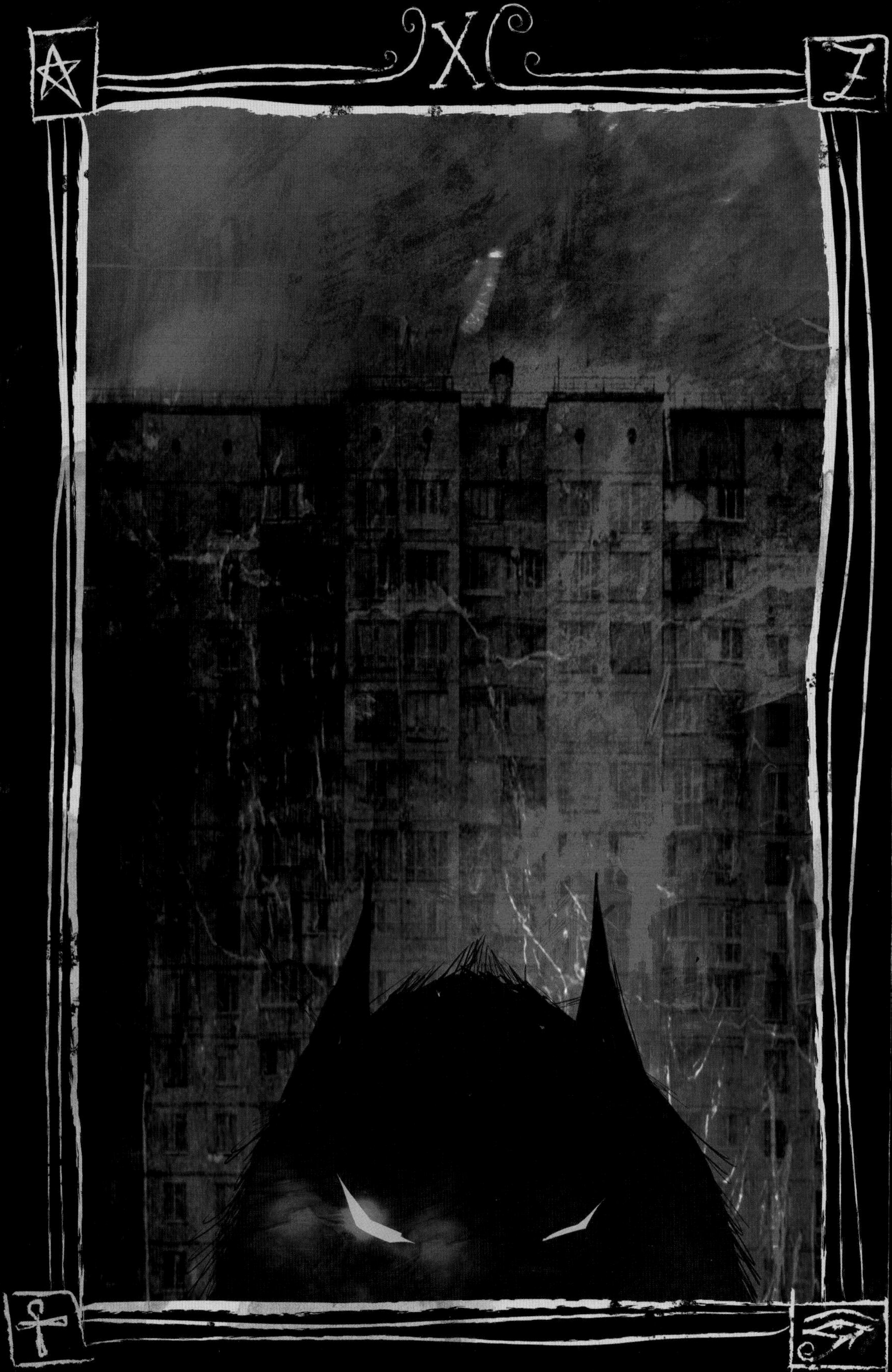
X

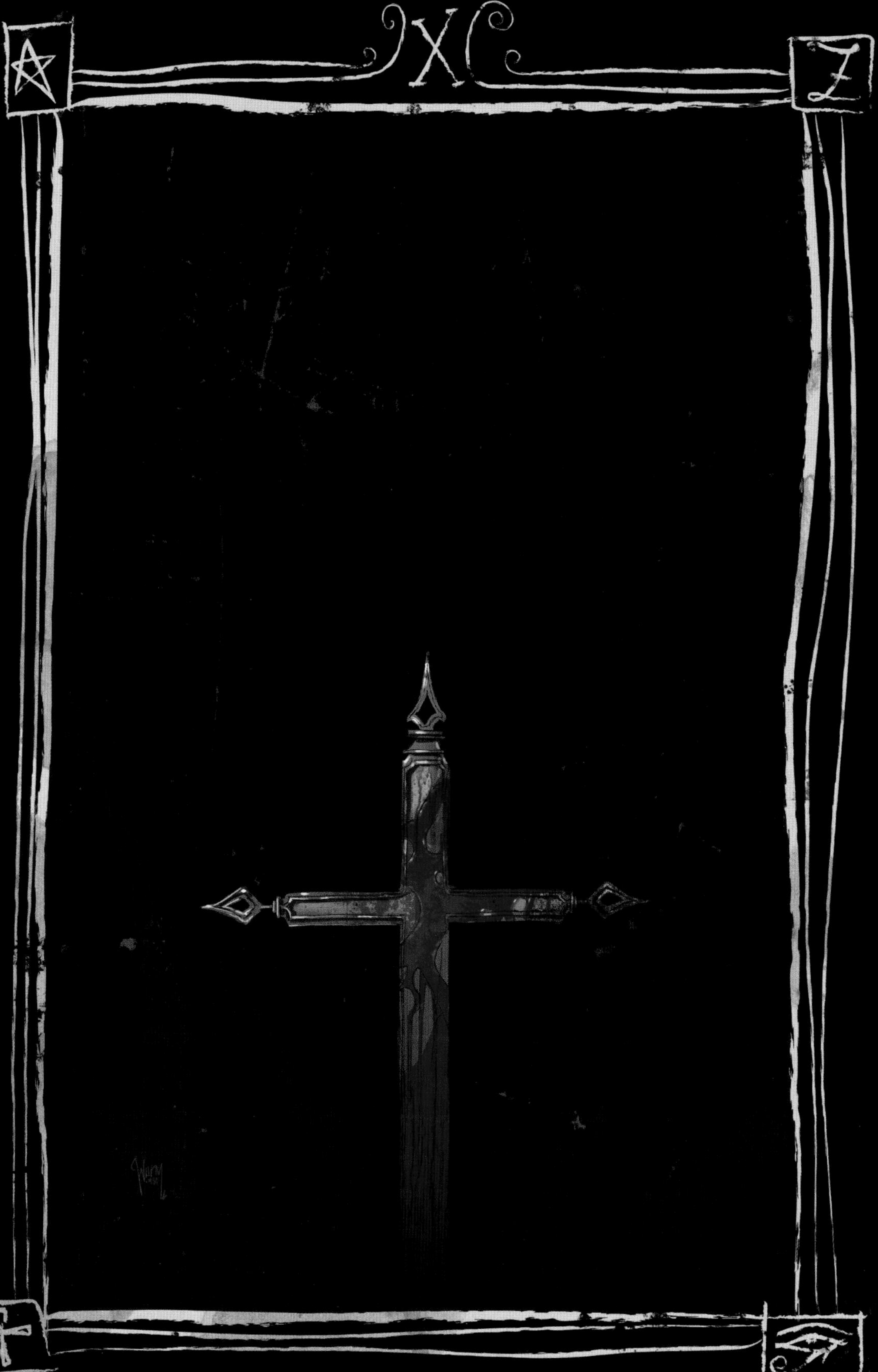

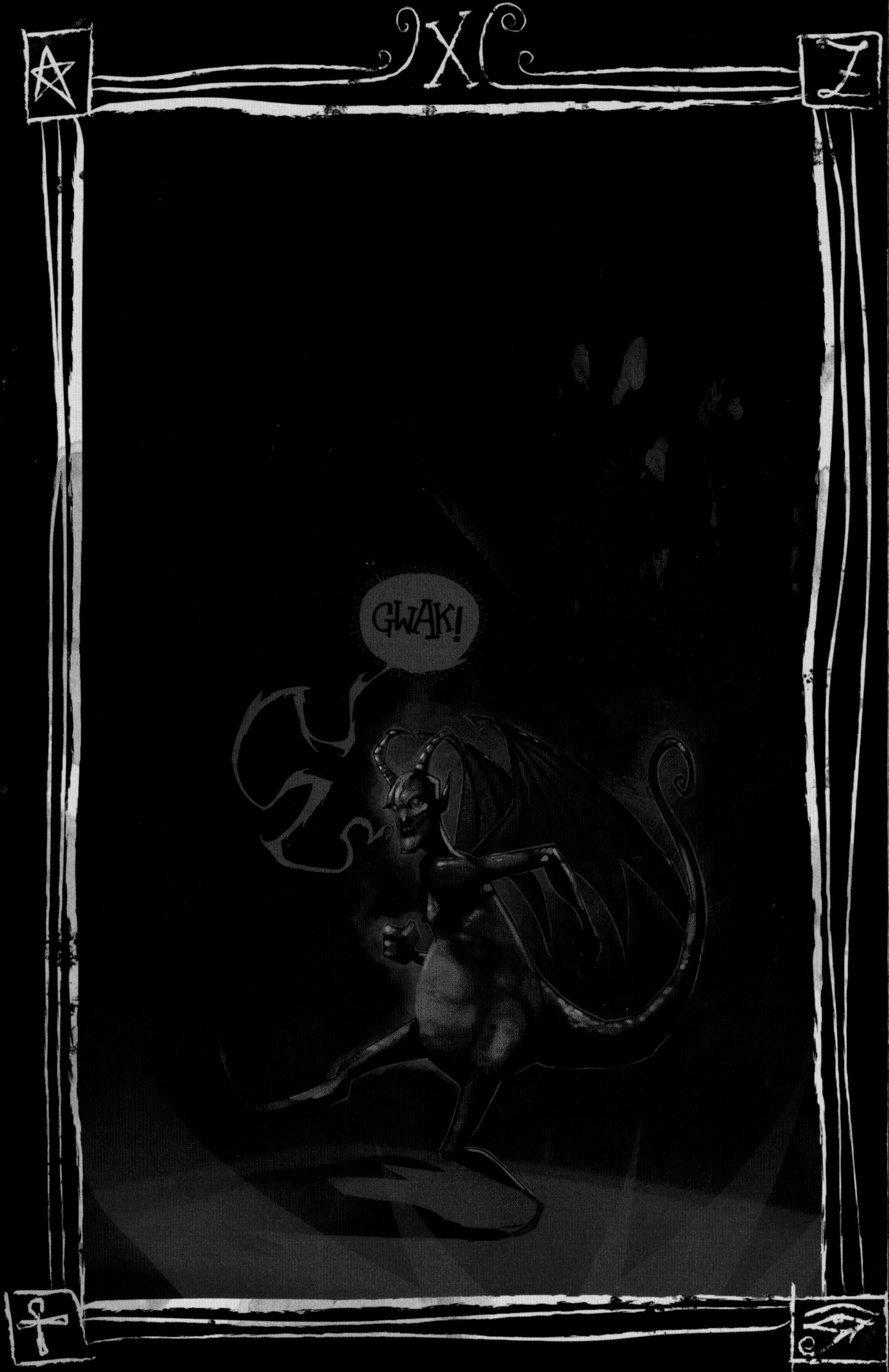
X
GWAK!

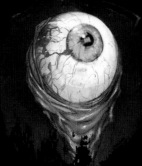

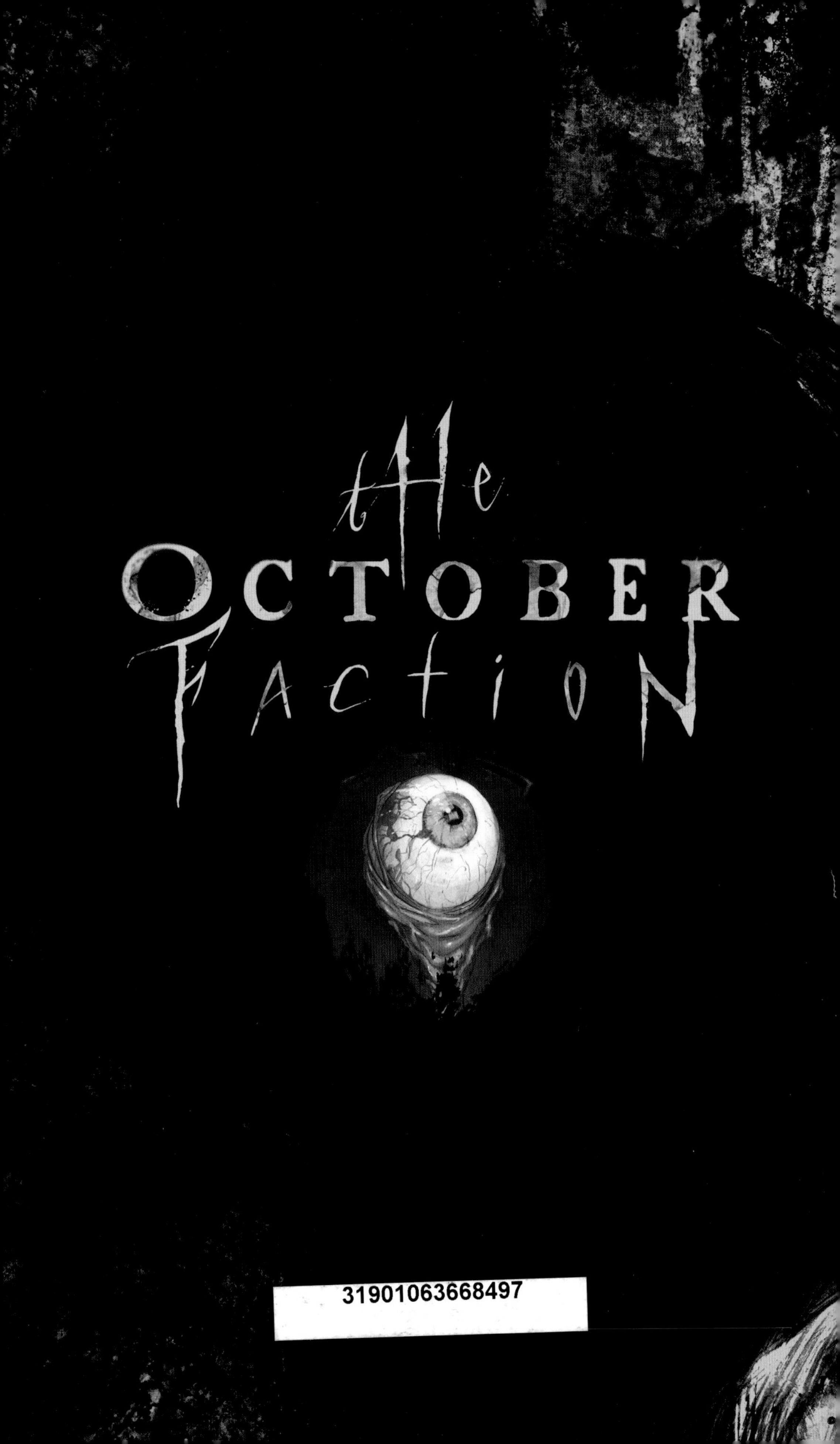

tHe
OCTOBER
FActioN